ARABIC GRAMMAR: A FIRST WORKBOOK

D0328137

ARABIC GRAMMAR

A FIRST WORKBOOK

G. M. WICKENS

Professor of Middle East and Islamic Studies, University of Toronto

CAMBRIDGE UNIVERSITY PRESS

CAMBRIDGE

LONDON · NEW YORK · NEW ROCHELLE

MELBOURNE · SYDNEY

Published by the Press Syndicate of the University of Cambridge
The Pitt Building, Trumpington Street, Cambridge CB2 1RP
32 East 57th Street, New York, NY 10022, USA
296 Beaconsfield Parade, Middle Park, Melbourne 3206, Australia

© Cambridge University Press 1980

First published 1980

Photoset in Malta by Interprint Limited

Library of Congress Cataloguing in Publication Data

Wickens, G. M.
Arabic grammar.

1. Arabic language–Grammar. 1. Title.
PJ6307.W48 492'.7'82421 77–82523

ISBN 0 521 21885 3 hard covers
ISBN 0521 29301 4 paperback

ACKNOWLEDGEMENTS

Among those critics whose comments have been particularly useful are: my colleague Professor J. R. Blackburn, who took over Introductory Arabic teaching for me at Toronto (see Introduction); Emeritus Professor F. V. Winnett, who was mainly responsible for the teaching of Arabic at Toronto before I arrived in 1957; my candid and high-principled friend, Professor George Makdisi, of the University of Pennsylvania; my colleague Professor L. M. Kenny, whose excellent knowledge of modern style was particularly useful; my colleague Professor M. E. Marmura and his sister Ella, cultured, sensitive users of their own language in the best tradition; and finally, in a list comprising only my known and most notable benefactors, my one-time secretary Miss E. M. Burson, who typed the whole text, Arabic script included, and reproduced it innumerable times for class use.

G. M. W.

CONTENTS

The numbers in parentheses refer to paragraph numbers

INTRODUCTION

This introduction to the major practical realities of Standard Arabic, covering as far as possible both "Classical" and Modern styles, was first put together in the early 1960s. About that time I became obliged, by the growth of my University department and of my general administrative and teaching responsibilities, to hand over the arduous task of teaching Introductory Arabic to another colleague. It was felt desirable to maintain an exact standard of method and coverage which could be counted upon by all the other Toronto instructors teaching the Islamic languages or using Arabic in their "disciplinary" classes. During the last fifteen years or so the material, in xeroxed form, has not only been used regularly at the University of Toronto in this way, but also read and commented on by colleagues in the Arabic and related fields at Toronto and elsewhere. These commentators were generally favourable, most to the point of urging publication. The present version takes account of their criticisms as well, and of those made by the readers designated by the Cambridge University Press.

The book makes no claim to have removed, or even to have fully elucidated, all the difficulties normally encountered in starting Arabic; nor to have provided the ultimate methodological tool which renders all earlier work redundant. In some respects it is quite traditional, in others "modern", in yet others original and innovative. What it *does* consciously attempt is to address itself, more than is usually the case in such works, to the hard, recurring realities of the language itself, especially in the related matters of sight-reading and syntactical structure; to the particular problems Arabic in actual use presents to English speakers; and to the general linguistic knowledge and skills present-day learners may (or, more likely, may not) bring to their task. In this last connection, it has become ever safer to assume that a majority of one's students will understand virtually nothing about language as a "system" or an organic reality, and absolutely nothing about traditional grammatical concepts. As a reaction sets in against the fashion for unstructured and non-humanist education, however, it seems (at least to judge by recent experience at Toronto) that this situation may improve somewhat, but the results will still take several years to work through the educational system and society at large.

All this being so, no attempt is made to present a comprehensive, quasi-synchronic, normative, "homogenised" review of Classical Arabic on the lines of, say, W. Wright's standard *Arabic Grammar*, or even in the fashion of A. S. Tritton's *Teach Yourself Arabic*. Indeed, any feature of (e.g. Koranic) style that does not recur regularly in the post-Classical or the Modern language is avoided as far as possible, or relegated to a footnote and so designated. Traditional pre-occupation with the rare or even unique occurrence (*hapax legomenon*), beloved of both Arabic and Western grammarians, is considered to have no place here.

Similarly, the purely scholarly tone is avoided, on the assumption that most learners nowadays have neither strict scholarly training nor scholarly ambitions – at least to become in any sense classical philologists or historians. Learners of Arabic today often know no other language at all well, if at all; they are almost always totally innocent of Latin and Greek. They usually want Arabic for a variety of reasons other than intellectual or philological interest: to read news-papers, or political or business documents; to study Islamic sociology, or the history of philosophy, religion or science; to use the Standard as a yardstick of reference for the practical learning of one or more colloquials – which they may eventually meld with it in varying degrees, as do educated or partly educated Arabs themselves. And so on.

A different type of approach that is handled with equal restraint here is that of modern linguistics. It cannot be questioned that modern linguisticians have brought some liberating and efficient attitudes to the study of language (though many individual teachers had seen the light long before it became a blinding glare). But much of the new operation, like that of the so-called "New Mathe-matics", is at the philosophical rather than the practical level. Moreover, the linguisticians have created new obfuscations of their own: in particular, a highly specialised terminology in phonetics and syntax, and a reluctance to enunciate principles that may not be universally applicable or ultimately valid, however useful for the study of a particular language or family of languages. Because an inexact concept such as "word" is difficult to accommodate in some languages and not acceptable within the full rigour of linguistic analysis, for example, there is no good reason to eliminate it from the practical study of a language like Arabic, particularly at the introductory level. Again, though the spoken word is undoubtedly primary in the Aristotelian sense, and in time and volume, one must not ignore the fact that Standard Arabic (whatever it may eventually become) has always been essentially the high-culture vehicle of a literate society, not a spe-cialised and refined form of everyday speech. (Striking evidence for this is the relatively low idiomatic content of the Standard, at least until modern times, as compared with the colloquials or with the "living" languages like Persian and Turkish.)

On the positive side, this work presents the basic "facts" of Arabic in some sort of pragmatic order (e.g. verbs before nouns in the first instance), and as they are likely to occur in actual use (e.g. Broken Plurals ahead of Sound Plurals). One major consequence of the latter consideration is that the student is urged from the outset to read unvowelled (unvocalised) texts. This is not simply a case of "sink-or-swim" treatment: the nature of written Arabic is such that one not only *must* learn to vocalise correctly, but *can* usually do so as an integral part of structural understanding. Offering fully or partially vocalised texts distracts and confuses both eye and mind. It also fosters permanent dependence on someone else's supposedly superior knowledge of the language: one of the results of introducing vocalisation in some modern Arabic books (though not all, and never in newspapers or journals), together with a fundamentally un-Arabic and unnecessary punctuation, is that even some educated Arabs nowadays never advance beyond a sort of partial literacy. One of the greatest risks with vocalised texts is that they may contain numerous errors, due either to editorial ignorance or to incompetence on the part of the printer.

As an élitist language, written Arabic has been so idiosyncratically developed and analysed that, wherever possible, it is best presented in its own terms. This is, of course, a cliché of the more flexible lingustic thinking, but it needs stressing in the case of a language which has both its own "classicism" and its own original "linguistic science". Accordingly, while avoiding the extreme Latin or "Common European" grammatical approach on the one hand, and the rigid modern linguistic and phonetic systems on the other, I have combined the Arabic categories (e.g. for verb "tenses") with my own *ad hoc* purely practical explanations, hints and short cuts. (Some of these are very much of the "*i* before *e* except after *c*" variety, and will need to be modified at an advanced stage.) If such a method irritates established scholars, it will surely help those faced with the difficulties of actually learning the language or of explaining its peculiarities, simply and effectively, to those who want to (as one of my students has said) "get a handle on it" as quickly as possible.

In short, the purpose of the work is to get the beginner into Arabic and over the hurdles that often daunt him before the race has begun. Above all, it is to instil confidence that there are systematic "tricks of the trade" for tackling the basic problems, and that these can be acquired within a reasonable time (say, one year) by practice and repetition.

Because the book is directed alike to teacher, student and self-teacher (as well as because it arose out of "live" classroom experience), it has a personal style that may annoy those who prefer the traditional detached cataloguing of phenomena. The grammatical explanations and analyses (*Vocabulary and remarks* sections) are worded very much in this spirit, with constant stressing of essential features, reminders of earlier occurrences of the same phenomenon, relation of the actual occurrence to the basic general explanation, and so on.

The philosophy behind the book's methodology is set out in the various sections of para. 12. Much more exercise and drill material could have been included, especially in the early chapters, as well as more elaborate follow-up advice for later work. In both cases, however, this would not only have drastically increased the size and cost of the book, but also imposed a framework of action and reference on its users both cramping of initiative and inappropriate to the situation. Virtually all the Arabic passages, short or long, are real, not made-up material.

It is hoped to follow this grammar with a reader more or less geared to it, which would offer a second year of moderately intensive work. Concentrating on largely pre-Modern Arabic (for the modern period is well provided for, particularly by American publications), it too would present genuine, "undoctored" specimens of the language, irrespective of their agreement or otherwise with the normative rules of the Classical grammarians. Substandard material is, of course, to be avoided, but there is no warrant for trying to improve on what educated writers have done at different times.

Once the "reader" year is over, the time for "monumental", printed guidance is past. The student will then be at grips with cultural and other problems, often in highly specialised and advanced areas. Sometimes he may be lucky enough to work under the guidance of "live" experts; sometimes he will have to shift for himself, because there may be no experts, or at best only a few, in the field of his interest. It is perhaps all too often not realised that, despite heroic work done over the last 150 years in Arabic and Islamic studies, in both East and West, any serious student soon reaches the frontiers of understanding in his field and becomes his own pioneer.

1

On learning languages in general

1. *Language-learning is a technical training.* To learn a foreign language even reasonably well requires an acceptance of the discipline governing any technique; it also demands considerable staying-power. Yet the task is often approached with an attitude that is both casual and naïvely hopeful: it is inevitable that frustration and failure should rapidly follow on such beginnings. Moreover, most students (and even some teachers) ignore not only the problem of psychological preparation, but also the need to set a series of goals that are both clear and practically attainable.

2. *Language-learning can never by easy.* Any serious effort to learn a foreign language is bound to be exacting in some measure, for the following reasons among many:

(*a*) The learner has to condition his mind to a whole new way of looking at reality, and in many cases to a completely new set of intellectual norms. This might be called the "flexible-mentality hurdle", one that is certainly beyond the capacity of some individuals.

(*b*) The learner must memorise a large number of words and phrases (both naturally in context and deliberately in isolation), if he is ever one day to become reasonably free of the tyranny of the dictionary. In some languages he will also need to memorise mechanically a minimum of variant forms, often conveniently arranged in tables. (It is for the teacher, and to some degree for the learner himself, to choose all of these items intelligently, with a view to economy, logical sequence and usefulness.) We are here taking for granted that the learner is an adult (or at least an adolescent), with both an adult's handicaps and an adult's advantages. The fashionable ideal of trying to "learn languages as a child learns its mother-tongue" sounds attractive; but it presupposes conditions that can never normally be duplicated to any real extent, once childhood is over and once the mother-tongue has been learned and the habit of literacy become second nature. Very few adults learn a foreign language in a setting where all needs, for every hour of the waking day, must be expressed only orally, and only in the language concerned, if they are to be expressed at all. Moreover, in learning a new language, no normal adult can entirely obliterate the native speech-habits of a lifetime (though he may gradually learn to suppress them), whereas the child's mother-tongue comes to fill a veritable speech-vacuum. Again, no language-learning adult normally disposes of the ten or more years that a child takes to gain its (often quite uncertain) grasp on its own language by natural, hit-and-miss methods. Above all, of course, the adult mind lacks the spontaneity and the absorptive capacity of the infant mind. But it has, by compensation, such very usable assets as stamina, conscious purpose, mental discipline, a developed power to compare, abstract and generalise, the ability to keep a written record, and so on. This, then, might be called the "memory hurdle" or the "drudgery hurdle": psychologically, it is often the most daunting of all when once experience reveals something of its size.

(*c*) The attainments referred to in (*a*) and (*b*) have eventually to be combined in a sort of reflex skill: one needs to apply the principles and produce the correct forms more or less instinctively when speaking or writing; and one must be able to recognise them readily when listening or reading, endowing them instantaneously with something approaching their intended meaning. This may be called the "co-ordination hurdle": unwearying practice and cheerful humility are needed here, but the proficiency eventually achieved, and the time taken in achieving it, will vary greatly according to individual temperament. Perfection, even after years, remains an ideal.

3. *What modern methods can do.* None of the many modern aids to language-learning (tape-recorders, language laboratories, situation-games, topical and "scientifically" chosen material, streamlined methods, and so on) can of itself eliminate or greatly reduce these difficulties: the latter are inherent in all deliberate, "artificial" study of languages. Good and efficient techniques (linguisticians would claim) can save much time-wasting, many false starts, and insidious and recurrent mistakes: but they cannot do the learner's work for him; they cannot make the normal, average-to-good student into an outstanding one; and they cannot make the occasional "language-blind" or "language-deaf" student into even a moderately good linguist. It may be added that, in general, few people can ever learn a language, for any purpose, from a book, with no personal guidance at all: the exceptions are the very few with a special flair, or the not many more with wide experience (though even these can hardly learn to *speak* well in this way). But even if superlatively good books were more plentiful than they are in language work, a teacher would normally be absolutely indispensable for the vast majority of students.

4. *"Who really "knows" a language*? If learning a language is not easy, it is not totally beyond the capacity of most people of average intelligence, education and industry, so long as they face the problems involved realistically from the outset. Above all, they need to define as clearly as possible their own purpose or purposes in studying a particular language. One might illustrate the problem by posing the question: What does it mean to "know" a language? Clearly, a man who says "Me come see you you house two week" has some right to feel that he knows English, but by the same token he could not claim to know English very well! Quite apart from questions of accent and intonation, it will be obvious to any English-speaker that such a man is foreign, or is pretending to be so. But what of the man who says "May I call on you at your home in a fortnight's time?" His formula expresses the same idea, perhaps with no greater clarity, but with what the same judge would instantly recognise as faultless, even polished, English usage. English may or may not be the speaker's mother-tongue; but even if it is, we should be unable to say for certain, on the evidence of this one remark, that he could express himself equally well on other matters: for example, he might have nothing of English legal or medical terminology, he might be unfamiliar with political or religious usage in English, he might know little of English literature, and he might well be severely embarrassed if asked to make a speech of congratulation or write a letter of sympathy. If his incapacity is proved in one or all of these areas, can he still be said to "know" English? Obviously, for practical purposes the answer might still be that he does, especially if English is his mother-tongue. It is more likely to be the foreign learner who, failing to meet such tests, would be accused by the native-speakers, by his own kind, and even by himself, of not having learned the language properly! The fact must be accepted, especially by the learner, that there is a general, imprecise but well-recognised, level of linguistic proficiency that must be attained before one can speak of "knowing" a language at all; but that once this is reached, specialised skills in an infinite number of more advanced areas may either never be acquired or at least be deferred for indefinite periods. This first stage, put at its very lowest, normally takes a year, or some 100 hours of fairly intensive instruction with at least another 200 hours of private study: the figure may be much higher for some languages, but will never be lower.

5. *The rewards of language-learning.* For the student able and willing to persevere through repeated falls at the above three hurdles, and through an often overwhelming sense of depression and futility, the rewards are satisfying indeed: even at the individual, non-social level, they may justly be compared to those of having learned to play a musical instrument, to fly or skate, to paint or dance, and so on. Again, as with all these, the hard-won linguistic skill must be kept in constant practice to be held at "concert pitch", let alone deepened as it should be. With all these considerations, it may be evident that no prudent person should try to learn more than a very few languages really well. Statements that a man "knows twenty languages" or "speaks ten languages like a native" can practically never be taken at face value, even in an approximate and practical estimate like the one above. Multilingual guides and waiters usually achieve their virtuosity in a very limited subject area; very few persons are even bilingual in the sense of having two identically developed mother-tongues, both equally apt to a wide range of needs; and, as we have seen above, no speaker really "knows" his mother-tongue in anything more than a relative sense of being accepted by some fellow speakers in certain situations.

6. *Reasons for learning languages.* It is generally accepted nowadays that the primary purpose and value of language-learning are for conversation with native speakers. Yet very few people travel or live for long enough periods in foreign-speaking communities to justify such effort as described above. At the same time, if the person who has learned largely in order to converse does not do so constantly, he will soon lose his sole skill in greater or lesser degree. To be able to converse, to speak with a good accent and rhythm, to have an oral–aural "feeling" of the language: these are always desirable and useful goals in language-learning. But they are in themselves limited and elusive goals as compared with skill in reading. The latter offers intellectual and cultural satisfactions that are far more easily achieved and far more surely retained in almost all situations: nor does it expose a by no means small class of learners to what they feel to be intolerable embarrassment and humiliation. In our own experience, the person with a really good grasp of a written language can usually learn to speak easily enough when both necessity and opportunity press upon him for any length of time; on the other hand, the person who (especially in a language like Arabic or Persian) has learned to speak only for practical purposes may never be able to make headway with the written language. The present course, though properly concerned with good pronunciation, intonation and rhythm, is primarily aimed at initiating literates into the technique of *reading* Arabic. In the case of this language, as will become apparent in the next chapter, there are very special reasons why one needs to limit one's immediate aim *at the outset* to either reading or conversing; and conversation cannot be learned from a book.

2

The nature of Arabic and the character of this course

7. *Common misconceptions.* It is necessary to try to clarify immediately what the word "Arabic" does and does not mean. In our experience, most prospective students of the language expect no problem here at all. Leaving the totally ignorant generality on one side, we may divide the merely misinformed into two groups: those who think of Arabic as the language of all Muslims, a language otherwise apparently known as "Persian" or "Turkish" or "Urdu", and so on; and those who define it, with less inaccuracy, as "the language of the Arabs" or "the language of Arabia". Unfortunately, the true situation is considerably more complicated: yet certain general principles must be grasped from the outset.

8. *Arabic is essentially a formal, written language.* As used by Arabic-speakers themselves, the term "Arabic" properly refers only to the formal language – a language that can be, and is, uttered vocally by those educated to do so, but one most often employed in written form. As such, it is the standard language of the whole so-called "Arab world" from Arabia to Morocco; it is also, however imperfectly understood, the official religious language of the Islamic faith, from Indonesia to West Africa, from Central Asia to Zanzibar. *But no Arab, and no non-Arab Muslim, uses Arabic as his normal vehicle of speech*: the latter would use one of the several languages (Persian, Turkish, Urdu, Malayan, and so on) that have borrowed much vocabulary from Arabic and are sometimes written in its script; the Arab (to continue using a term that is itself the subject of much controversy) would employ one of several related tongues that might be called, taking only the main groupings, Iraqi, Arabian, Syro-Palestinian, Egyptian-Sudanese, North African, and North-West African. These languages – variously termed "colloquial", "common", "popular" or "vernacular" – seem to have existed, side by side with the formal or written language, for at least 1,400 years past. They have borrowed freely from it, as well as influencing it in return, at least locally. Though related both to it and to each other, they are not mutually comprehensible with any ease, especially where they are widely separated geographically (e.g. North-West African and Iraqi). But, above all, they cannot be effectively written down, though this is attempted in a somewhat makeshift way in newspaper cartoons and jokes, and sometimes in drama and "realistic" dialogue, using the standard script of Arabic.

9. *A crucial distinction.* It is essential that the student should not minimise the importance of these contrasts. All languages make some distinction between written, formal expression and verbal, informal utterance; but such distinctions do not normally question the basic unity of the language concerned. In the case of Arabic and the colloquials, however, the cleavage is one of identity, and it has far-reaching implications for international affairs, as well as for political, social and cultural activities. To take a few examples: an Iraqi peasant cannot really converse with his Moroccan counterpart (though both may be Arabs) unless one learns the colloquial of the other, or unless both learn Arabic – and this contingency is most improbable, since they will both normally be illiterate. On the other hand, an Iraqi professor or ambassador could converse easily with the Moroccan equivalent in Arabic, even though their respective pronunciations and intonations would quite likely be affected by their colloquial mother-tongues; indeed, one might say that they not only *could* converse in Arabic, but that on academic or diplomatic subjects they would be *obliged* to do so, for neither colloquial (even if the other had learned it for some reason) would easily suffice to carry such conversations. Even with a given speech-area, e.g. Egypt, two civil servants or two scientists would be obliged to supplement their common colloquial with a good deal of Arabic, at least if they were discussing economic development or atomic fission rather than, say, the state of the weather or the price of meat! At times, moreover, two such persons might find it simpler to go over entirely to Arabic. Again, an Arabic newspaper, book or play written in Syria is understood by all educated Arabs throughout the Arab world: but even if the same newspaper or book were read aloud, or the play acted, it would not be properly intelligible to poorly educated (to say nothing of illiterate) Arabs, whether in Syria or elsewhere. At the same time, if the Syrian author used the Arabic alphabet to represent his own colloquial speech (supposing that this were adequate to the ideas involved), his book or play or news items would be intelligible to his fellow-countrymen only if they knew enough Arabic to read the letters, or if someone who could do so were to read aloud to them; non-Syrian Arabs, however, would suffer varying degrees of incomprehension in either event. Finally, in this all too short list of instances and implications, an Iraqi political leader, making an important speech, has often to choose whether he wishes to be wholly intelligible to all educated Arabs everywhere or to all of his own countrymen, or in varying degrees to both: in which case he will speak, respectively, Arabic or Iraqi colloquial or an amalgam of the two.

10. *Egypt's special position.* In its search for unity, the Arab world is confronted linguistically with two basic choices: either Arabic must become the general speech, as well as being the standard written language and the official vehicle of important utterance and of the Islamic faith; or one colloquial must receive definitive written form and be accepted by all Arabs as standard for virtually all purposes. Either choice, put thus, is somewhat utopian; the first is favoured by the spread of education, but the second would meet with all-too-certain local hostility and cultural and religious opposition. Some ultimate blending is no doubt to be expected, but the event may well be far distant. Meanwhile, Egyptian colloquial is gaining a special prestige of its own inasmuch as Egypt's leading position in the Arab world draws thither many non-Egyptian Arab students, political figures and others, who often reside in the country for years on end: clearly, while such persons often use Arabic, pure or mixed, in their professional concerns, they have no choice but to learn the Egyptian colloquial for everyday affairs, and this means that that speech-form is steadily being disseminated (at least among intellectuals) throughout the whole Arab world. Indeed, a similar process appears to be developing throughout the non-Arab, and even the non-Islamic, worlds of Africa and Asia as more and more Afro-Asians, of all races, languages and religions, come to regard Egypt as a leading centre of "non-Western" civilisation. Egyptian pre-eminence in the entertainment industry (cf. the USA's role in the English-speaking world and beyond) is also a powerful instrument here. The recent accord with Israel is, of course, bound to prejudice Egypt's cultural position in the Arab world, at least temporarily.

11. *The language of this course.* As has already been suggested at the close of para. 6, this course is designed to take adult, literate students through the first major stage of learning to read Arabic. It has no immediate concern with any colloquial language (though students who have worked through the course may find themselves at some advantage if they later try to learn a colloquial form, either under specialised guidance or in the region concerned). Something more must now be said about Arabic itself. In its present form, the language has been written and articulated for some 1,400 years, over an area extending at different times from China to Spain, from Central Asia to Central Africa. It has, moreover, been used for an even wider variety of purposes: religious, historical, philosophic, geographical, poetic and scientific (to name only some more important categories); at a somewhat more trivial level, in many cases, it has also been employed for keeping records and accounts, notebooks and travel diaries, as well as in newspapers, magazines and pamphlets, and in radio and television programmes. But through all these ages, places and purposes, it has preserved a general unity and uniformity quite unparallelled in, say, English or French or German. Obviously, each of the main categories listed above will have its special style and technical vocabulary; equally evident is the fact that a modern television programme on the space age will use some words either unknown to a tenth-century Spanish Arabic love-poet or to a fifteenth-century Egyptian historian, or at least holding a different meaning for them. But all these types of Arabic form one language in a way that the languages of *Beowulf*, *The Canterbury Tales* and a Churchill speech do not. It is the *essential character of this one language* that will be drawn in the present course. We shall not concern ourselves with any of the rarer and more abstruse usages of the so-called Classical Period (roughly AD 600 to 1800 in its widest assessment), nor shall we burden the student with some of the Modern Period's more turgid styles or ephemeral items of vocabulary. What we shall do, rather, is to present a sufficient sampling of real, representative, basic, "neutral" Arabic to enable a learner to proceed more surely and speedily towards a chosen field of specialisation at the end of the course.

12. *Various practical counsels*

(*a*) Trust this course entirely, at least until you are well along in it. It differs in many important respects from all other courses, and premature comparisons will lead only to confusion.

(*b*) Treat everything in the course as essential. It represents in every detail an absolute minimum.

(*c*) If you cannot grasp the first explanation of a *principle*, do not worry overmuch: try to do so on some subsequent recurrence. But if you do not learn the "*memory material*" as it comes, you will soon lose your way and become frustrated.

(*d*) For convenience and variety, most chapters will contain some grammatical ideas, some "memory material", and some genuine Arabic on which to practise. The learner, however, will probably find it most useful to himself (and a great aid to learning) to group the material ultimately under such headings as: Grammatical Ideas (or Syntax); Variant-Form Tables (or Morphology); Vocabulary (under Roots: see para. 18); and Arabic Texts.

(*e*) Getting to know a language is an organic process. Constant and patient watering, hoeing, pruning and weeding, so to speak, are essential: you cannot work satisfactorily in fits and starts, or make last-minute spurts. You cannot miss out or neglect essential steps and expect all to come out well. Remember, too, that language-learning is not always a logical or an intelligent process: a gifted mathematician may be able to work much out for himself, a quick-witted philosopher or social scientist may succeed by sheer quality of mind; but these things will not help you in language work if you have not absorbed the language into yourself by long and steady effort.

(*f*) Collaboration between teacher and student is unquestionably essential, but it is not an equal or symmetrical partnership. Class time is primarily for guidance: drill, practice and repetition are primarily the student's responsibility, to be undertaken in his own time.

(*g*) Be prepared to feel embarrassed and annoyed at your own blunders, but do not let them deter you from continuing to participate. Be ready, too, for recurrent feelings of panic and depression: they should grow less frequent after the first six months or so.

(*h*) Remember that in most cases your teachers will have gone through all your experiences long before you did: follow their steps, but do not expect *them* to come back to *you* and sit commiserating with you by the wayside on the difficulties of the job you are both trying to do!

(*i*) Try to approach the language humbly and without prejudice. Ask yourself constantly *what* the users of Arabic do, and *how* they do it: to ask *why* they do it is to ask a question that is not really valid linguistically, though it may be of legitimate concern to psychologists, anthropologists, social scientists and philosophers. Remember that *all* languages are equally peculiar, though their native users tend to think of them as thoroughly normal and efficient. Some users of Arabic even regard it as "God's own language": at least aim at appreciating its wonderful structure and economy.

3

Arabic script; The alphabet; Roots and patterns; Layout and punctuation

13. *Difficulties of the script.* For students accustomed only to the Latin alphabet some difficulties immediately present themselves. First, the Arabic script is written from right to left – though this problem sounds more alarming than it really is. Secondly, it is a cursive script, i.e. there is still no special "print" or "inscription" form, in which the individual letters stand detached. (In consequence, Arabic printing and typing is somewhat cumbersome; but even though every effort is made there to reproduce the cursive, written hand, a keen-eyed student will often notice minute breaks between the letters, which are imposed by practical, mechanical limitations; a more important result, both in writing and machine reproduction, is that most of the letters necessarily undergo various distortions of shape according to their position in a word and the shape of the letters to which they are connected.) Thirdly, several of the letters, representing quite different sounds, are identical in shape, being distinguished only by one, two or three dots (or points) placed above or below them. Fourthly, there are, and have long been, in use several different *styles* of script: while they vary only in minor details, they often appear disconcertingly different to the learner when he first meets them. The script used in this course will be either a "neutral", clear hand (much too clear for use in ordinary fast writing) or the standard typeface found on most typewriters. When the student is thoroughly accustomed to both of these, he should lose no opportunity of trying (preferably with the time-saving help of someone more experienced) to familiarise himself with other variations: in most cases, he will be agreeably surprised at the small number of differences, their relatively trivial nature and the speed with which it is possible to master them. (We are speaking, of course, of scripts that are in any case legible in themselves: some handwriting in particular is bound to be almost or completely illegible, and the student need not be ashamed of being unable to do in Arabic what he likewise cannot do in the case of his own mother-tongue!)

14. *The alphabet.* The Arabic alphabet derives from the same ultimate origin as our own, but the passage of time has wiped out any resemblances that might be helpful to the learner. The 28 basic letters are *all consonants*, with the exception of the first (*alif*), which has no fixed value of its own, but serves in combination (actual or hypothetical) with other signs to indicate a variety of sounds. Omitting the *alif* for the time being, we shall first work through the other 27 letters in the order they normally assume (which must, of course, be learned for consulting dictionaries and other alphabetically arranged reference works): for the most part, these letters will be found to run in "families", differing (as mentioned in para. 13) only by the placing of points.

15. *Non-alphabetic signs.* There is in Arabic a whole series of non-alphabetic signs, added above or below the consonant letters to make the reading of the word either less ambiguous or absolutely certain. It must be emphasised at the outset that writers of Arabic never normally use these signs without very special reasons: the sacred Koran is always fully "signed" to avoid any misreading, and the same is often true of poetry, and sometimes of foreign or unfamiliar words, and of beginners' manuals (at least in the early stages). In the present course, we shall defer a systematic study of these signs until we have covered the whole consonantal alphabet.

16. *Vowels.* The majority of these non-alphabetic signs relate to vowels, and the warning given in para. 15 applies particularly to these. The *writer* of Arabic does *not* ordinarily provide the reader with *any short vowels at all* (an example of a short vowel is *oo* in "soot"): it is the *reader's* need and duty to *supply* these as he reads, either by writing them in, or (more conveniently) by inserting them aloud or in his mind. Long vowels (an example of a long vowel is *oo* in "boot") and diphthongs (i.e. double vowels like *ou* in "house" or *i* in "sign") are not normally written either – at least, they are not written *expressly*, though certain consonants (particularly *w* and *y*) are regularly used to "hint" at them, but always with some measure of ambiguity.

17. *Consonantal Arabic is normal Arabic.* Since the overwhelming majority of Arabic texts, throughout the ages and at the present day, consist only of consonants, this course proposes to teach students to read (as far as possible from the very outset) only consonantal Arabic. A student who depends on the kindness of the writer to mark the vowels for him will be able to read small children's books or other specially prepared material, but he will never read normal Arabic with even approximate ease. Learning to animate the consonants (or, as Arabic says, "to move" them) is a long apprenticeship, and the learner cannot begin too early to subject himself to it. If he delays too long, he may lose his nerve altogether.

18. *Roots and patterns*. One basic aid to reading with at least practical accuracy of vowelling is to have trained oneself to understand quickly, by a grasp of structure, the probable *function* of a given word in a sentence. We shall therefore pay much attention to examining the limited, stereotyped structure-categories into which most Arabic sentences can be fitted. There is also, however, another aid, which is peculiar to Arabic itself (or at least to the Semitic family of languages to which Arabic belongs). This is a knowledge of "roots" and "patterns". Nearly all Arabic words, no matter how long and how complicated (or how short and apparently simple), can be theoretically reduced to "roots" consisting of three "radical" consonants: for example, *mutakallimūna* is reduced to KLM and *qif* to WQF. Thus the radicals KTB, in this order, invest the Arabic words in which they are found with the idea of "writing": *maKTaB* ("office"), *KāTiB* ("clerk"), *maKTūB* ("written" or "document"), and *yaKTuBu* ("he writes") are all patterns based on this same tri-radical root. Moreover, these patterns, and hundreds more like them, are valid for a virtually unlimited number of other similar roots: so, if KTB connotes "writing", and QTL "killing"; and if *KāTiB* means a "clerk", then one is not surprised to learn that *QāTiL* means a "murderer". Similarly, to take the other three patterns as given above, *maQTaL* means "a place where somebody was slain" ("scene of the crime", or some such term in English); *maQTūL* means "killed" or a "slain man", "victim"; and *yaQTuLu* means "he kills". As we have just said, there are literally hundreds of these patterns, all endowed with a special shade of meaning in varying degrees of precision. This seems at first to the beginner to represent a formidable tax on the memory, and it is certainly true that he must begin to memorise the most essential patterns from the very first days of his study of Arabic, maintaining this practice through something like two years. There are, however, two large compensations for this labour: one has just been described, namely the ability to diagnose often by pattern alone the probable pronunciation, function and meaning of the word in context; the other is that one is time and again spared memorising a great many disparate items of vocabulary – the Arabic words for "remedy", "hospital", "healer" and "clinic", for example all come from the same root and are formed according to well-established patterns. It is not true to suggest, as some enthusiasts do, that one can be almost mathematically certain about these matters (assuredly, one must not "make up" one's own words by patterns); but there is no question that the system of patterns in the long run makes the learning of Arabic easier than many other languages, as well as providing in itself an interesting intellectual experience. One might add that, as matters stand at present, an ability to deduce the root from the pattern, and to decide which pattern has been imposed on the root, is a prerequisite skill for the use of an Arabic dictionary; in the latter, words are commonly arranged not in continuous alphabetical order, but in alphabetical order of the roots from which they derive.

19. *Layout and punctuation*. Until fairly recently, most Arabic books and other writings were not arranged in paragraphs, and they had little or no punctuation. In recent years, however, it has become fairly general to try to arrange Arabic texts in much the same way as is done in the West. As far as paragraphing is concerned, this innovation is welcome, since it places far less strain on the eye, and enables one to locate a given passage much more quickly than was possible formerly. Punctuation, however, is a less distinct blessing to written Arabic. Developing without punctuation, the language has over the centuries come to accommodate itself to this lack, and to use certain other devices that fulfil the same function. In many cases, Western students find that they can make neither head nor tail of a modern Arabic writer's attempt to punctuate his text, and they often discern his meaning more easily by ignoring the punctuation completely. However, punctuation has doubtless come to stay in Arabic, and may in time have its own effect on the construction of Arabic sentences. The learner can perhaps do no better than to proceed warily with punctuation, being always ready to try disregarding it if he finds that the text seems to be making little sense by observing it.

20. *Revision.* The learner is advised to re-read this chapter (and also Chapters 1 and 2) more than once, for it treats of a number of basic principles inherent in the Arabic language which will be referred to again and again throughout the course.

4

The families B, J, D and R

21. *Scheme of treatment*. Before combining these families, and ultimately others, in some real examples of Arabic words (this being the central purpose of the present part of the course), each family of consonant letters will be described in terms of the following:

(*a*) The *several pronunciations* signified by the different members of the family: note the standard latinised forms (certain variations are possible) used to transliterate the Arabic symbols. Since this is not necessarily a course for specialists, indications of the pronunciation will be approximate and non-technical only.[1] Ultimately, for pronunciation, nothing can replace the guidance of an Arabic-speaker, or preferably several Arabic-speakers, but it should be remembered that any individual's colloquial speech may tend to "colour" his pronunciation and

[1] References to "English speech" normally denote Standard Southern British.

intonation of Standard Arabic (cf. paras. 8 and 9). Films, radio, television and recordings are all more or less satisfactory substitutes for live contact.

(*b*) The *essential shape* of the letter-family. (It may here be remarked that there is no distinction in Arabic between capitals and small letters.)

(*c*) The *main modifications* effected by the position of any particular shape within a given word (see para. 13). On the face of things, it will be obvious that *three* positions are involved (the student should remember constantly to think, as well as to write, from right to left): at the beginning of a word (*initial*), in the middle (*medial*), and at the end (*final*). However, probably to avoid confusion with other similarly shaped letters, 6 of the 28 *do not join to the left*, and two further consequences flow from this: first, when the non-joining, broken letter occurs as the last-but-one letter in a word, the last letter itself needs a *fourth* modification, the *isolated* shape (many final and isolated shapes have an extra "flourish" to indicate that the word is complete); secondly, the non-joining, broken letters themselves have effectively only *two* shapes – the isolated (found *always initially*, and also both medially and finally after another non-joining letter) and the final (found both medially and finally after a joining letter). This sounds complicated, but examples below will show its complete logicality. (See also Note after para. 27.)

(*d*) The *placing of the point or points* that alone may distinguish one member of the family from another (cf. para. 13). It will become obvious that what ultimately distinguishes each of the 28 letters from its 27 fellows is a fluctuating combination of factors (*b*), (*c*) and (*d*), with sometimes one, sometimes the other assuming overwhelming, or total, importance.

22. *The* B *family*

(*a*) The *members* are *b*, *t*, *th* (and also *n* and *y*, though these have become separated from the rest of the family and placed towards the end of the alphabet, where they will be treated in their proper place). Acceptable *pronunciation* of the first two sounds involved may be conveyed by reference respectively to the English words "boy" and "toy"; the third sound is pronounced as in the English word "thing", but variations may be heard throughout the Arab world ranging from a *t* sound to that of *s* (cf. poor French or German pronunciation of this English word itself, "ting", "sing", "zing" etc.). In general, it may be said that Arabic enunciation of consonants is sharper than in most varieties of English speech: in particular, the Arabic *t* is pronounced with the tongue behind the upper teeth, and not behind the upper gumridge as in most English speech-forms.

(*b*) The *essential shape* of this family is the simplest in the whole alphabet: a short vertical, or left-leaning, stroke above the line; but, being simple and small, it is very easily overlooked or confused with other signs, and hence the vital importance in this family of the distinguishing points (see sub-para. (*d*) below).

(*c*) The *four positions modify the shape* of this family as follows:

Initial 

Medial

Final  (shallow, dish-like curve)

Isolated  " " "

(*d*) Of the three letters involved, *b* places *one* dot immediately *below*; *t* has *two* immediately *above* (usually side by side); and *th* has *three* also immediately *above* (usually arranged in a triangle). Since in each case only one letter from other families shares each of these arrangements of points (respectively *j*, *q* and *sh*), and as each of these other letters is in Arabic very different from the "short vertical, or left-leaning, stroke" just described, it follows that these dot-placings virtually serve *in themselves* to identify *b*, *t* and *th*. Thus, they compensate in large measure for this family's lack of essential character.

23. *The* J *family*

(*a*) The *members* are *j*, *ḥ* and *kh*. A standard *pronunciation* can be indicated for *j* by reference to the English word "just", but Egyptians and others commonly pronounce the sound as *g* ("gust") and Syro-Palestinians and others like the sound of *s* in "pleasure". The sound transliterated by *ḥ* refers to a *heavy, smooth* breathing, not easily found in most varieties of English speech. The sign *kh* represents a *heavy, scraped* breathing, a sort of throat-clearing, as in the Scottish word "loch" or the German "Dach". It must be realised that this is one sound, not two, though two Latin letters are commonly used to transliterate it.

(*b*) The *essential shape* of this family is that of a crocodile's jaws facing to the left, on or slightly above the line, as:

It cannot easily be mistaken for the essential shape of most other families.

(*c*) The *four positions modify the shape* of this family as follows:

Initial 

Medial  (often led into from *above*)

Final  (hangs below line; often led into from *above*)

Isolated  (hangs below line)

(*d*) Of the three members of this family, *j* places *one* dot midway *below* the letter (or in the centre of the final and the isolated flourishes); *ḥ* has *no dot at all* in Arabic, and *kh* places *one* dot *above* the letter. In this family, it will be seen that the dots serve to distinguish the members from each other rather than from the rest of the alphabet, since the family shape is characteristic.

24. *The* D *family*

(*a*) The *members* are *d* and *dh*. The first is *pronounced* more or less as in English, but with the tongue behind the upper teeth rather than behind the upper gumridge; the second is either like the initial sound of the English word "then" or varies with different speakers from *d* to *z* (cf. these remarks to those on *t* and *th*, their unvoiced equivalents, in para. 22 (*a*)).

(*b*) The *essential shape* of this family may be described as like two sides of a small equilateral triangle open to the left, thus:

د د د

This family is properly written on or above the line, but some confusion often arises with other letters (notably members of the *R* family) which should always hang below the line.

(*c*) The *D* family is one of those having only *two modified forms* (see the explanation in para. 21(*c*)). The *isolated* form is roughly thus: د and the *final* form appears thus: ـد.... (Read Note after para. 27.)

(*d*) Of the two members forming this family, *d* has *no dot at all*, while *dh* places *one* dot *above* the short sloping upright.

25. *The* R *family*

(*a*) The *members* are *r* and *z*. The *pronunciation* of both is not unlike those usually given to these letters in various types of English, save that the *r* is trilled as in "northern" or Scottish speech. Furthermore, *r* tends to "thicken" accompanying vowels.

(*b*) The *essential shape* of this family is that of a crescent or scimitar hanging below the line (cf. para. 24(*b*), as:

ر

Not only is this family liable to some confusion with the preceding one, but it is even more similar to the one-family representative *w*, near the end of the alphabet.

(*c*) Once again, we are dealing with a family having only *two modifications* to the shape. The *isolated* form is roughly ر , the *final* form appears as ـر . (Read Note after para. 27.)

(*d*) Again, of the two members of this family *r* carries *no point at all*, while *z* carries *one* point immediately *above* the top of the stroke.

26. *Some words formed from the families* B, J, D *and* R

Handwritten	Typeset	Consonants used	Possible pronunciation (including vowels and double consonants)	Meaning
بحر / بحر	بحر	bḥr	baḥr	sea
حرب	حرب	ḥrb	ḥarb	war
درب	درب	drb	darb	lane, narrow pass, defile
حرث	حرث	ḥrth	ḥuritha	it was ploughed
حدث	حدث	ḥdth	ḥadatha ḥadutha	it happened he was young
جدد	جدد	jdd	jaddada	he renewed
جد	جد	jd	jadd jidd	grandfather seriousness
خرج	حرج	khrj	kharaja	he went out
خبر	خبر	khbr	khabar	news
حجر	حجر	ḥjr	ḥajar	rock, stone
تجر / تجر	تجر	tjr	tajara	he traded
درر	درر	drr	durar	pearls
بر	بر	br	barr birr	dry land piety
بحث / بحث	بحث	bḥth	baḥth	research investigation
ثبت	ثبت	thbt	thabbata	he confirmed
رد	رد	rd	radda	he rejected
زبد	زبد	zbd	zabada	he churned (milk)
بزر	بزر	bzr	bazara	he sowed (seed)
خرب	خرب	khrb	khariba	it became ruined
خبز	خبز	khbz	khubz	bread
جذب	جذب	jdhb	judhiba	it was dragged
جزر	جزر	jzr	jazara	he butchered

27. *Remarks on above word-table.* A few remarks should be made about the above list (and those that come later). First, it is only a *sample* of possible combinations of these families to make some ordinary words, some of which might be memorised. Secondly, stress is not shown (it will be discussed in Chapter 8), since all the above words are either of one syllable only or have their stress on the first syllable. Thirdly, it should be understood that the full, vowelled reading in the fourth column, and hence the English meaning in the fifth, represent only the most plausible and useful choices: even where alternatives are actually shown, still other readings and meanings are usually possible. (Remember that while these words appear exactly as they would in a real text, when you actually come to read Arabic you will be helped by context, by experience, by a grasp of grammatical function, and by a knowledge of patterns: at the moment, you are expected only to read, with difficulty, the consonantal "skeleton".) Fourthly, attention should be paid to a slight alternative writing-deviation, three times used in the first column, where the *B* family precedes the *J* family. Fifthly, the learner should compare the discrepancies apparent between handwriting and typing, trying to become used to both. Sixthly, the repetition of several "patterns" (cf. para. 18) should be noted in the fourth column: you do not "know" these patterns yet, but you may notice already that they endow Arabic with a certain monotony (in foreign eyes and ears) or a wonderful wealth of rhyme and assonance (in Arab opinion). Seventhly, remember to try to "thicken" the vowels immediately associated with *r*: *a* and *u* both tend towards *o*, and *i* towards the vague English *io* in "vision" or the indistinct *e* in "talent". Finally, note that where most typefaces lie more or less along a straight line, in some handwriting *each word* tends to slope from NE to SW, so that the overall effect (exaggerated) is something like this:

 (imaginary line from right to left)

(Traditionally, Arabic script does not space letters and words as precisely as do scripts like Latin, which have evolved along the lines of printed and inscriptional texts.)

NOTE: Where a non-joining letter is immediately followed by a joining letter in any other position than at the very end of a word (where the isolated form would be required, as explained), then the joining letter must necessarily begin the new sequence in its initial form (see for example the word for "he churned" in para. 26), not in the medial form, which requires joining both ways.

5

The families S and thick Ṣ/Ṭ

28. *The* S *family*

(*a*) The *members* are *s* and *sh*, both *pronounced* much as in English, but (as always) with sharper enunciation.

(*b*) The *essential shape* of this family is that of three short teeth or prongs above the line, as: ...سـ...ـسـ. However, in many styles of writing these teeth are flattened into one long stroke; this is easily recognised if prolonged sufficiently, but may sometimes be overlooked or misread by a learner.

(*c*) The *four positions modify the shape* as follows:

Initial	...سـ	
Medial	..ـسـ..	
Final	ـس..	(hangs below line)
Isolated	س	" " "

(*d*) *S* has *no dot* at all, *sh* places *three dots triangularly above* the body of the shape. (Cf. the remark at the end of para. 22(*d*).)

29. *The thick* Ṣ/Ṭ *family*

(*a*) The members are *ṣ* and *ḍ*; and *ṭ* and *ẓ*. Compared with the "ordinary" sounds of *s*, *d*, *t*, and *z*, as given in paras. 22, 24, 25 and 28, the present *sounds* are not "spat out", but retained "plummily" in the middle of the mouth: this has a characteristic "thickening" effect on the vowels (cf. para 25(*a*)), so that while for example *saif* sounds something like the English "safe", *ṣaif* sounds more like "soyf".

(*b*) The *essential shape* of the family is a sort of poised egg, as: ـصـ . But whereas the thick-*Ṣ* branch completes the ellipse with a "hook" to the left (ـصـ), the thick-*Ṭ* branch keeps the line smooth, but dangles a loose, thin, vertical stroke over the shape, not always in contact (ط).

(*c*) *The four positions modify the shape thus:*

	Thick-Ṣ branch		*Thick-Ṭ Branch*
Initial	...صـ		....طـ
Medial	...ـصـ...		...ـطـ...
Final	ـص...	(hangs below line)	ـط...
Isolated	ص	" " "	ط

(*d*) Thick ṣ and thick ṭ themselves carry *no dots*. Thick ḍ and thick ẓ each carry *one above* the shape, somewhat to the left.

30. *Some words formed from the families so far*

Handwritten	Typeset	Consonants used	Possible Pronunciation (including vowels and double consonants)	Meaning
درس	درس	drs	darasa dars	he studied lesson
جسر	جسر	jsr	jisr	bridge, embank-ment
سرج	سرج	srj	sarj	saddle
بصر	بصر	bṣr	baṣar	sight
صبر	صبر	ṣbr	ṣabr	patience
خطر	خطر	khṭr	khaṭar	danger
حطب	حطب	ḥṭb	ḥaṭab	firewood
حضر	حضر	ḥḍr	ḥaḍara	he was present
ضرب	ضرب	ḍrb	ḍaraba	he struck
ضرر	ضرر	ḍrr	ḍarar	damage
خط	خط	khṭ	khaṭṭ	line, handwriting
حظ	حظ	ḥẓ	ḥaẓẓ	luck, share
شرب	شرب	shrb	shariba	he drank
بشر	بشر	bshr	bashar	human-being(s)
شرط	شرط	shrṭ	sharṭ	condition, requisite

31. *Remarks on above word-table.* Virtually all the above words have some degree of vowel-thickening due to the presence of at least one thickening-consonant. Re-read para. 27 in so far as it applies here.

6

The families '/F and K

32. *The '/F family*

(*a*) The *members* are: ' and *gh*; and *f* and *q*. The third member is pronounced much as in English; but something needs to be said about the *pronunciation* of the other three, for they have few or no parallels in English. The first, ', represents a voiced form of *ḥ* (see para. 23(*a*)), a sort of throaty gulp. (A teacher or a native-speaker is virtually indispensable to help with this sound.) The second, *gh*, is a sort of voiced form of *kh* (see again para. 23(*a*)), and it represents the Parisian throat-rolled "r", also heard in certain forms of Scottish-English speech. *Q* is a "k" sound, well back in the throat, sharp and without scrape: by contrast with the "simple" *k* sound (to come in para. 33), it thickens the vowels most noticeably.

(*b*) It is difficult to speak of the *essential shape* of this family, but it might be described as a small, squashed or broken, circle above the line.

(*c*) The *four positions modify the shape* as follows:

	'-branch		*F-branch*	
Initial	...عـ		...ٯـ	
Medial[1]	...ـعـ...		...ـٯـ...	
Final	ـع...	(hangs below line)	ـڡ... ـٯ...	(dish-like for *f*,
Isolated	ع	" " "	ڡ ٯ	deeper for *q*)

(*d*) The letter ' itself takes *no dot*, *gh* takes *one dot above* the shape; *f* takes *one dot above*, and *q two dots above* (though various North African-Moorish styles follow other schemes for these last two letters).

33. *The* K *family*

(*a*) The *members* are *k* and *l*, both *pronounced* somewhat as in English speech: the *l* must be clear and light, not tending towards *w* as in some less acceptable English speech forms, e.g. "buw" for "bull".

(*b*) The *essential shape* of the family is a long vertical, or left-leaning, stroke above the line.

(*c*) The *four positions modify the shape* only minimally, and *no dots* are used to distinguish the two members. However, various other devices employed render it necessary to show the commonest forms of the two members in two separate tables:

[1] There is a risk of confusion here between the two branches.

	K		*L*	
Initial	كـ....	(note pennant above)	لـ...	
Medial	....ـكـ....	" " "	...ـلـ...	
Final	....ـك	(note pennant dropped	...ـل	(hangs below line)
Isolated	ك	and inset squiggle)	ل	" " "

34. *Some words formed from the families*

Handwritten	Typeset	Consonants used	Possible pronunciation (including vowels and double consonants)	Meaning
عرب	عرب	‘rb	‘arab	Arabs
غرب	غرب	ghrb	gharb	West
صعب	صعب	ṣ‘b	ṣa‘b	difficult
قرب	قرب	qrb	qurb	nearness
بقر	بقر	bqr	baqar	cattle
فرق	فرق	frq	farq	distinction
ثقل	ثقل	thql	thiql	weight
قل	قل	ql	qalla	it diminished
شجر	شجر	shjr	shajar	trees
عصر	عصر	‘ṣr	‘aṣr	era, late afternoon
تل	تل	tl	tall	hill, "tell"
ظل	ظل	ẓl	ẓill	shade
شكل	شكل	shkl	shakl	form, shape
سلك	سلك	slk	silk	wire
طلق	طلق	ṭlq	ṭallaqa	he divorced
رطل	رطل	rṭl	raṭl	name of weight of varying value, "ratl", "rotl" (example of attempt to indicate vowel-thickening)
فلك	فلك	flk	falak	sky, heavens
لطف	لطف	lṭf	luṭf	kindness, graciousness

Handwritten	Typeset	Consonants used	Possible pronunciation (including vowels and double consonants)	Meaning
فرس	فرس	frs	faras	horse, mare
فرش	فرش	frsh	farsh	carpeting, furnishing
شرف	شرف	shrf	sharaf	nobility, honour
شرق	شرق	shrq	sharq	East
سفر	سفر	sfr	safar	journey
صغر	صغر	ṣghr	ṣaghura	he was small
رعد	رعد	r'd	ra'd	thunder
صفر	صفر	ṣfr	ṣifr	zero
فرع	فرع	fr'	far'	branch
غفر	غفر	ghfr	ghafara	he pardoned
غفل	غفل	ghfl	ghafala	he was careless

35. *Remarks on above word-table.* Remember once more to try to thicken the vowels where appropriate in the above list. Once again, re-read para. 27 and apply it here.

7

The orphans and rejects

36. *Remainder of consonantal alphabet*. In this chapter we shall examine the remaining five consonants, three of which belong to no family at all, while the other two have been displaced from the *B* family. All five have one or more peculiarities apiece to be noted.

37. *The pronunciation of the letter* m. This is much as in English. Its *essential shape* is that of a "blob" or a "bump" above the line: as a general rule, beginners may assume that any letter they tend to overlook or cannot place is an *m*. Its *four modifications* are as below:

Initial ...مـ
Medial ...ـمـ...
Final ـم...
Isolated م

The question of *dots* does not arise.

38. *The pronunciation of the letter* n. This is also much as in English. Its *essential shape* is that of the *B* family, but it has a deeper *modified curve* than the standard dish-shape of that family in the final and isolated forms:

Initial ...نـ
Medial ...ـنـ...
Final ـن
Isolated ن

It will be observed that *one dot* is placed *above*.

39. *The pronunciation of the letter* h. This is, again, much as in English. It has *no one essential shape*, varying from a small circle above the line, through a "lip" below the line, to a "butterfly" lying either above or both above and below. Its *four modified forms* are shown below in typical styles, but the student may meet others:

Initial ...هـ ...هـ
Medial ...ـهـ... ...ـهـ...

Final	ـه	ـه
Isolated	ه	ه

There are normally *no dots*, but see Chapter 9 for a special final use of this letter with two dots above (the "feminine ending" or "bound-*t*").

40. *The pronunciation of the consonantal* w. This is much as in English "wet" (its other, more extensive uses will be discussed in Chapter 8). Its *essential shape* is akin to that of the *R* family (cf. para. 25) but it has a "head" and forms a fuller curve below the line, thus:

Isolated	و
Final	ـو

Once again, it will be observed, we are dealing with a non-joining letter, having only *two modifications*. There are *no dots*. (Read Note after para. 27.)

41. *The pronunciation of consonantal* y. This is as in English "yes" (its other, more extensive uses will be discussed in Chapter 8). Its *essential shape* is that of the *B* family, but it has unique *modified curves* of its own in the final and isolated forms:

Initial	يـ	
Medial	ـيـ	
Final	ـي	ـي
Isolated	ي	

It will be observed that *two dots* are placed *below* the letter. These dots *may* often be casually omitted below the unmistakable final and isolated forms. (In Chapter 8 we shall see that the dots under these two forms *must* be omitted in certain special circumstances; while in Chapter 9 we shall meet one situation where the dots are normally omitted also under the initial and medial forms.)

42. *Further words from all the consonant families*

Handwritten	Typeset	Consonants used	Possible pronunciation (including vowels and double consonants)	Meaning
وجد	وجد	wjd	wajada wujida	he found; it was found, it existed
لهم	لهم	lhm	la-hum	for them (men)

Handwritten	Typeset	Consonants used	Possible pronunciation (including vowels and double consonants)	Meaning
لهن	لهن	lhn	la-húnna	for them (women)
نصر	نصر	nṣr	naṣr	victory
نسر	نسر	nsr	nasr	eagle
مغرب	مغرب	mghrb	maghrib	West
مشرق	مشرق	mshrq	mashriq	East
لك	لك	lk	la-ka la-ki	for you (masc.) for you (fem.)
لكم	لكم	lkm	la-kum	for you (men)
لكن	لكن	lkn	la-kúnna	for you (women)
فهم	فهم	fhm	fahm	understanding
هلكتم	هلكتم	hlktm	haláktum	you (men) have perished
وجهه	وجهه	wjhh	wajhu-hu	his face
منزلهم	منزلهم	mnzlhm	manzilu-hum	their home
ذرو	ذرو	dhrw	dharw	dispersal, scattering
تمر	تمر	tmr	tamr	dates (fruit)
ثمر	ثمر	thmr	thamar	fruit
يبس	يبس	ybs	yabisa	it was dry
بني	بني	bny	buniya	it was built
سير	سير	syr	suyyira	he was sent

43. *Remarks on above word-table.* Two new things should be noted: first, the stress-mark on the transliteration of three words, these being the only cases so far of polysyllabic words not stressed on the first syllable (stress will be discussed in Chapter 8); and secondly, the hyphens used in several transliterations, to indicate that what appears as a single unit *in Arabic* is really made up of interchangeable components.

The student's attention may be drawn at this point to the fact that several letters involving small circles (ʻ, *gh*, *f*, *q*, *m*, and so on) will be found to have the circles sometimes clear, sometimes blocked in: whatever correct practice may once have been in each case, the variation now is unimportant: where letters are blocked in it is often because the type is old or dirty!

Once again, re-read para. 27 and apply it here.

8

The vowels in Arabic

44. *Short vowels and their sounds.* As already indicated (paras. 15–17), the *short vowels are never normally written,* while the long vowels and diphthongs are only hinted at ambiguously. The student will have noticed for himself from the transliteration that all the words so far used have only short vowels, and that these seem to be only three in number: *a*, *i* and *u*. (Approximate equivalents for these may be found thus: for *a* in the English[1] words "bat", "but" or "bet", depending on general vowel-colouring, but often a compromise falling between all three; for *i* in "bit", and for *u* in "book".) However, it will be remembered that several consonants (para. 25 onwards) have a thickening effect on neighbouring vowels, and this extends the range of *vowel-sounds* very considerably. Thus, with such consonants *a* and *u* both tend from different sides *towards* something like English "o" as in "hot": for example while *kalb* sounds rather like *kelb*, the word *qalb* is more *qolb*; contrast likewise *fulk* (with the sound *foolk*) and *qufl* (with the sound *qofl*). With the same thickening consonants, *i* may either become like an English "e" (e.g. *silm* is as it would be read in English, but *'ilm* sounds rather like *uh-elm*), or it may tend towards the "vague" vowel of English (thus the *i* in *ṣifa* sounds like the unstressed vowel in "pleasure" (*plezh?*), "vision" (*vizh?n*) or "Saint Joan" (*S?nt*)).[1] Remember that these distinctions between thick and thin are not just a frill, but vital to differentiating the meaning of quite unrelated words: *kalb* above means "dog", *qalb* is "heart"! The difference in sound seems as obvious to an Arabic-speaker as that between "boat", "boot", "bit", "beat", "bet" etc. to our ear. Bear in mind, too, that the indications given here are crude and unscientific: phoneticians and linguists have an almost exact way of describing these sounds, just as musicians can describe musical notes. It is assumed here that the learner has no such background and cannot, for the time being, profit by native-speakers.

45. *The marking of short vowels.* If absolutely necessary, short vowels (irrespective of actual pronunciation) are marked thus: *a* by a short, thin, right-leaning stroke above the preceding consonant; *i* by a similar stroke *below* the preceding consonant; and *u* by a small comma (a tiny *w*, in fact: see para. 40) *above* the preceding consonant. Where it is, again, absolutely essential to indicate that a

[1] As stated earlier, "English Speech" here denotes Standard Southern British.

consonant has *no vowel*, a minute circle or near-circle may be placed *above* the preceding consonant. Here are samples marked on a thick *ṭ*:

طَ *ṭa*
طِ *ṭi*
طُ *ṭu*
طْ *ṭ* (and definitely no following vowel)

Practise these marks on the words in the lists following the various families (paras. 26, 30, 34 and 42). *One word of warning*: in some styles of writing, two dots are indicated by a thickened bar and three dots by a mark something like the no-vowel sign; remember that the vowel-signs themselves are rarely written and should be thin, so that risk of confusion is not great. In ornamental script, particularly in book titles, the vowels are often put in amid a great deal of functionally superfluous material: reading Arabic book titles is a fairly advanced art, so the beginner should not be discouraged!

46. *Diphthongs.* These are sounds made of two vowels combined. Some languages have a wide variety of them (English, particularly Cockney English, has virtually no single vowels at all, as normally spoken!). Arabic has only two, albeit each has a thin and a thick variation: *au* (sometimes written *aw*), varying between English "cow" (or German "Haus") and "mow"; and *ai* (sometimes written *ay*), varying between English "bait" and "bite". In the thickened forms, *au* sounds more as in English "bought", and *ai* as in "toy". In writing, *au* is normally indicated merely by placing a *w* after the appropriate consonant; *ai* is normally indicated merely by placing a *y* after the appropriate consonant. In the abnormal, fully vowelled text, the appropriate consonant would also carry an *a* mark, and the *w* or *y* a no-vowel mark. It will be seen from para. 48 why we have used such terms as "hint" and "ambiguity".

47. *Long vowels (pronunciation).* These are ideally vowels "prolonged for twice the time of short vowels", but they will often seem in fact to have also a somewhat different "quality" from their short equivalents. To short *a* corresponds long *ā* (note transliteration), which is roughly the sound in the English "sad"; the thick variation is roughly as in English "tar" (with no "r"sound, of course!). To short *i* corresponds long *ī*, with roughly the sound in English "meet"; the thick variation of this is almost "ui" or "wee", as in "suite" or "sweet". To short *u* corresponds long *ū*, somewhat as in "root"; variations between thick and thin may be ignored for *ū*.

48. *Long vowels (writing).* (*a*) Long *ī* is normally written as is *ai*, that is by a *y* after the appropriate consonant; in the abnormal, fully vowelled text, however, the appropriate consonant carries an *i* mark as well, but the *y* should never carry a no-vowel mark in this situation. Long *ū* is normally written as is *au*, that is by a *w* after the appropriate consonant; in the abnormal, fully vowelled text, however, the appropriate consonant carries an *u* mark as well, but the *w* should *never* carry a no-vowel mark in this situation. *Valuable hint*: in a normal text, *w* and *y* may each mark a consonant, a diphthong or a long vowel; only experience, practice and a knowledge of patterns will help you to be reasonably sure which is involved. If the *w* or *y* bears a no-vowel mark, it is being used as a diphthong-indicator.

(*b*) Long *ā* is indicated by using what is usually treated as the first letter of the alphabet, *alif*, which we have not so far considered (see para, 14), since it is not a consonant, and has in itself no fixed value. This is a non-joining letter, a long vertical stroke above the line (something like *l*, with which it should not be confused), thus:

Isolated	ا
Final	ـا...

In normal, unvowelled texts *ā* is shown by placing *alif* after the appropriate consonant: while this cannot be confused with any diphthong, *alif* does have other common functions (which will be mentioned in Chapters 9 and 10). In the abnormal, fully-vowelled text, the appropriate consonant carries in addition an *a* mark, but the *alif* itself carries no mark at all. *Valuable hint*: *Alif* may indicate a long *ā*, but not necessarily.

(*c*) In certain words, which will be noted as we come to them, long *ā* at the *end* of the word is written with undotted *y* and not with *alif*. If any suffix is added to such words, the *y* normally reverts to *alif*; but in some cases, principally such prepositions as *ilà* (up to) and *'alà* (against, upon), the *y* remains and is treated as a diphthong-indicator. Thus *ramà* (he pelted) joined with *-ka* (you) becomes *ramāka*; but *ilà* with *-ka* becomes *ilaika*. (Notice how *ā* as *y* is sometimes transliterated *-à* for purposes of distinction.)

49. *Stress in Standard Arabic*. (*a*) There are three sorts of syllable in Arabic: *short-open*, a consonant followed by a short vowel, as *ka-ta-ba* (he wrote); *short-closed*, a consonant followed by a short vowel followed by an unvowelled consonant, as *kun-tum* (you were); and *long*, a consonant followed by a long vowel or diphthong, as *fī-nā* (in us) or *nā-dai-nā* (we called). *Valuable hint*: with very few exceptions, which will be noted as they occur, there is *no such thing as a long-closed syllable* in Arabic: *ya-qū-lu* (he says) ought in certain situations to be *ya-qūl*, but Arabic cannot tolerate this and makes *ya-qul* instead. (In many cases where the principle seems to be violated, it is simply because the final vowel has not been written, but could be if desired.) *This is perhaps the most useful single principle you can learn to help you understand a mass of seemingly arbitrary changes in Arabic verbs.*

(*b*) Stress in Arabic normally recedes from the end of the word towards the beginning in search of a *long* or a *short-closed* syllable; if it meets neither, it falls on the first, but in practice it never recedes beyond the third from the end. Thus, compare *mutakallimúna* with *mutakállim*, and *kalimất* with *kálima*. There are a few, well-established exceptions to this principle, and we shall point them out as we meet them. Beware, too, of the native-speaker, who will often be unable to prevent the obtrusion of his colloquial stress-pattern: thus, the word for "bridge", *qánṭara*, will almost certainly be stressed by an Egyptian on the second syllable rather than the first; speakers from North-West Africa will, on the other hand, often tend to elide syllables altogether; and so on. Where stress *appears to be on* the last syllable (*kalimất-*), that syllable also *seeming* to be long-closed, a final vowel has been omitted in both writing and speech (see Chapter 10 under noun case-endings, paras. 70ff.).

50. *The "sound" of Arabic.* Arabic is often described as a "guttural" language. In a sense this is true, but try to notice the following much more characteristic features: the contrast between the "metallic" thin sounds and the "plummy" thick ones; the heavy dwelling on long vowels, diphthongs and doubled consonants (compare *qatala* with *qattala* or *qātala*, for example); and the clipped truncation of short vowels, particularly in open syllables. "Staccato" might better describe the language than "guttural"!

51. *Reading-practice lists*

Handwritten	Typeset	Consonants used	Possible pronunciation (including vowels and double consonants)	Meaning
صوت	صوت	ṣwt	ṣaut	voice
فول	فول	fwl	fūl	beans
ذوو	ذوو	dhww	dhawū	men possessing (some quality)
ذوات	ذوات	dhw/alif/t	dhawất	women possessing (some quality)
صير	صير	ṣyr	ṣayr	becoming
سير	سير	syr	sayr[1]	going
قِيلَ	قيل	qyl	qīla (only possible reading)	it is said
ميل	ميل	myl	mīl	mile
مَيْل	ميل	mẏl	mail (only possible reading)	inclination

Handwritten	Typeset	Consonants used	Possible pronunciation (including vowels and double consonants)	Meaning
يكاتب	يكاتب	yk/alif/tb	yukā́tibu	he corresponds
يكاتبون	يكاتبون	yk/alif/tbwn	yukātibū́na	they correspond
يتكلمون	يتكلمون	ytklmwn	yatakallamū́na	they speak (men)
يتكلمن	يتكلمن	ytklmn	yatakallámna	they speak (women)
نصارى	نصارى	nṣ/alif/ry	naṣā́rà	Christians
نصاراها	نصاراها	nṣ/alif/r/ alif/h/alif	naṣārā́-hā	the Christians of it (a city)
على	على	‘ly	‘alà	against
عليهم	عليهم	‘lyhm	‘alái-him	against them

[1] cf. para. 42, last item

52. *Remarks on above word-table.* Pay particular attention both to thickening and to stress (often marked). All the apparent cases of long-closed syllables at the end of words are because the final vowel is not shown or heard. Re-read para. 27 and apply here.

9

A final review of sounds and signs

53. *Hamza.* (*a*) While a few signs still remain to be mentioned (most of them as rarely used in practice as the vowel-marks), there is one last *sound* to which we have so far given no attention: *hamza.* This is a consonant in its own right, a light glottal stop, a catch in the breath, often a division between vowels not already divided by a "bold" consonant; sometimes, especially at the beginning or end of a word, it is practically inaudible to foreign speakers, who would say that the word began or ended with a vowel. In the middle or at the end of words, it is transliterated by an apostrophe (not to be confused with the reversed apostrophe ‘ of para. 32); at the beginning it is usually "assumed". Thus: *'akala* ("he ate"), which we shall henceforth write merely as *akala*; *sa'ala ("he asked"); jaru'a* ("he dared"); *shai'* ("a thing"); and so on.

(*b*) There is little difficulty about recognising or pronouncing *hamza*. The real problem lies in the writing of it. This is partly a historical problem, for the pronunciation and marking of *hamza* in Standard Arabic seems to have been an innovation, added in recorded times to an already established *hamza*-less alphabet. Accordingly, it has never been properly absorbed into the alphabet, but stands as a small ء either in mid-air; or over *w* or *y* (the latter without dots usually in all positions); or over or under *alif*. *Valuable hint*: when *hamza* is found in conjunction with any of the last three letters, disregard the letters themselves and pronounce the *hamza*, with or without an appropriate vowel according to the pattern. Thus, the words given above are written: أكل سأل جرؤ and شيء. The two *alifs* and the *w* are mere "bearers" or "supports" of *hamza*; in the last word it has no "support".

(*c*) The rules usually given for writing *hamza* are very numerous, and many an aspiring Arabist's career has been cut short trying to master them! The purpose of the present course is primarily to learn to read, so that the problem is less acute. However, the following simplified rules will cover most cases: *in general*, pronounce the hamzated word without the *hamza*, write it accordingly, and then insert the *hamza* relative to the appropriate *w*, *y* or *alif*;[1] *however*, initially *hamza* is always associated with *alif* (written below it with *i* and above for *a* and *u*); after long *ā*, *hamza* at the end of a word is normally written unsupported, as سماء (*samā'*); after long *ā* in the middle of a world, *hamza* often occurs with *i* and is written over initial-form *y* (without dots), as قائل (*qā'il*). Where *hamza* occurs amid a seemingly conflicting vowel-pattern, the relative strengths determining the "bearer" are (in declining order) *i* (demanding *y*), *u*(*w*) and *a*(*alif*): thus, *su'ila* is سئل but *ba'usa* is بؤس . Remember, these are *general guides*: there are exceptions and variations, as we shall later point out.

54. ***Madda***. In the formation of certain Arabic patterns containing *hamza*, one is sometimes faced, at the beginning of a word or syllable, with the following combinations: *hamza* (supported, of course, by *alif*: see para. 53(*c*)) plus *a* plus *alif* indicating long *ā*: أَ + ا ; or *hamza* (still supported by *alif*) plus *a* plus *hamza* without vowel: أَ + ءْ . *Both* such combinations are normally written thus: آ, and pronounced simply as an initial long *ā*. Accordingly, *qur'ān* (Koran) is not written قرأان , but قرآن ; and *'a'mana* is not written أءمن, but آمن and pronounced *āmana*. This "horizontal *alif*" is called *madda* (literally, "extension").

[1]This represents a practical application of the historical process described above in sub-para. (*b*). So, *fu'ād* may be pronounced *fuād*, then naturally *fuwād*, and written فؤاد , to be re-pronounced *fu'ād*.

Valuable hint: whereas all vowels apparently found at the beginning of a word or syllable really follow a *hamza*, long *ā* in this position has its own special form of writing.

55. *Waṣla*. Initial *hamza* (as always supported by *alif*) and its vowel in *certain* common words and patterns has no real root connection with the word at all, but has been "stuck on" to make a (for Arabic-speakers) difficult cluster of consonants more pronounceable. Thus, *nkisār* ("breakage") is written, and pronounced, *'inkisār*. This type of *hamza* (called *hamzat al-waṣl*, "joining *hamza*") is *best never written*, even when all the other signs are being inserted for some reason. Moreover, as soon as the word beginning with this type of *hamza* is used in a sentence, and hence usually follows some other word, the final vowel of the previous word is "run into" the hamzated word in pronunciation, displacing the initial *hamza* and its vowel (the supporting *alif* remains *in writing*, but has no function).[2] Thus, if *'inkisār* follows *min* ("from"), we get *mini-nkisār*, not *min 'inkisār* (*min* is even given an extra, "false" vowel for this purpose!). When this running-on takes place *in fully vowelled texts*, the solitary remaining, useless *alif* has a sign placed over it called *waṣla* ("junction"): مِنِ ٱنْكِسَار . Remember that none of this applies to the initial *hamza* forming an *essential* part of the word. *Valuable hint*: learn the few words and forms having *hamzat al-waṣl* as you come to them; treat all others as *hamzat al-qaṭ'* ("definite *hamza*"), and always write this latter *hamza*, even though many Arabic texts omit initial *hamza* in *all* situations. Better omit than put in wrongly if you cannot remember which situation obtains.

56. *Shadda*. When it is particularly desired to indicate that a consonant is doubled, that is repeated without an intervening vowel, a minute sign like a small *s* is placed over the consonant: *kunna* is written كُنَّ . Remember that this sign is not always inserted in Arabic texts despite its occasional vital importance for identifying a pattern. It is also known as *tashdīd*, both names signifying "reinforcement". It cannot, of course, be used where a vowel intervenes between the repeated consonants: *sunan is* سُنَن; سنّ would probably be read as *sinn*, "tooth".

57. *Feminine ending (bound-t)*. As indicated in para. 39, the final or isolated form of *h* is used, with two dots above, to indicate many feminine nouns and adjectives, but not verbs. This ending normally has in itself no pronunciation, but always presupposes a preceding *a* vowel: "king" is ملك *malik*, "queen" is ملكة, written *malika* or *malikah* or *malika(h)*,[3] However, when it precedes a vowel or a *hamzat*

[2] If the last vowel of the previous word is long, e.g. *fī* or *'alà*, these are shortened in pronunciation to *fi* and *'ala* before *hamzat al-waṣl*.

[3] Pedantic older texts even have *malikah̄*, an attempt to combine *h* and *t*, as the Arabic does.

al-waṣl (see para. 55), it is commonly pronounced as *t*: a good example is that very term itself, which comes from *hamza*, and should strictly be written and pronounced *hamzatu--l-waṣl*. (In *transliteration* we often find it more convenient to leave the words unjoined, i.e. not "run into", since it saves printing problems.) *Valuable hint*: while all words ending in bound-*t* are grammatically (and often sexually) feminine, not all feminine words end in bound-*t*. We shall say more about this in Chapter 12 and subsequently.

58. *Arabic names of the consonants*. The following are the names of the consonants, in the order used for dictionaries and other reference works (some Arab regions, and some "non-Arabic" Muslims, vary order and pronunciation slightly; some of the latter also add extra letters):

alif	*rā'	ghain
bā'	*zāy	fā'
*tā'	*sīn	qāf
*thā'	*shīn	kāf
jīm	*ṣād	*lām
ḥā'	*ḍād	mīm
khā'	*ṭā'	*nūn
*dāl	*ẓā'	hā'
*dhāl	'ain	wāw
		yā'

Those marked with an asterisk are called "sun-letters", and they will be referred to in the next chapter in discussing the definite article, "the" (*al-*). Sometimes *lām* followed by *alif* is treated as an extra letter, *lām-alif*. It is written thus, and does not join to the left: final ـلا..; isolated لا (they do *not* hang below line like *l*).

59. *Arabic names of the vowels*. The vowels and the no-vowel sign are called as follows:

a: fatḥa(h)	*u*: ḍamma(h)
i: kasra(h)	no-vowel: sukūn

60. *Remarks*. All the technical terms and names given in this chapter will be used subsequently for greater convenience. Practise writing them in Arabic.

10

Standard Verb in māḍī; Standard Noun

61. *From script to grammatical principles, forms and words.* (*a*) We have now covered all but a very few, and very minor, aspects of the basic problems relating to the Arabic script (and these other details will be dealt with as they arise). However, the student will be doing well if he can yet identify the consonants readily, not to mention the less important signs: it will be weeks, and even months, before he feels "at home" with the script in its simplest form, and for easy decipherment of some more difficult and more artistic forms, years are often not enough. Above all, the student who has thoroughly digested Chapter 3 will realise that is is *never* possible to speak of "reading" Arabic in the same sense that he might, even at the present stage, read Italian or Russian: anyone who has learned the *almost fully explicit relationship* between sign and sound in these languages can effectively pronounce any word in them, whether or not he understands that word's meaning or function: it is never possible to say this of Arabic, unless it be artificially adorned with the vowel-marks and other signs.

(*b*) While the student is slowly but steadily strengthening his hold on the script,[1] we must begin rapidly to lay the foundations of grammatical understanding; the student himself must also memorise all the forms and vocabulary used from now on, but grammatical understanding is at this stage the real key to progress, and it remains indispensable. Anyone who cannot understand certain basic principles to be enunciated in this chapter, and who has not memorised the forms, form-tables and words given in it, should not try to proceed further: each step follows from earlier ones, but without the first no advance is possible. Remember that this operation at three levels will be difficult, even painful: do not worry too much about occasionally forgetting, if you have honestly tackled the problems and are willing to keep "picking up the broken pieces".

62. *The Arabic verb in general.* The old-fashioned, inexact definition of a verb as a "doing-word" is more or less adequate to Arabic, especially at this stage. A verb does not name or describe a person or thing or idea (like "John", "table", "suffering", "young", "wooden" or "continuous"); it does not simply indicate relationships (like "and", "with", "to" and "because"); it tells us what some-

[1] For a short time we will accompany the Arabic by Latin transliteration, abandoning this as soon as we start serious reading.

body does or has done to him (like "comes", "went", "will write" and "is killed"). In English a verb is usually very closely tied to the idea of time: in other words, it has tenses ("comes, will come, came, has come, had come, did come, would have come" etc.) which fairly exactly define the time of the action, either in relation to the speaker or in respect of another action. *In Arabic the verb in itself carries only a very limited idea of time.* There are two basic divisions (we shall call them "Aspects" rather than "tenses"), the *māḍī* and the *muḍāri'*: it is true that in the comparatively rare cases where either of these is encountered *alone, with no other indications*, the former is normally taken to refer *generally* to the "past", while the latter carries the *general* suggestion of the "present" or the "immediate future". For this reason, we shall render the *māḍī* in grammatical discussion by the past ("he did"), and the *muḍāri'* by the present ("he does");[2] but as soon as we actually use the Aspects in real Arabic sentences, it will be seen that other important "pointers" (which we shall call "time-indicators") lead us to translate either of them by virtually any one of the many varied tenses commonly used in English. Time-indicators, some of them obvious, some easily overlooked, are of extreme importance to a real understanding of Arabic.

63. *Tabulation of forms, particularly verbs.* The English verb "come" used in para. 62, however varied the use to which it is put, itself suffers few changes: *come, comes, came, coming.* This is largely true of the modern English verb system generally, the changes being roughly parallel, though not identical in all cases (cf. the verbs "break", "be", "have" and "do"). These changes, accordingly, can be learned quickly without drawing them up in table form, though they often need to be considered separately for each verb. In Arabic, however, the changes are both numerous and varied, although they remain essentially the same from verb to verb. It therefore seems worth while to tabulate this mass of data for easier learning and reference; this we shall do, but only to the minimum extent necessary. In drawing up our verb tables we shall subdivide into *singular* (one thing or person only being involved), *plural* (several persons, but not usually things), and *dual* (two persons or things); further, into *masculine* (a man, or an object conventionally regarded for grammatical purposes as "male") and *feminine* (a woman, or an object conventionally regarded for grammatical purposes as "female", and often plural things). In the case of verbs only, we shall also subdivide as between *first person* (the speaker, I, we), *second person* (the one addressed, you: nowadays covering both singular, dual and plural in English usage, but distinguished in Arabic); and *third person* (the one spoken of, he, she, it, they). Proceeding from the simple to the more complicated, the Arabic grammarians usually tabulate from the third to the first person, con-

[2] The Arabic names mean literally "past" and "similar". The latter is said to be so called because its end-vowels "resemble" those of nouns. Try to think of the names, Arabic or English, as mere "labels" without real significance.

trary to "Western" practice. We shall follow the Arabic usage. The following abbreviations stand for the words italicised above: s., p., d.; m., f.; 1, 2 and 3. One further abbreviation, c., will be used for "common", i.e. the same form shared by both m. and f.

64. *"Past" of standard root KTB*

3 m.s.	كتب	kátab	a	he wrote
3 f.s.	كتبت	kátab	at	she ″
2 m.s.	″	katáb	ta	you ″
2 f.s.	″	katáb	ti	″ ″
1 c.s.	″	katáb	tu	I ″
3 m.p.	كتبوا	kátab	ū	they wrote
3 f.p.	كتبن	katáb	na	″ ″
2 m.p.	كتبتم	katáb	tum	you ″
2 f.p.	كتبتن	katab	túnna	″ ″
1 c.p.	كتبنا	katáb	nā	we ″
3 m.d.	كتبا	kátab	ā	they (two) wrote
3 f.d.	كتبتا	kátab	atā	″ ″ ″
2 c.d.	كتبتما	katáb	tumā	you ″ ″

65. *Comments on above word-table.* We use the root KTB, because it is simple and presents no pronunciation problems for a learner, but the Arabic grammarians themselves normally use F'L (associated with the basic notion of "doing") here and in all patterns. Note the movement of stress (marked) in accordance with para. 49. Observe, and *remember as permanently important*, the fact that four of the five *written* patterns in the singular are identical in their normal *unvowelled* appearance. Pay no attention to the extra, functionless *alif* on the end of 3 m.p.: it is commonly found terminating m.p. verbs (in some places in 2 as well as 3), but disappears when a suffix is added. Note that there is no Dual form for 1. Try to think of the endings standing to the right of the vertical line as often characteristic of the relevant person, gender and number: you will meet them again. Finally, note that the verb often contains its own subject: because *kataba* and *katabtum* are so distinct, we do not need to add the Arabic equivalents of "he", "you" etc., save for extreme clarity or special emphasis.

66. *Root; 3 m.s.; Infinitive.* It will be noticed that 3 m.s. *māḍī*, as normally written, without vowels, corresponds with the root itself; and it will be remembered (para. 18) that the root (and hence the 3 m.s. *māḍī*) is used as the reference point for words in a dictionary. Accordingly, on analogy with dictionary practice in English, French, German etc., Western grammars often refer to 3 m.s. *māḍī* as the "infinitive" and say "(to) write" instead of "he wrote". This, however, is a mere convenience and has no bearing on the real meaning.

67. *Applicability of table.* This table is directly applicable to thousands of Standard or semi-standard verbs (i.e. verbs not having *w* or *y* as the second or third radical, for these will be treated specially: even to them, it is *substantially* applicable, especially as regards endings). Many Standard Verbs have the vowel *i* on the *second* radical letter, and several have *u*. Thus, شرب *shariba* ("to drink"); حسن *ḥasuna* ("to be handsome, beautiful, nice"). It is best to learn the middle vowel naturally as one learns the verb (the dictionary always shows it). *As a rough general rule*, if you forget the middle vowel, ask yourself if the verb is transitive (i.e. has an immediate object of the action): if it is, the verb is *more likely* to be like *kataba* than like *shariba*; it cannot go like *ḥasuna*, which is reserved for permanent states or qualities. An intransitive verb is *more likely* to resemble *shariba* or *ḥasuna*; but note that *shariba* itself is transitive (i.e. you drink *something*), while *saqaṭa* ("to fall") is intransitive!

68. *The Arabic noun in general.* At this stage, it may be said that a noun, for the purposes of Arabic, is a name or a describing-word for a person, a thing or an idea (examples will be found at the beginning of para. 62). This more or less blurs the common distinction drawn between nouns and adjectives, since the two function in precisely the same way in Arabic, and are most often interchangeable. As with the verb (see para. 63), the English noun normally undergoes few changes in use: most, like "boy", for example, simply add an "s", with or without an apostrophe before or after it. The standard Arabic noun has *six* different endings, depending partly on its function and partly on the degree of "definiteness" attaching to it. (It should perhaps be stressed that the term "definiteness" is here used grammatically, not metaphysically, i.e. it refers merely to whether the noun has the so-called "definite article" ("the": Arabic *'al-*)[3] attached: in a non-grammatical sense, "an apple" or "one apple" can be just as definite as "the apple"!)

69. *Functions of the Arabic noun.* The Arabic noun may be the subject of a statement, i.e. the person or thing or idea which does, suffers, or is, whatever is spoken of: it is then given an ending referred to as the Nominative Case. Secondly, it may be the *object of a statement*, that is the person or thing or idea which directly suffers the action done by the subject: it is then given an ending referred to as the Accusative Case (this case also has a wide range of use in Arabic for which English has no real parallel, but this will be discussed in due course). Thirdly, the

[3] A most important instance of *hamzat al-waṣl* (see para. 55)!

Arabic noun may stand either *after a preposition* ("to the boy", "in a book") or in a *possessive or genitival relationship* to another noun ("the book *of the boy*, the *boy's* book"): it is then given an ending referred to as the Genitive Case. The following table sets these endings out (or "declines" them) for both the Definite and the Indefinite forms of the Standard Noun (other, non-standard types will be met later), using the masculine noun *walad* ("boy").

70. *Standard-Noun endings*

	Definite		*Indefinite*	
Nominative	الولد	al-waladu[4]	ولد	waladun
Accusative	"	al-walada[4]	ولدا	waladan
Genitive	"	al-waladi[4]	ولد	waladin

71. *Comment on above word-table.* Notice first that, while the definite and indefinite forms respectively can be distinguished (even in ordinary, non-vowelled script) by the presence or absence of *al-*, the only form which is *visibly distinct in itself* is the Indefinite Accusative: this carries an unpronounced *alif* at the end but not after bound-*t* (para. 57), and could be mistaken for a standard *māḍī* 3 m.d. (para. 64). *Valuable hint*: *alif* at the end of a word may indicate either of these possibilities, and also others not yet reached; this is where a sense of pattern and function becomes important.

72. *Indefinite endings*: tanwin. While the *definite* endings can obviously be indicated by the use of the three vowels, *ḍamma*, *fatḥa* and *kasra* (para. 59), the student will doubtless wonder how to indicate the *indefinite* endings. The short answer is: by the same three vowels doubled, as:

Nominative Indefinite		وَلَدٌ	(*or* وَلَدٌ *or* وَلَدٌ)
Accusative	"	وَلَدًا	(again note *alif*, but not after bound-*t*)
Genitive	"	وَلَدٍ	

This doubling of the vowels to give an effect of "vowel plus nasal *n*" is known in Arabic as *tanwīn*, which means "n"-ing or "nūn"-ation. We shall use the Arabic term itself.

73. *Dropping of endings.* Once again, it should be emphasised that these endings are not normally written, the only identifying mark of the Standard Noun's cases

[4] If the noun begins with a sun-letter (para. 58), one pronounces e.g. *at-tājir* not *al-tājir* ("the merchant"), though it is often convenient to transliterate by *al-* in all cases. In Arabic writing this is signified *if desired* by putting *shadda* (para. 56) over the sun-letter and by *never* writing *sukūn* (para. 59) over the *l* of the article. Thus, اَلْوَلَدُ but اَلتَّاجِرُ

being the redundant (but obviously useful) *alif* in the Indefinite Accusative (albeit not with bound-*t*). There is a similar tendency not to *pronounce* these endings, with the marked exception of the same Indefinite Accusative (including bound-*t*); this tendency is not so general as in writing, however, since the ear has less time and opportunity than the eye to work out relationships, and accordingly often needs aids of this kind. The ear knows that a noun following a preposition will be in the Genitive, in any case; but in a complicated sentence it is not always so easy for it to recognise the subject without the Nominative ending. Do not fall into the common habit of thinking of the word for "boy" as *waladun*: "boy" is *walad*, and the endings relate to the noun's *function in an actual sentence.*

74. *Assignments and drill.* The student may wonder why at this stage he has no exercise assignments. These will come from Chapter 12 onwards, but at the moment there is nothing for him to exercise on! His three present tasks are to practise identification of script, to memorise the tables and vocabulary in this chapter, and to try to understand the principles and implications explained at length in the various "discussion" paragraphs.

11

Plurals; Sentence types

75. *Formation of plurals.* Arabic plurals are formed in one of two ways: either by adding certain prescribed endings, like the English *-s* or *-en*; or by breaking up the singular pattern, and building an entirely new pattern on the same radical letters. The latter type of plural is called "broken", the former by contrast is known as "sound" or "intact". While the Sound Plurals are easy to learn, they apply only to a comparatively small range of nouns; we shall therefore defer consideration of them till later. The Broken Plurals, applying to the vast majority of Arabic nouns, need to be learned automatically as one learns the noun itself. They vary from noun to noun, but certain *broad* areas of predictability can be made out: generally speaking, and within limits, *the shorter the singular, the more uncertain the plural.* Some nouns have more than one Broken Plural, or both a Sound and a Broken Plural (or plurals): sometimes one predominates. Experience, and constant reference to dictionaries, are the only guides here.

76. *Three common Broken Plurals.* The following are the commonest Broken Plurals formed from *three-consonant nouns with one or two short-vowels* (using KTB for basic radicals): 'aKTāB, KuTūB and 'aKTuB. The word for "month", *shahr*, most commonly takes the last two, *shuhūr* and *ashhur* (remember that we do not usually bother to transliterate the *hamza* initially, since it *must* be there if the word appears to begin with a vowel – see paras. 53(*a*) and 54). The word for "pen", *qalam*, normally takes only the first type of plural, *aqlām*, as does also the word for "boy", *walad* becoming *awlād* (*aulād*: see para. 46). The word *bait* or *bayt* (see para. 46) means both "house" and "line of poetry": in the former sense its plural is *buyūt*, in the latter *abyāt*. Not all three-consonant nouns with one or two short vowels behave like this (e.g. *kalb*, "dog", forms *kilāb*), but the vast majority do; this is true of most of the nouns given in the practice-lists after the letter-families, but you will not yet know which of the three they take for certain. *Two rough guides*: the two patterns *aktāb* and *kutūb* are more common than *aktub*; and singulars of the KaTaB pattern, or those having a *w* in them, commonly take the 'aKTāB plural. *These three plurals all take the same endings as the singulars in para. 70.*

77. *The Verbal Sentence.* The commonest type of sentence in Arabic is one containing a verb (not all Arabic sentences do!), which is normally placed first, before its subject (assuming that the latter is mentioned expressly). This is called a Verbal Sentence. It cannot be too heavily emphasised that in the Third Person this verb will virtually always be *singular* (and often singular masculine), whatever the number of the subject: it may be plural or Dual only when it contains a plural or dual subject within itself (i.e. when the subject is not expressed), or when it follows the subject (when we no longer really have a Verbal Sentence as just defined: see para. 81). See how these principles work out in the following very primitive sentences:

The boy wrote	كتب الولد	kataba al-waladu
	الولد كتب	al-waladu kataba*
The boys wrote	كتب الأولاد	kataba al-aulādu
	الأولاد كتبوا	al-aulādu katabū*
They wrote (of males)	كتبوا	katabū (pl. only possibility)

The renderings marked with asterisks are the less usual ones, and will be discussed in para. 81. Remember to "join" the *hamza* of the article (paras. 55 and 68), that is, to say *kataba--l-walad*, and so on; note, once more, the idle *alif* at the end of the plural verbs. A further aspect of these problems is discussed in para. 84.

78. *Adverbial displacer in Verbal Sentence.* While in Verbal Sentences the verb commonly occurs as the first word or element, it *may* be displaced by an adverb or an adverb phrase (particularly where the adverbial elaboration relates to time). The following sentence is a standard Verbal Sentence:

دخل الأجناد القدس وقتلوا السكان

dakhala al-ajnādu al-qudsa wa-qatalū al-sukkāna
The troops entered Jerusalem and killed the inhabitants

In the first half, the subject (a Broken Plural of the *'aktāb* pattern from *jund*) takes the Definite Nominative ending, and follows a standard *māḍī* 3 m.s.; the object takes the Definite Accusative ending. In the second half (after *wa-*, "and"), something of the same structure is repeated, but this time the subject has either preceded or may be regarded as included in the verb ("they killed"), and so the verb is *māḍī* 3 m.p.; the object is another Broken Plural pattern, *kuttāb. Now,* I may add to this sentence the adverb ثم *thumma* ("then"), which would necessarily preceded *dakhala* or *qatalū* (probably removing *wa-* in the latter case). Or I could add a more elaborate adverbial phrase, for example في تلك السنة *fī tilka al-sanati* ("in that year"),[1] when the choices would be wider: it could either precede *dakhala* or *qatalū* (not removing *wa-* this time), or it could follow *al-qudsa* or *al-sukkāna. In the former two cases,* we are getting rid of the phrase early, suggesting it is not particularly important, these being some more of the things that happened "in that year": the place they entered, or the people they killed, are more important. On the other hand, *in the latter two cases,* the phrase "in that year" assumes greater importance, so to speak, than the objects of the actions. This may lead you to suspect (quite rightly) that position is more important in Arabic than in English, where emphasis can just as easily be suggested by tone or stress; also that the "interest" of an Arabic sentence rises towards the end (which is largely true). But, for the moment, you need only grasp the principle of displacement in a Verbal Sentence: that is, *do not necessarily always expect the verb to be right at the beginning of your Verbal Sentence.*

79. *Nominal Sentences.* These form the other broad category of sentence structure in Arabic. Such sentences have *no verb,* and they predicate that "A is (not expressed) B", or that "A is (not expressed) in" a certain place or state. Examples of the two types are:

الولد صغير	al-waladu ṣaghīrun	The boy (is) small
الولد في الشارع	al-waladu fī al-shār'i	The boy (is) in the street

It will be noticed that the subject in both cases is a definite noun; and that the predicate is either an Indefinite *Nominative* noun-adjective, or an adverbial phrase. These are examples of the ideal Nominal Sentence, the classic type.

[1]This phrase is made up of a relation-word, the preposition *fī* ("in"), followed (para. 69) by two "nouns" in the Genitive, "that" and "the year": the first is not visibly so, the second ends according to the table in para. 70.

80. *Deviant types of Nominal Sentence.* (*a*) Sometimes, in the case of the "A is B" type, deviations occur that are liable (for reasons that will become increasingly obvious) to make immediate recognition of the Nominal Sentence difficult. These are: the subject may need to be Indefinite ("*a* boy (is) sick"); the predicate may need to be Definite ("the boy (is) *the* criminal"); or, with or without these difficulties, subject or predicate (or both) may be long and unwieldy, making the transition from one to the other hard to recognise ("the tall young Arab with the long beard whom you met last night (is) the cousin of my brother-in-law on my sister's side"). In all these three cases, subject is normally marked off from predicate by inserting the word "he" (or "she", "it", "they", as the case may be): "a boy *he* (is) sick", "the boy *he* (is) the criminal", "the tall young Arab . . . *he* . . . ."

(*b*) In the case of the "A is in . . ." type of Nominal Sentence, the first sort of deviation may also occur, namely the indefinite subject. In this case, subject and predicate are reversed: "in the street (is) a boy". (Contrast this with the displacer of para. 78: an adverbial phrase followed by a verb introduces a Verbal Sentence; but followed by a noun, it almost always introduces a deviant Nominal Sentence of the "A is in . . ." type.) The second deviation (the Definite predicate) obviously does not apply to this type of Nominal Sentence. The third deviation (lengthy or indistinct subject and/or predicate) is treated as in the same situation for the "A is B" type, by the insertion of "he" etc.

81. *Nominal Absolutes.* A common device in many languages, for dealing with an unwieldy or important subject of a sentence, is to place it at the beginning, and then to leave it hanging, carrying on with the sentence as though the original subject did not exist. This is often done in conversational English, though it is not officially approved of in most cases. We do not normally say: "Mr Jones, the baker, who lives at the end of the third street on the right as you leave the town going east, is sick", but rather: "(You know) Mr Jones . . . (well,) *he is sick*". Arabic does this constantly, not only with official approval, but as a characteristic mark of style. In the case of Verbal Sentences, we have already met examples of this in the asterisked sentences in para. 77: taking these very simple cases, then, *al-waladu kataba* really means "the boy: he wrote"; and *al-aulādu katabū* really means "the boys: they wrote". (This is why the verb appears to agree with the subject: in fact, the verb in itself re-states the subject, and hence may go beyond the mere 3 m.s. normally demanded of standard Verbal Sentences.) In the case of Nominal Sentences, the method used for circumventing all the deviations of the "A is B" type and the second deviation of the "A is in . . ." type, namely inserting a "he", "she" etc., will be seen as examples of the same thing. *Valuable hint*: the fact that a sentence appears to begin with a noun or a noun-complex does not necessarily mean that it is a Nominal Sentence: this may be a Nominal Absolute, introducing either type of sentence, Nominal or Verbal. In such a case, it is harder, sometimes virtually impossible, for the verb of the Verbal Sentence to be "displaced" (para. 78) or for the Nominal Sentence to "deviate" (para. 80).

82. *Summary.* Try to accustom yourself to the idea that you must tackle all Arabic sentences by first classifying them as Verbal or Nominal; that either of these may be introduced by a Nominal Absolute; that the Verbal Sentence may suffer initial adverbial "displacement"; and that the Nominal Sentence is of two types ("A is B", and "A is in . . ."), with both first and second types sometimes having a central divider or marker, and with the second type alone being sometimes inverted. This is the framework on which all Arabic syntax is built, however complicated it may become.

12

Agreement; The Construct

83. *Agreement.* This is the term commonly used to cover the relationship between verbs, nouns, pronouns (i.e. general noun substitutes like "he", "she" etc.) and adjectives. It means little or nothing in modern English; but it is a most important principle in languages like Arabic, which differentiate rigorously for number, gender and case. With one most striking exception, the Arabic scheme of agreement is in normal practice reasonably logical (always bearing in mind the important notion of the *precedent Third-Person singular verb in a Verbal Sentence* (para. 77)): where rational beings, or near-rational, or supposedly rational beings (i.e. humans and the higher animals) are concerned, agreement is virtually complete, number agreeing with number and gender with gender (case *always* agrees). But practically *all non-rational and inanimate beings* (i.e. the lower animals and "things") are generally regarded as *grammatically feminine singular when they occur in the plural,* irrespective of the conventional gender in the singular and Dual. Thus "a book", *kitāb*, being masculine, is treated as a singular or dual male in respect of verb, pronoun and adjective; but "books", *kutub* (Broken Plural of new pattern!), are referred to pronominally not as "they" (m.p.) but as "she" (f.s.), and the verb and adjective accompanying them are accordingly f.s. The Dual, which has yet to be discussed outside of verbs, has virtually complete agreement.

84. *Gender of the precedent Third-Person singular verb.* In a Verbal Sentence the precedent verb is not only 3 s., but commonly 3 *masculine* singular. The only situation where the verb *must* be 3 f.s. (according to a dominant school of Classical Arabic grammarians) is where the *subject is truly female and follows immediately on the verb.* However, the principle enunciated in para. 83 (lower animals and "things" occurring in the plural are grammatically *feminine* singular in most cases) has long tended to outweigh here. Thus we have the following main variations:

The men fell	وقع الرجال	waqaʻa al-rijālu
The women fell	وقعت النساء	waqaʻat al-nisā'u
The girl fell	وقعت البنت	waqaʻat al-bintu
The books fell	{ وقع / وقعت } الكتب	{ waqaʻa / waqaʻat } al-kutubu
The apple fell	{ وقع / وقعت } التفاحة	{ waqaʻa / waqaʻat } al-tuffāḥatu

In pronouncing the above, remember to "join" the *hamza* of the article (paras. 55 and 68), even giving *waqaʻat* a "false vowel" (*i*) for this purpose: *waqaʻati--l-kutub* etc. (cf. also para. 73). Do not forget the "sun-letters" (para. 70 and footnote).

85. *Adjectives and agreement.* (*a*) The qualifying adjective immediately follows its noun in Arabic, and agrees with it in "definiteness" (see para. 68) and, of course, in case. "A good book" is expressed as "a book a good"; "the good book" is "the book the good", and so on. This is an important indicator for distinguishing the mere subject of a Nominal Sentence from a complete statement in Nominal-Sentence form. Thus: "the book the good" is an incomplete statement, probably the subject of a Nominal Sentence: but "the book a good" means "the book (is) good" (cf. para. 79).

(*b*) In addition the adjective agrees with its noun (whether it qualifies the latter immediately or serves as the predicate of a Nominal Sentence) in gender and number, *as indicated in para. 83.* To state this in positive detail: *masculine (including male) singular nouns* have masculine singular adjectives, that is the standard form as found in the dictionary; *feminine (including female) singular nouns* have feminine singular adjectives, often but not always formed from the masculine by adding a bound-*t* (para. 57); *male plural and female plural nouns* take corresponding forms of adjectives (which you do not yet know how to make, and which are sometimes identical for both genders in Broken Plural forms); *masculine and feminine plural nouns, when not male or female,* usually take feminine singular adjectives as described above (but they sometimes take a Broken Plural form as an alternative, where one exists). Remember that the Dual, which has yet to be discussed outside of verbs, has more or less exact agreement wherever possible.

86. *The Construct.* Where two nouns are closely associated (either because one possesses the other, or for example because one is made of the other), languages often mark the association by some outward sign. Thus, in English, if the words "book" and "boy" are put together, without modification of any kind, it is not immediately obvious what their connection may be; even if we add "the" or "a" to either, we have still established no visible relationship. But, if we say "the book *of* the boy" or (more normally, in English) "the boy*'s* book", we have made clear that the one *possesses* the other; similarly, in expressions like "a bar *of* gold", "a book *of* verse" or "a bottle *of* milk", we have established relationships of *substance* or *content* (still others are possible). Various names are possible for such structures of relationship: the native Arabic term is *iḍāfa* ("annexation"), but Western Arabists have traditionally spoken of the Construct, the Construct Case, or the Genitival Relationship. All are really little more than labels, and we shall use whichever seems convenient in a given situation.

87. *Basic peculiarity of the Arabic Construct.* From the last of the terms just mentioned, it may be apparent that the normal way of indicating this relationship in Arabic is by putting the possessing noun in the Genitive Case (see paras. 68 to 72), a process closely resembling English usage. However, Arabic usually has a peculiarity of its own, one which can lead to disastrous misunderstandings if not properly grasped in all its implications. *The first of the two elements in an Arabic Construct may not normally have the article (al-); but it takes the "Definite" endings* (para. 70) *and should in most cases be translated as Definite* (i.e. as though it had "the" or some equivalent). The second of the two elements (i.e. the possessing noun) can be Definite or Indefinite as occasion demands. However, if a series of Constructs is built up ("the book of the son of the ruler of the country", to take an extreme example), the first principle operates for *each element except the very last*: in the foregoing English phrase, an Arabic translation would remove the article, but not its force, from every noun except "country". (We shall see later that the *virtual absoluteness of the statements in this paragraph needs to be modified somewhat when we come to the "improper" Constructs*, i.e. the "non-possessing" relationships, particularly in the Arabic equivalents of phrases like "white of hair", "hard of heart", and the growing quasi-compound forms of the modern language, such as "police of passage" ("traffic-police"): however, for normal, "possessing" Constructs the principles here stated are so important as to warrant emphatic generalisation!)

88. *Typical examples of the "proper" Construct and some implications*

وجه الرجل	wajhu al-rajuli	*the* face of the man, the man's face
وجه رجل	wajhu rajulin	*the* face of a man, a man's face

لون وجه الرجل	launu wajhi al-rajuli	*the* colour of *the* face of the man, the colour of the man's face
لون وجه رجل	launu wajhi rajulin	*the* colour of *the* face of a man, the colour of a man's face

The above four phrases cover the whole effective range of the "proper" Construct, that marking possession. Certain shades of English meaning not apparently covered by these (e.g. "*a* daughter of the king": not necessarily *the one and only* daughter) are not normally capable of expression in Arabic by the Construct at all, but must be conveyed in other ways: "a daughter *belonging to* the king", "a daughter *from among the daughters* of the king", and so on (we shall meet examples of these later). Remember that *a Construct should never be broken:*[1] if you wish to qualify the first element by an adjective, the *adjective must follow the whole Construct*, agreeing by Arabic standards with its noun in gender, number, case and definiteness (i.e. it must take the article in this situation). If the first phrase above had been "the *handsome* face of the man" or "the man's *handsome* face", the Arabic would be:

وجه الرجل الحسن wajhu al-rajuli al-ḥasanu

Note, further, that the normal unvowelled Arabic is often ambiguous in such situations, particularly where both nouns have the same gender and number, and where the "possessor" is Definite: in this phrase, the adjective could have been read *al-ḥasani* (Genitive, qualifying the second element *al-rajuli*), giving the sense "the face of the handsome man" or "the handsome man's face". Clearly, with a *series* of Constructs, putting an adjective right at the end would be hopelessly confusing: once again, other structures than the Construct have to be used, such as "the book the little *belonging to* the son of the ruler of the country". It should perhaps be emphasised that while we have above conventionally given the *first elements* Nominative endings (*u*), they could equally well be Accusatives or Genitives, depending on their function in the sentence:

نظر وجه الرجل naẓara wajh*a* al-rajuli he caught sight of the man's face

The beginning student often finds a sentence like this last thoroughly confusing. He asks himself how one is to know, in normal unvowelled texts, that *wajh* is not the subject and *al-rajul* the object, giving "a face caught sight of the man"! The only honest answer is that one proceeds partly by the sense, partly by a cultivated awareness that an apparent noun with no article followed by a noun with article is nearly always an instance of Construct. The next stage is for him to wonder, if this is so, why one could not regard this phrase as a compound Construct with

[1] Modern Arabic sometimes does this in phrases like "the son and daughter of the king", but careful writers still preserve the old usage "the son of the king and his daughter".

three nouns in relationship: once again, one has regard partly to sense (this might be made to give something like "the glance of the face of the man"), partly to the fact the first element in most (though not all) Arabic sentences is a verb.

89. *Practice sentences.* Translate as quickly as you can "by impression" the sentences given under this paragraph number in the separate section (p. 105). Then try to put vowels on the words and pronounce them in accordance with the function you have given them in your translation. It will take you probably much longer than you expect to make absolutely sure, but the more you persevere the sooner you will be able to take sentences like this in your stride. If you cannot square your reading with the rules, it is wrong, no matter how plausible it sounds! Remember to differentiate Nominal and Verbal Sentences, then try to clarify the subject in each case (*every sentence must have a subject, expressed or implied*). Compare the verbs with the verb-table, the nouns with the noun-table, and make sure your translation would allow the actual forms these have. Keep checking the rules for factors like agreement and Construct, so as to ensure that your translation falls within the limits of these. Revise some of the writing problems: remember the ambiguous verb forms in the *māḍī* singular, the significance (possibly) of a final *alif*, the places where that *alif* does not occur, and so on. Every point in these sentences has been thoroughly covered, often more than once, in the twelve chapters past; but a few small reminders are given in the vocabulary following the sentences. Frequently, a look at the vocabulary will give you the illusion that the work has really been done for you; but remember that it is much more important in the long run to see that, for example, *qaṭa'a* is *māḍī* 3 m.s. than to discover from the vocabulary that it means "to cut". Ideally, the right reaction to the first sentence, at this stage, is to realise (before ever looking at the vocabulary) that it means: "He something-ed the something with a something", or preferably: "He verb-ed the object with a something"!

13

Standard Verb in Muḍāri'; Independent and attached personal pronouns

90. *The Arabic verb in general.* The student should here re-read the paragraphs on verbs in Chapter 10 (pp. 37ff.) Assuming that what was said there is clearly understood, we shall now proceed to tabulate the *muḍāri'*. This table should be learned immediately, being just as vital as the *māḍī* table for the recognition of common Arabic structures.

91. *"Present-future" of standard root KTB*

3 m.s.	يكتب	yá	ktub	u	he writes
3 f.s.	تكتب	tá	ktub	u	she "
2 m.s.	"	"	"	"	you write
2 f.s.	تكتبين	ta	ktub	ī́na	" "
1 c.s.	أكتب	á	ktub	u	I "
3 m.p.	يكتبون	ya	ktub	ū́na	they write
3 f.p.	يكتبن	ya	ktúb	na	" "
2 m.p.	تكتبون	ta	ktub	ū́na	you "
2 f.p.	تكتبن	ta	ktúb	na	" "
1 c.p.	نكتب	ná	ktub	u	we "
3 m.d.	يكتبان	ya	ktub	ā́ni	they (two) write
3 f.d.	تكتبان	ta	ktub	ā́ni	" " "
2 c.d.	"	"	"	"	you " "

92. *Comments on above word-table.* First, it should be remembered that, as for the *māḍī*, this table is valid for *all* standard verbs and *substantially applicable* for all others. It is essential to have it completely mastered as a basis for many further discussions and elaborations to come. It should be noted that, unlike the *māḍī*, the variations here are in terms of both prefix and suffix; once again, the combination of the two has important associations for number, person and gender, and it will be seen that several of them correspond with (or generally echo) the *māḍī* forms. Note the ambiguities, one in the singular and one in the Dual; and also the forms that differ only as between prefixed *y* and *t* in all three numbers. Finally, attention should be paid to the *middle vowel*, here *u* as against *a* for the *māḍī* of KTB; *just as one should learn the plural together with the noun, so the middle vowel of the muḍāri' should be learned as one learns the verb.* If one forgets it, recourse may be had to the dictionary; but the following *general principles* may be found useful: *u* in the *māḍī* gives *u* in the *muḍāri'*; *i* gives *a*; *a* in the *māḍī* (unfortunately, the most numerous class!) can give all three, but most commonly gives *u* or *i*, save where the second or third radical is *ḥ* or *'ain*, when it normally gives *a* (*raja'a, yarji'u*, "to return, come back", is a notable and important exception to this last remark). We shall henceforth show the middle vowel of the *muḍāri'*, in the vocabularies, after the verb in brackets.

93. *Use of the* muḍāri'. As remarked in para. 62, the *muḍāri'*, in default of specific time indications, is normally rendered by the English present or the near future.

However, one of its most characteristic functions in Arabic is that of a "tense-prolonger". Consider the English sentence: "he struck him on the head and killed him". It might be thought that this could be easily enough rendered into Arabic by two *māḍī* (i.e. "past") verbs in succession; this could in fact be done, but the tendency would then be to understand the statement as referring to two successive, and not necessarily related, actions: he struck him on the head on one occasion, and actually went so far as to kill him on another! What would be much more normal in Arabic would be to render: "he struck (*māḍī*) him on the head, kills (*muḍāri'*) him". It will be noted that the "and" normally disappears in such constructions, leaving something akin to our own alternative phrasing: "he struck him on the head, killing him". *Valuable hint*: where two or more actions, in whatever "time", are closely related or virtually simultaneous, Arabic commonly sets the "time" in the first verb and follows with *muḍāri'* forms, omitting "and" at the first juncture (though not subsequently). Conversely, remember that in Arabic a succession of *māḍī* verbs, linked by "and", suggests a series of *separate* past actions; and a succession of *muḍāri'* verbs, *all* linked by "and", would suggest a series of *separate* present–near-future actions. Obviously, as so often in languages, borderline cases can easily arise; and, in any event, the appropriate English rendering will often be (as in the original example above) quite ambiguous.

94. *Independent personal pronouns.* These are "whole" words, that is they are not attached to other words as suffixes. While they correspond, broadly speaking, to the English words "I", "you", "he" etc., they have functions that are best understood in terms of Arabic itself. *First*, and most important, they replace a noun as the subject of a Nominal Sentence; thus, in the examples in para. 79, the masculine singular subject *al-waladu* could be replaced by any masculine singular independent personal pronoun (though the most likely one would, of course, be "he", *huwa*). Similarly with other possible variations of gender and number (case does not enter into the matter here, only the Nominative being possible): however, *remember the principle discussed in para. 83* – that is, the pronoun replacing "ships" or "teeth" or "books" would normally be "she", not "they"! *Secondly*, these independent pronouns may be used in Nominal Sentences as "dividers" between subject and predicate (see para. 80), a use often difficult to distinguish in practice from that where the pronoun "re-starts" a Nominal Sentence after a Nominal Absolute (see para. 81). *Thirdly*, these independent pronouns are used for special emphasis, particularly in Verbal Sentences where the subject is implied in the verb: if *kataba* means "he wrote" (with emphasis, if anywhere, on the action more than the person), *kataba huwa* means only "*he* wrote". *Huwa kataba* (a rare usage) is an example of a Nominal Absolute followed by a Verbal Sentence (cf. again para. 81).

95. *Independent personal pronoun table*

3 m.s.	هو	huwa	he, it
3 f.s.	هى	hiya	she, it, they
2 m.s.	أنت	anta	you
2 f.s.	"	anti	"
1 c.s.	أنا	ana (alif redundant)	I
3 m.p.	هم	hum*	they
3 f.p.	هن	hunna	"
2 m.p.	أنتم	antum*	you
2 f.p.	أنتن	antunna	"
1 c.p.	نحن	naḥnu	we
3 c.d.	هما	humā	they (two)
2 c.d.	أنتما	antumā	you (two)

Before *hamzat al-waṣl* those marked with an asterisk take *u* as false vowel, *humu* only, not *huma* or *humi*.

96. *Attached personal pronouns*. These are not whole words, but short suffixes attached to verbs, nouns and prepositions. Once again, while they correspond to such English words as "me", "my", "him", "his" etc., it is essential to try to understand their functions within the operations of Arabic itself. *First*, they can replace an Accusative noun, Definite or Indefinite, as the object of a verb: *qaṭa'a al-khubza* ("he cut the bread") becomes *qaṭa'a-hu* "he cut *it*", m.s.: there is no hyphen in Arabic, so that this is written as one word. *Secondly*, they can replace a Genitive noun functioning as the second element of a Construct: the first two phrases in para. 88 could be re-fashioned as *wajhu-hu* ("his face"). *Thirdly*, they can replace a genitive noun following a preposition: *min al-waladi* ("from the boy") becomes *min-hu* ("from him"). It will be noted that while the *independent* pronouns normally substitute for the *Nominative* functions of nouns, the *attached* pronouns cover three basic uses of the other two cases; at the same time, their endings do not vary as between Accusative and Genitive, Definite and Indefinite, as would be the case with the nouns they replace. (Remember that, as with the first element in a Construct, the noun qualified by these pronouns becomes Definite in sense and needs a Definite form of the adjective: *wajhu-hu al-ḥasanu*, "his handsome face".)

97. *Attached personal pronoun table*

3 m.s.	ـــــــ ـه	—hu*	
3 f.s.	ـــــــ ها	—hā	
2 m.s.	ـــــــ كَ	—ka	
2 f.s.	ـــــــ كِ	—ki	
1 c.s.	ـــــــ ى	—ī	see next para.
	ـــــــ نِي	—nī	
3 m.p.	ـــــــ هم	—hum*	
3 f.p.	ـــــــ هن	—hunna*	
2 m.p.	ـــــــ كم	—kum	
2 f.p.	ـــــــ كن	—kunna	
1 c.p.	ـــــــ نا	—nā	
3 c.d.	ـــــــ هما	—humā*	
2 c.d.	ـــــــ كما	—kumā	

NOTE: No translations are given this time, because with such particles meaning depends on use.

The four forms marked with an asterisk all change their *u* vowel to *i* when *directly* following an *i*, or a *y* serving to indicate *ī* or *ai*: thus *min-hu*, but *fī-hi*. (This is a rhyming effect only, and has nothing to do with case: in both these examples the suffix is technically a Genitive after a preposition!)

98. *Remarks on above word-table.* Note the few exact correspondences (two in the plural, one in the Dual), and the several similarities, with the independent pronouns; moreover, as suggested in discussing the verb-tables, certain "echoes" and associations of number, person and gender constantly recur in connection with such affixes. As with the independent pronouns, 3 m.p. and 2 m.p. take a false vowel *u* before *hamzat al-waṣl*. In the case of 1 c.s., the -*ī* ending is normally attached to nouns and prepositions only, and the -*nī* ending to verbs (but also to some particles[1] ending in -*n*, if desired): *qatala-nī* ("he killed me"), but *kitāb-ī* ("my book"). Two further points should be noticed about the -*ī* ending in 1 c.s. In the *first* place, unlike the other attached pronouns, it "swallows up" the noun's case-ending: *kitābī* is "my book" in all three cases, whereas "his book" is *kitābu-hu*, or *kitāba-hu* or *kitābi-hi* (rhyme-change only!), depending on the

[1] A convenient term for virtually everything that is not a noun or pronoun, or a verb, i.e. (in English terms) prepositions, conjunctions etc.

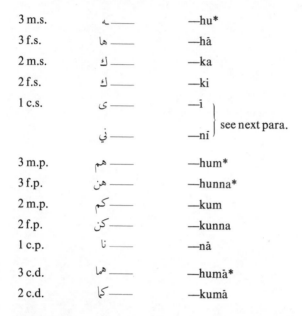

noun's function in a sentence. *Secondly*, where *-ī* directly follows *ī*, *ai* or *ā*, it takes the form *-ya* (with appropriate script adjustments: thus *kitābai-ī*, "my two books" (Accusative Dual, not yet studied) becomes *kitābai-ya*, written كتابيّ ; "in me" is not *fī-ī*, but *fī-ya*; written فيّ, or exactly as for *fī* without vowel marks!). The preposition *li-* ("to, for, for the sake of") becomes *la-* before all these suffixes except *-ī*: *li-waladin* ("for a boy"), but *la-hu*. The 2 m.p. of the *māḍī*, *katabtum*, becomes *katabtumū-* before *all* these endings. Finally, remember that while we have listed these suffixes in the initial alphabetic form,* their actual appearance in fact depends on the word to which they are attached: دره *durruh-u* ("his pearls"), but كتابه *kitābu-hu*. A small number of other, less common, peculiarities relating to these attached pronouns will be dealt with as they occur. However, the student is here reminded, once more, of the remark made in para. 65 – that the functionless *alif* appended to certain masculine plural verb-forms is dropped before these suffixes: كتبوا *katabū*, but كتبوه *katabū-hu*.

99. *Practice sentences.* Treat the sentences given under this paragraph number in the separate section (pp. 106f.) according to the instructions you applied in para. 89.

14

Sound Plurals; Dual nouns; Subjunctive and Jussive verbs

100. *Use of Sound Plurals.* Sound Plurals were defined in para. 75. It was also pointed out there that their use is considerably restricted by comparison with the Broken Plurals. In fact the *Masculine* Sound Plural is associated principally with the "*professional*" *or* "*habitual*" noun pattern KaTTāB (*fallāḥ*, "peasant, cultivator"; *'akkāl* "glutton(ous)"), with the related-adjective ending *-īy* (*miṣrīy*, "Egyptian"; *ḥalabīy*, "from Aleppo"), and with *participles*, though there are exceptions even here (we shall introduce participles in Chapter 15). The *Feminine* Sound Plural is associated with *nouns ending in bound-t*, though not by any means all of these, and with *certain unpredictable masculine or feminine nouns*, particularly foreign words imported into Arabic (an example of the first class is *malika(h)*, "queen", though *madīna(h)*, "city", commonly takes one of two Broken Plurals; examples of the second class are *ḥayawān* (see vocabulary to para. 99, p. 107); *tilifūn*, "telephone"; *sijill*, "register, record" (from Latin or

*Items 1, 3, 4 and 5 are shown for convenience in the final or isolated forms, but the caveat still applies.

Italian)). We shall add minor categories to these as we come to them. It will be noted that, while the Masculine Sound Plural is virtually limited to male beings only, the Feminine Sound Plural is not so limited.

101. *Sound Plural Masculine.* This is formed from the singular by adding the ending *-ūna* for the Nominative Case, and *-īna* for both the Accusative and the Genitive. (Remember that, as usual, the last vowel is almost never seen and rarely heard!) Unlike the singular, these endings do not vary as between Definite (with the article *al-*) and Indefinite. However, if a Sound Plural Masculine is the first element in a Construct, or has an attached personal pronoun (which is essentially the same thing), the endings are reduced to *-ū* and *-ī* respectively. In the following table we use the word "peasants" (see para. 100) in all these situations:

	Indefinite	Definite	In Construct	With pronoun
Nom.	فلاحون	الفلاحون	فلاحو العراق	فلاحوها
Acc./Gen.	فلاحين	الفلاحين	فلاحى العراق	فلاحيها
			(the peasants of al-'Irāq (Iraq)	(its peasants, i.e. Iraq's)

102. *Sound Plural Feminine.* This is formed from the singular by deleting the "*a* plus bound-*t*" ending (if there is one), and adding *-ātun* for the Nominative case, and *-ātin* for both the Accusative and the Genitive. (The *-un*, *-in* endings here represent *tanwīn*: see para. 72.) Apart from the fact of a two-vowel range instead of a three-vowel one, these endings behave exactly as does the Standard singular noun in all situations; however, since there is naturally no *alif* to point to an Indefinite Accusative *-an* (see para. 71), one normally never sees anything more than the basic *-āt* to indicate that one is dealing with a Sound Plural Feminine, the case to be determined by sense and structure. In the following table we use an example we have already met: *banāt* (somewhat irregularly formed from a singular *bint*: see vocabulary to para. 89, p. 106):

بنات	banātun, banātin	daughters
البنات	al-banātu, al-banāti	the daughters
بنات النيل	banātu / banāti al-nīli	the Daughters of the Nile (an Egyptian women's society)
بناته	banātu-hu / banāti-hi (see para. 98)	his daughters

103. *Dual nouns.* These are formed, whenever needed, from both masculine and feminine singulars by adding the ending *-āni* for the Nominative case, and *-aini* for both the Accusative and the Genitive. Unlike the Sound Plural Feminine, these endings do not eliminate any "*a* plus bound-*t*" ending, merely changing the latter to an ordinary *t*. (Remember to think of these endings as basically *-ān* and *-ain*, without end vowels!) As regards Definiteness and Indefiniteness, as well as Construct situations and attached pronouns, these endings behave in a way that exactly parallels the remarks in para. 101 on the Sound Plural masculine. Contrast the following table with that of para. 101:

	Indefinite	Definite	In Construct	With pronoun
Nom.	فلاحان	الفلاحان	فلاحا العراق	فلاحاها
Acc./Gen.	فلاحين	الفلاحين	فلاحى العراق	فلاحيها

The second line is identical in appearance (though not in pronunciation) with the Sound Plural Masculine.

104. *Specialised modifications of the* muḍāriʻ. The form of the *muḍāriʻ* which we have so far reviewed is commonly termed the *Indicative*: it is used, as we have seen, to make a statement about an action in the present or near-future; or about a series of actions that are independent but closely linked to an initial action, at whatever time the latter occurs. There are two other forms of the *muḍāriʻ*, only slightly modified from the Indicative, which Arabic reserves for uses more or less peculiar to itself (though many other languages exhibit similar operations, albeit modern English hardly at all). One of these forms is called the *Subjunctive* by Western scholars: its most common use is after verbs (and sometimes other words) of commanding, wishing, hoping, intending, fearing and the like; and it is usually found "linked' to these verbs by a particle (conjunction) *an*. This particle is sometimes translatable by the ambiguous English word "that": "he wishes *that* he goes" (Subjunctive) or "he wished *that* I go" (Subjunctive); but this is not particularly useful, since the normal English way of saying these things would be "he wishes to go" or "he wished me to go". The second of the modified forms is often called the *Jussive*: a common use of this in Arabic is in Conditional Sentences, that is sentences beginning with "if" or some equivalent. If the student can keep these two basic uses in mind, we will indicate refinements and additional complexities as we come to them.

105. *The appearance of the Subjunctive.* The student should here refer to the Indicative table in para. 91, noting the two very minor changes required to make the Subjunctive: the *-u* ending becomes *-a*; and the *-īna, -ūna,-āni* endings are all reduced to the respective long vowel *-ī, -ū, -ā*. (The simple *-na* ending of 3 f.p. and 2 f.p. is not affected.) It should be noted that this means that, in normal, unvowelled Arabic, the Indicative and the Subjunctive can be distinguished only in

2 f.s., 3 m.p., 2 m.p., and in the three Duals. There is obviously no point in tabulating such small discrepancies at full length.

106. *The appearance of the Jussive.* Where the Subjunctive converts the Indicative *-u* ending to *-a*, the Jussive replaces it by *sukūn* (see para. 59). In all other cases, the Subjunctive and the Jussive coincide. Once again, this has important implications for recognition: the six possible points of distinction mentioned in the previous paragraph in fact only separate the Indicative on the one side from the Jussive-Subjunctive on the other, but they do not separate the Subjunctive and the Jussive from each other. *Valuable hints*: in the Standard Verb the Subjunctive and the Jussive cannot normally be distinguished from each other at any point (as will be seen later, certain extra distinctions can be drawn for many non-standard verbs); again, in the Standard Verb, the Indicative is clearly distinguishable from the Subjunctive-Jussive forms at six points, not normally distinguished at five other points, and absolutely identical at two others.

107. *Ambiguities of the endings* alif, -w, -y *and* -t. The student will have noticed that these endings have appeared by now in several different places. It might be useful at this point to tabulate them, since even quite advanced scholars are often inclined to overlook some of the less immediate possibilities:

(*a*) Final *alif*, on present showing, may be: a mark of the Indefinite Accusative masculine (in which case it indicates the sound *-an*); a mark of *māḍī* verbs in the Dual; a mark of *muḍāri'* verbs, Subjunctive or Jussive, in the Dual; a mark of Dual nouns, Nominative, in Construct or with an attached pronoun; a mark of *māḍī* 3 m.p., where the letter has no sound value at all, and is dropped whenever a suffix is added; likewise, with the same limitations, a mark of *muḍāri'*, Subjunctive or Jussive, 3 m.p. and 2 m.p. It may, of course, also be a part of other words and endings, such as *humā* and *-hā*, particularly where Duals are involved. As we shall see later, even this does not exhaust all the possibilities; but the above need to be borne in mind, more or less consciously for a time, until identification becomes virtually instinctive. Remember that reference to "nouns" usually includes what English-speakers might regard as adjectives.

(*b*) Final *-w*, on the present showing, may be a mark of Sound Plural masculine nouns, Nominative, in Construct or with an attached pronoun. It must be remembered that while it is, phonetically as *-ū*, a mark of *māḍī* 3 m.p. and *muḍāri'* Subjunctive-Jussive 3 m.p. and 2 m.p., it does not appear *visually* in these places *as the final letter*: as just noted once more in sub-para. (*a*), silent *alif* does duty here, unless removed by the addition of an attached pronoun. Finally, remember that *wa-* ("and", the simplest and commonest of all Arabic conjunctions or statement-linkers) often becomes detached in practice from the beginning of the word to which it really belongs, and seems to belong (in the usual "cramped" writing or printing) to the end of a previous word. Once more, we shall meet final *-w* in other connections in due course.

(*c*) Final *-y*, on the present showing, may be a mark of: the attached pronoun 1 c.s.; the *muḍāri'* Subjunctive-Jussive 2 f.s.; Sound Plural Masculine nouns, Accusative-Genitive, in Construct or with an attached pronoun; Dual nouns, Accusative-Genitive, in Construct or with an attached pronoun. Once again, final *-y*, with and without dots, has several other significations, yet to be encountered.

(*d*) Remember that the endings *-ūna, -īna, -āni* may be found both in nouns and *muḍāri'* verbs, but *-aini* belongs to nouns alone. Until the ability to distinguish such occurrences becomes instinctive, it must be based largely on an understanding of pattern and structure. Occasionally, even the expert is deceived momentarily!

(*e*) Final *-t* may be a radical letter; it may mark one of four persons in the *māḍī* singular; it may mark feminine nouns singular or plural; it appears as bound-*t* only in some feminine singular nouns, and then only when they do not have attached pronouns added as suffixes.

108. *Practice material.* Work through the material given under this paragraph number in the separate section (p. 110), applying the same methods as for paras. 89 and 99.

15

Diptotes; Demonstratives; Imperatives; Participles and maṣdars

109. *Diptotes in general.* We considered the Standard Noun in paras. 70–2, and we have noted various deviations from the endings there given, in the cases of the Masculine Sound Plural, the Feminine Sound Plural, and the Dual. Some of these deviations were considerable and some involved variable factors of their own, but the general pattern of deviation was in the direction of replacing three endings by two. We now have to review a special type of noun which also takes two endings: so marked is this feature here that this class is known pre-eminently as the "two-ending" or "diptote" noun, in contradistinction to the Standard (or "triptote") Noun. This diptote noun forms a varied class, including Elatives (paras. 159–60) and many personal and place-names, as well as a high proportion of Broken Plurals. We shall note the individual instances and the several categories as they occur. The following are typical Diptotes, the first two being words we have already met:

Indefinite Nominative: *afḍalu* *aṣdiqā'u* (pl. of *ṣadīq*) *miṣru* (Egypt) f.
Indefinite Acc./Gen.: *afḍala* *aṣdiqā'a* *miṣra*

In this course, we shall always indicate Diptotes as such, leaving triptotes to take care of themselves. The student will almost certainly find it convenient to do the same.

110. *Diptotes: particular points.* It will be realised that the essential effect of the Diptote is to deprive the noun, in the normal unvowelled script, of the one permanent mark of distinction characteristic of the *Indefinite Accusative* in most cases, the redundant *alif.* Do not therefore doubt your structural analysis if a noun you have identified as Accusative does not appear to be so: it may be a Diptote, especially if it falls into the classes mentioned above. *Note particularly* (though the normal visible result is nil) that *when Diptotes are definite grammatically* (i.e. they have the article, or they are the first element in a Construct, or have the attached pronouns as suffixes) *they revert to triptote endings.* Thus, "the friends" (Genitive) is *al-aṣdiqā'i*, "his friends" (Genitive) is *aṣdiqā'i-hi*, and so on.

111. *Demonstratives in general.* When in English we wish to point to nearer or more remote locations respectively (either real, in space, or figuratively, in time or utterance), we use words like "this, these, the latter" or "that, those, the former". Such words are called Demonstrative Pronouns or Demonstratives. Arabic has counterparts to each set, but it tends to use the "this" set rather more freely than the "that" set as compared with English, except where a definite contrast needs to be drawn. The following are the Arabic forms in normal use, albeit several minor variations may be found in poetry or archaic texts generally:

	Masc. (all cases) sing.		Fem. (all cases) sing.		Plural (common gender) all cases	
THIS	هذا	hādhā	هذه	hādhihi	هؤلاء	hā'ulā'i
THAT	ذلك	dhālika	تلك	tilka	أولائك	ulā'ika

Note particularly the following points: the Arabic Demonstratives have no real case-endings, i.e. they are indeclinable; in four of the instances shown above the vertical *fatḥa* is used for *ā*, as explained under *allāh* (vocabulary to para. 99, p. 107); there is a discrepancy between the spelling and the pronunciation of the first vowel-length in *ulā'ika.* Remember that the feminine singular will often be used to cover inanimate or non-rational plural nouns (see para. 83). The "this" set has a Dual form which is sometimes met, and this declines as a regular Dual: *hādhāni (-aini)* in the masculine, and *hātāni (-aini)* in the feminine (all spelt with vertical *fatḥa* in the first syllable).

112. *Use of Demonstratives.* As in English, the Arabic Demonstratives can be used to replace a noun in virtually any situation (i.e. as pronouns), or they can qualify a noun directly ("this man", "those books" etc.). The former category presents no new problem. In the latter case, however, the Arabic Demonstrative normally precedes its noun in apposition: that is to say, it exercises no influence grammatically on its noun, but stands (at least theoretically here!) in the same case as that noun takes according to its function (cf. explanation under *nafs* in vocabulary to para. 99, p. 108). Moreover, the noun so used must take the definite article. Thus one finds, for example *hādhā* preceding *al-rajulu*, or *-a*, or *-i*, the sense in each case being "this man". The presence or absence of the article here is an important structural criterion for distinguishing the mere subject of a Nominal Sentence from a complete statement in Nominal-Sentence form: هذا رجل will normally be read as *hādhā rajulun*: but هذا الرجل is *hādhā al-rajulu* (or *-a* or *-i*), "this man", which may be the subject of a Nominal Sentence, or a Nominal Absolute (para. 81), or any of the several things a Definite noun can be in Arabic. If one wants to say "this is *the* man", one must insert a dividing *huwa* in accordance with what was said of the second deviant type of Nominal Sentence under para. 80(*a*).

113. *Further on Demonstratives.* What of the Demonstrative which must directly qualify a noun that cannot take the article – for example many proper names, the first element in a Construct, or a noun with an attached pronoun suffix? In such cases, the Demonstrative comes as soon *after* the noun as possible. Consider the following instances:

مصر هذه	this Egypt (f.)
كتاب الولد هذا	this book of the boy
كتاب ولد هذا	this book of a boy, this "boy's book"
كتابه هذا	this book of his, this his book
كتاب هذا الولد	the book of this boy, this boy's book

The first four cover the situations just mentioned. In the fifth example, it should be noted that we are not "breaking" a Construct (see para. 88): *kitābu* (or whatever the case may be) is in Construct with *hādhā*, and *al-waladi* is in apposition to the theoretically Genitive *hādhā*, as explained in para. 112. It is important to try to see all the distinctions, both implicit and explicit, between the second and the fifth examples, the second and the third, and the third and the fifth respectively.

114. *Imperative forms in general.* Many languages, including Arabic (but not normally including modern English) have a special form of the verb for giving orders, usually termed the Imperative. In Arabic, the Imperative is most conveniently formed from the Jussive 2 m.s., i.e. (in the case of the Standard Verb as we have so far considered it) from *taktub*. The first step is always to remove the personal prefix, leaving us here with *ktub*. Secondly, if the resulting form is unpronounceable *in Arabic as beginning with two consonants*, a *hamzat al-waṣl* is prefixed, with the following vowel-pattern: *u* if the vowel of the middle radical is *u*; *i* if it is *a* or *i*. Thus we have *uktub*, but *ishrab* and *irji'* ("write!", "drink!", "come back!"). It is important to remember that what is added is *hamzat al-waṣl*, so that the *hamza* itself should not be written (only the *alif*, usually without a vowel), while the vowel sound disappears wherever possible in connected speech. Moreover, as will be seen later, this *hamzat al-waṣl* is not needed for many non-standard verbs or for Standard Verbs in several of the so-called "derived forms": following the rules set out above, for example, would in such cases give you forms like *qul* and *saiyir* which offer no pronunciation problems.

115. *The persons of the Imperative.* The form we have been discussing is used for giving an order to one masculine person or thing. The process is commonly refined by adding the following Jussive endings as needed: 2 f.s. (*-ī*); 2 m.p. (*-ū*); 2 f.p. (*-na*); 2 c.d. (*-ā*). Arabic is quite rigorous in using these endings where appropriate, so do not regard them as frills. Try to collate these endings, as used here, with what was said in para. 107.

116. *Participles and* maṣdars. (*a*) *Active Participle.* There are three parts of the Arabic verb which, while two of them often still carry sufficient verbal force to govern objects, nevertheless have the form and the function of nouns or noun-adjectives. First, the *Active Participle*, which (in the Standard Verb as we have so far considered it) has the pattern *kātib* – a pattern of which we have already encountered such examples as *tājir* and *sālim*. The Active Participle (note that we should not speak of a "present participle", since no necessary idea of time is involved) names or describes the person, or the thing, performing the action in question: thus *tājir* might be translated "a merchant" or "engaged in commerce". It should be noted that in the first sense (which is, so to speak, technical and professional) the Active Participle commonly takes the Broken Plural *tujjār*, *kuttāb*, which we have already given. Where it is purely descriptive of males performing certain actions, however (and particularly where it exercises its verbal force), it tends to take a Sound Plural. The less common feminine parallel in bound-*t* is a little more complicated in the choice of plurals, and will be discussed as we come to it, though something of the same general principle obtains.

(*b*) *Passive Particles.* In the Standard Verb as we have so far considered it, this has the pattern *maktūb*, *mashrūb*, *maqtūl*. Examples we have encountered are *madhkūr* and *ma'rūf*. The *Passive Participle* (note that we should not speak of a "past participle", though time does naturally often tend to be implied here) names or describes the person, or the thing, affected by the action in question: thus *maktūb* might be "a letter" (i.e. something written) or simply "written";

mashrūb "a drink" or "taken as a drink, drunk"; and *maqtūl* "a victim, a martyr" or "slain, murdered". There can naturally be no real question of verbal force here, at least in the sense of governing. Where the reference is to a person, the Sound Plural Masculine is usual; where to a thing, either a special Diptote Broken Plural or sometimes the Sound Plural *Feminine*. The latter is of course also used to make a plural from the feminine form of the Passive Participle in bound-*t*, but confusion is in practice very rare.

(*c*) *Maṣdar.* This part of the verb, which is also sometimes referred to as the Verbal Noun or the Infinitive (by a rather misleading analogy with certain Western languages), has no single pattern in the Standard Verb as we have so far considered it. However, of the forty-odd patterns technically possible, only some ten or twelve could really be described as being in common use, and of these some half-dozen recur most frequently. Much the best course is to learn the *maṣdar* for the Basic Form of the Standard Verb, together with the middle vowel of the *muḍāri‘*, as one learns the *māḍī*; as will be seen later, it is not necessary to do this individually for the so-called Derived Forms, or even for the basic Form of many non-standard verbs. The *maṣdar* names the action of the verb or speaks of the fact of it. It corresponds to a number of different words or forms in English; in the following English sentences all the underlined forms would be rendered by the Arabic *maṣdar* form *qatl* (from *qatala, yaqtulu*): "*killing (the act of killing, to kill, murder)* is wrong"; "his *killing (being killed, murder)* was the work of a madman"; "his *killing* his father (*murder* of his father) was unpremeditated". It should be noted that the Arabic *maṣdar* is practically always Definite, either by way of the article *al-*, or as being the first element in a Construct, or through having an attached pronoun as suffix. In the first of the three types above, the article would be required in Arabic. As can be seen from the second of the above sentence types, the *maṣdar* sometimes carries passive as well as active implications, but the latter are more common. We shall discuss the *maṣdar*'s verbal force and the three main modes by which it governs when we come to actual instances.

117. *Practice material.* This, together with necessary analyses, will be found under the appropriate paragraph number in the separate section, p. 115.

118. *Translation into Arabic.* Though the primary purpose of this course is to enable students to *read Arabic*, it is occasionally useful to turn carefully selected English sentences into Arabic in order to strengthen and clarify one's mastery of vocabulary and principles of construction. The sentences given under this paragraph number in the separate section (p. 117) have this purpose in mind.

16

Derived Forms II–IV

119. *The Derived Forms in general.* The form of the Arabic verb we have been studying so far is the Base or Ground Form, that one which (theoretically, at least) expresses the essential notion of the verb at its simplest. In addition, however, every Arabic verb (both Standard and non-standard) is potentially capable of several pattern-modifications to indicate modifications of the essential meaning. Thus, while *qatala* is "to kill", *qattala* is "to kill violently or on a large scale" (i.e. "to slaughter", "to massacre"); and *qātala* is "to try to kill" (i.e. "to fight with"); *taqattala* and *iqtatala*, again, both mean "to fight (against each other)". While there are 14 such Derived Forms in addition to the Base, no verb has them all; some have none or one, but most have something between three and six such forms in common use. Western Arabists number the forms conveniently in an agreed sequence from I to XV, and we shall adopt this practice. The most important are numbers II to VIII and X.

120. *Advantages and limitations of the Derived Forms.* The Derived Forms are often spoken of as though they gave Arabic a sort of mathematical exactness, that is as if the exact shade of meaning of every verb in a Derived Form could immediately be recognised once one knew the relevant formula; or as if every student of Arabic could "make up" his own Derived Forms to suit his purpose. This is at the very least a gross exaggeration. Languages in normal use do not behave mathematically: as with all other human activities, the most one can hope for is a rough general area of assimilation and predictability. Accordingly, while we shall make some attempt to analyse the sense-modification (in some cases there is more than one) of each Derived Form as we come to it, the student should try to associate a *particular* English equivalent with the *particular* Derived Form of *any given verb*: thus, do not get into the habit of thinking of *istakhraja* (X Form of KHRJ) as "to cause to come forth for one's own benefit", but as the normal Arabic verb meaning "to extract" (e.g. minerals). Similarly, *akhraja* (IV Form) means essentially "to cause to go out": but it is the normal verb used for all sorts of situations where things or people are removed from within a "container", so that the proper rendering in any given instance might be "to expel, banish, send out, remove, dislodge, extract, produce etc." It will be appreciated that although this often tends to reduce the diversified volume of Arabic vocabulary a student needs to learn as compared with English, he has a corresponding obligation in the opposite direction to render a single Arabic word in a wide variety of ways according to the context. One incontestable advantage of the Derived Forms, from the learner's point of view, is that *all patterns are predetermined*: one need not, as in the Base Form, learn the particular middle vowels (*māḍī* and *muḍāri'*) or the *maṣdar* of any given verb, since these are all absolutely regular. Instead, one learns only the *patterns* of the *māḍī* and the *muḍāri'*, and of the *maṣdar*, for each Derived Form (the Derived Form participles are formed direct from the *muḍāri'*, by a process that remains constant throughout). The *suffixes* of the various numbers, genders and persons of the *māḍī* and the *muḍāri'*, in the Derived Forms, are exactly the same as in the Base Form. The *prefixes* of the derived *muḍāri'* are *essentially* the same, though the vowel is *u* in *some* forms instead of *a*: *yaktubu* I, but *yukattibu* II, *yuktibu* IV, *yatakattabu* V, *yastaktibu* X etc. All of this obviates the need for lengthy tabulation of these forms. We shall simply show the *māḍī* and the *muḍāri'*, 3 m.s., and the *maṣdar* of each Derived Form, indicating the rule for making the participles in the case of the Second only and leaving it to the student to apply the rule to all the other Derived Forms. We shall continue to use KTB *to illustrate the pattern*, even though that root does not in fact have some of the Derived Forms in use.

121. *The Second Form (appearance).* The basic features here are the doubling of the second radical, and the vowel-pattern *u-a-i-u* of the *muḍāri'*. The commonest *maṣdar* is very easily recognised, being quite peculiar in itself:

Māḍī	*Muḍāri'*	*Maṣdar*
kattaba	yukattibu	taktīb(un)

In the Second, as in all the Derived Forms, the Active Participle is formed from the *muḍāri'* by substituting *mu-* for the prefix (here *yu-*) and replacing the final *-u* by the Standard Noun endings: *mukattib(un)*. The Derived Passive Participle differs from the Active only by the substitution of *-a-* for *-i-*: *mukattab(un)*.

NOTE: In all the Derived Forms of the Standard Verb, in the normal unvowelled script, the Active and Passive Participles *look* exactly alike. In the Second Form, unless the *tashdīd* is actually written in, the *māḍī* and the *muḍāri'* cannot be distinguished from those of the Base Form (at least in the Standard Verb); as will be seen later, the *muḍāri'* II can also be confused with that of IV, where the *tashdīd* and other signs are missing. The Imperative here needs no prefixed *hamza* as in the Basic Form.

122. *Form II (common shades of meaning)*

(*a*) *An intransitive verb is made transitive.* Thus, *waqafa (i)* I is "to stand, to come to a halt", but *waqqafa* is "to stop *or* halt (someone), to arrest".

(*b*) *An already transitive verb is made doubly transitive* (i.e. causative): *'alima al-ḥisāb(a)*, "he knew arithmetic"; *'allama-hu al-ḥisāb(a)*, "he caused him to know arithmetic", (more normally) "he taught him arithmetic". In the latter case, the verb now has two objects, the pupil and the thing studied. (Note, once again, that the internal vowel-pattern in the Derived Forms is independent of that in the Base Form.)

(*c*) *A verb (transitive or intransitive) is intensified or extensified; kasara (i),* "to break", but *kassara*, "to smash to pieces"; *qatala*, "to kill", but *qattala*, "to slaughter, massacre".

(*d*) *A verb may be made from a noun* (the "denominative" use): *jild*, "skin, leather, binding", gives *jallada*, "to bind (of books)". Note that such Derived Forms really have no Base Form, although an apparent Base Form may exist in some other sense. Here, for example, *jalida* I is "to freeze, become frozen", giving once more *jallada*, "to freeze, make frozen" (cf. (*a*) above); and *jalada* (*i*) is "to flog" (possibly related in sense).

(*e*) *A "verb of opinion" (the "estimative" use) may be made from a verb or a noun-adjective: qabuḥa*, "to be loathsome", or *qabīḥ*, "loathsome", give *qabbaḥa*, "to find loathsome, to loathe". This use is often shared with the X Form.

123. *Form III (appearance).* The basic features are the insertion of *-ā-* after the first radical, and the vowel-pattern *u-ā-i-u* of the *muḍāri'*. There are two *maṣdars*, both fairly common, but not all verbs use both:

Māḍī	*Muḍāri'*	*Maṣdar*
kātaba	yukātibu	mukātaba(h)
qātala	yuqātilu	muqātala(h)
		qitāl

NOTE: Since the added *-ā-* demands a written *alif*, this form can always be easily recognised, however sparse the use of signs. The first of the two *maṣdars* is exactly identical in pattern with the Passive Participle feminine, and identical in its unvowelled appearance with the Active Participle feminine also. The Imperative here needs no prefixed *hamza* as in the Basic Form.

124. *Form III (common shades of meaning)*

(*a*) *The notion of reciprocity is introduced.* Thus, where *kataba* I is "to write" (i.e. something which no one necessarily reads or answers), *kātaba* is "to correspond with" (implying an exchange of writings). As a result, where Form I may or may not use a preposition to govern (*kataba ilà*, "to write to . . ."), Form III virtually always governs directly in the accusative.

(*b*) *The notion of endeavour (the "conative" use) is often implied*, without necessarily excluding the idea of reciprocity. Thus, *qatala* I is "to kill", but *qātala* is "to try to kill", usually being translated by "to make an attack on, to fight with".

125. *Form IV (appearance).* The basic features here are the prefixing of *'a-* (*hamzat al-qaṭ'!)* in both the *māḍī* and the Imperative,[1] with *sukūn* on the first

[1] This makes the Imperative of Form IV the only one deserving of special mention. All the others are formed in accordance with para. 114: i.e. nothing is added to the "mutilated" Jussive for II, III, V and VI; and *i-* (*hamzat al-waṣl*) is added for VII, VIII and X.

radical; and a vowel-pattern *u-sukūn-i-u* in the *muḍāri'*. The *maṣdar* also has prefixed *'i-*, again *hamzat al-qaṭ'*, and with *sukūn* on the first radical:

Māḍī	*Muḍāri'*	*Maṣdar*
aktaba	yuktibu	iktāb

126. *Form IV (shades of meaning).* This form duplicates Form II in the series given in para. 122 under (*a*), (*b*) and (*d*). (Sometimes a verb can be used, more or less identically and arbitrarily, in both forms; sometimes there is a subtle distinction between II and IV; sometimes one is preferred to the other.) Examples of three uses indicated under II are:

(*a*) KHRJ (u) I, to go out; IV, to expel

(*b*) SHRB I, to drink; IV, to cause to drink (e.g. to administer a potion, to saturate, imbue)

(*c*) JLS (i) I, to sit; IV, to seat, install

(*d*) *maṭar*, "rain"; *amṭara*, to rain

NOTE: Form IV, and indeed most other Forms, often exhibit, in any given instance, subtleties of sense not easily reducible to categories. Form IV is usually, though obviously not in the case of (*d*), transitive in operation.

127. *Practice material.* Read the three stories under this paragraph number in the separate section, p. 118. From this point on, explanations in the vocabulary will not be repeated at length.

17

Derived Forms V and VI; WĀW of Circumstance; Negatives

128. *The Fifth Form (appearance).* The characteristic feature here is the prefixing of *ta-* to what is essentially Form II. However, the vowels in the *muḍāri'* are *a-a-a-a-u*. Thus, *'alima* gives (as we have seen in para. 122 (*b*)) *'allama* in II, but *ta'allama* in V. It should be noted that this characteristic *ta-* is not normally affected by the presence of prefixed *ta-* indicating Second Person *muḍāri'*. The following are the "key" parts:

Māḍī	*Muḍāri'*	*Maṣdar*
ta'allama	yata'allamu	ta'allum

NOTE: Despite the series of *fatḥa* vowels in the *muḍāri'*, the Active and Passive Participles continue to be distinguished in the usual way: *muta'allim* as against *muta'allam*.

129. *Form V (shades of meaning)*

(*a*) Essentially, Form V is a reflexive of Form II – that is the transitive action of Form II is "bent back" upon the subject rather than affecting another person or thing (though it may do this also). Thus, *'alima*, "to know", gives (as just recalled) *'allama*, "to teach"; its Form V, *ta'allama*, is "to teach oneself" or (in more normal English) "to learn".

(*b*) This meaning, whether derived from an actual Form II or from a noun-adjective, is also often associated with the idea of "representing oneself as being . . . "; not infrequently, this shade of meaning carries an overtone of ridicule or contempt: *takabbara* is "to pretend to bigness", "to give oneself airs", "to be haughty"; *tanaṣṣara* (from *naṣrānīy*, "Christian") is "to become a Christian" (as a simple statement of fact) or "to turn Christian, put on Christianised manners".

(*c*) Often, the exact shade of meaning is difficult to define theoretically, especially in relation to the other forms: *kallama* is "to speak to", "to address", whereas *takallama* is simply "to speak".

130. *Form VI (appearance).* The characteristic feature here is the prefixing of *ta-* to what is essentially Form III. However, the vowels in the *muḍāri'* are *a-a-ā-a-u*. Thus, *qatala* gives (as we have seen in para. 124(*b*)) *qātala* in III, but *taqātala* in VI. It should be noted that this characteristic *ta-* is not normally affected by the presence of prefixed *ta-* indicating Second Person *muḍāri'*. The following are the "key" parts:

Māḍī	*Muḍāri'*	*Maṣdar*
taqātala	yataqātalu	taqātul

NOTE: Despite the series of *fatḥa* vowels in the *muḍāri'*, the Active and Passive Participles continue to be distinguished in the usual way: *mutaqātil* as against *mutaqātal*.

131. *Form VI (shades of meaning)*

(*a*) Essentially, Form VI is a reflexive or a "mutualiser" of Form III. Thus, while *qātala* is "to fight with", taking a direct object, *taqātala* is "to fight against each other", with subject and object being virtually indistinguishable. It may be noted that the subject of such a verb will of necessity normally be Dual or plural, though the verb itself may by the rules of agreement be singular in the appropriate situation.

(*b*) Even more than Form V, Form VI often carries the idea of "outward representation", not to say "pretence". Thus, *tashāghala*, "to give the appearance of being busy"; *tanāwama*, "to feign to be asleep".

132. *The* wāw *of Circumstance.* Arabic commonly uses the particle *wa-* (i.e. "and", "but", "for" etc.) in a way that, while not without parallel in certain other languages, is seldom so characteristic and fully developed as here. Consider the following sentence:

كان يلْبَس عمرُ وهو خليفة لباسا من الصُوف

"'Umar, when he was Caliph, used to wear a garment of wool."

For practical purposes at this point, the sentence may be grammatically analysed as follows: A Verbal Sentence ("Used to wear 'Umar . . . a garment of wool") enclosing a *Nominal Sentence introduced by "and"* (. . . "*and* he (is) a Caliph" . . .). Note the compound verb at the beginning (we have already had examples, cf. para. 108, of the *māḍī* of *kāna* preceding the *muḍāri'* of another verb to give the sense "used to do", "was doing"); and also the Diptote proper name – common phenomenon (especially in the case of place-names, feminine personal names, and non-Arabic names, though none of these applies here).

Now consider the following sentence

أسلم عمر وقد كان كافرا

"'Umar was converted to Islam after having been an infidel."

This sentence may be grammatically analysed as a Verbal Sentence linked to another Verbal Sentence by *wa-* and *qad*. A literal rendering might be: "'Umar Islamised (note Form IV) and he had been (note force of *qad*, again as explained in para. 108) an infidel." As with *laisa*, the predicate of *kāna* is Accusative.

Both these specimen sentences are classic examples of the use of the *wāw* of Circumstance: in the first type, the Circumstance accompanies (and often dovetails into) the main action; in the second type the Circumstance precedes (but usually only to a limited extent) the main action, though it is the clause expressing the latter that is put first. It should be noted that there is a wide variety of ways of rendering these constructions into English, but "while" (or some equivalent) will usually be found useful to render the *Accompanying* Circumstance, and "after having done . . ." (or some equivalent) for the *Preceding* Circumstance.

133. *Negatives in Arabic.* Various Arabic particles perform the functions of the English words "not", "no", "neither", "nor" etc. Since they are most often used as "time-indicators" (cf. para. 62), it is convenient to consider them as far as possible under the headings of Past, Present and Future.

134. *Negative Past.* The past is negated by the particle *mā*[1] with the *māḍī* or *lam* with the Jussive. Thus, *mā kataba* or *lam yaktub* both mean "he has not written, did not write, had not written" etc., through the whole range of past tenses normally found in English. In addition, *lammā* with the Jussive adds the idea of "yet" to the negative pastness of *lam*: *lammā yaktub*, "he has not yet

[1] Do not confuse with *mā* meaning "what".

written", "did not yet write", "had not yet written" etc. *Note*: Do not confuse this *lammā* with the one found in para. 99: *lammā kataba* means "when he wrote . . .".

135. *Negative Present*. The Present (including the Near-Future) is negated by *mā* or *lā* followed by the *muḍāriʿ*: *mā* (or *lā*) *yaktubu*, "he does not write", "is not writing", "will not write" etc. Of the two particles, *lā* is less closely tied to time than *mā*, and negates the action in a general way. Thus, *lā yaktubu* could well mean "he does not write", "is not given to writing". *Note*: The peculiar verb *laisa* (para. 117) negates those normally present-tense statements which we call Nominal Sentences: *huwa walad(un)*, "he is a boy", but *laisa walad(an)*, "he is not a boy". See also Chapter 21.

136. *Negative Future*. What might be called the Solemn Future, or the Formal Future, is negated by *lan* followed by the Subjunctive. Thus, "he has gone away and he will not return", might be rendered: *qad dhahaba wa-lan yarjiʿa*. *Note*: The Future can be similarly emphasised in important *positive* statements by the use of *sa-* or *saufa* before the simple *muḍāriʿ*: a solemn declaration or threat, "I will return", would almost certainly be rendered into Arabic as "*sa-arjiʿu*" or "*saufa arjiʿu*".

137. *Special uses of the negative* lā. This particle has three common uses in addition to those mentioned already:

(*a*) It combines with the Second Person of the Jussive to form "prohibitions", i.e. Negative Imperatives (cf. paras. 114 and 115). Thus *uktub*. "write", but *lā taktub*, "do not write". Any of the Second Person numbers or genders can be made negative in this way. One may *not* simply prefix a negative particle to the ordinary Imperative, as in many languages.

(*b*) It directly negates an indefinite noun, in the Accusative Case and without *tanwīn*, to make a statement of absolute negation. The most celebrated example of this is found in the first part of the Muslim profession of faith: *lā ilāh(a) illā allāh(u)*, "there is no god but God!", "there is no deity except God (Himself)". Remember in pronouncing this to say "*illa-llāh*", not as we have just written it for convenience and clarity. On the other hand, the word *ilāh* begins with *hamzat al-qaṭʿ*.

(*c*) Where there is a string of negative verbs, one may use *lā* with the appropriate Aspect once the time of the action has been established at the beginning of the sentence by *mā* or *lam*. Thus, the English sentence "he neither read nor wrote", "he did not read or write" might be put into Arabic as *mā qaraʾa wa-lā kataba* or *lam yaqraʾ wa-lā yaktub* (cf. para. 134).

138. *Practice material*. Translate the English and Arabic passages under this paragraph number in the separate section, p. 121.

18

Derived Forms VII, VIII and X; Positive time-indicators

139. *Form VII: appearance and meaning.* The characteristic feature here is the prefixing of *in-* to Form I, with middle vowel regularised as *-a-* in the *māḍī*. The *hamza* involved is of *waṣl*, disappearing in the *muḍāri'*, which has the vowel-pattern *a-sukūn-a-i-u*. The *maṣdar* (and that of VIII and X) has a characteristic long *ā* in the final syllable. Thus from Form I *kasara*, we find Form VII *inkasara, yankasiru, inkisār*. Note that the stress never falls on this prefix. Note, too, that this form rarely if ever occurs in verbs with an initial radical "unsympathetic" to *n*, for example *hamza, r, l, n, w*, and *y*. The sense of this form is somewhat hard to define precisely; however, it commonly renders a transitive Form I intransitive, quasi-reflexive or "neuter". Thus *kasara* I is "to break (something)", but *inkasara* is "to break, become broken", with some degree of ambiguity as to whether or not an agent may have been responsible. Again, *hazama* (*i*) is "to rout, put to flight", while *inhazama* is "to decamp, take to one's heels". The VII often doubles or interchanges with V, but it cannot take an explicit object.

140. *Form VIII: appearance and meaning.* The characteristic feature here is the "enclosure" of the first radical by prefixed *i-* (*hamzat al-waṣl*) and postposited *-ta-*, the first radical itself taking *sukūn*. In the *māḍī*, the *muḍāri'* and the *maṣdar*, the vowel-pattern echoes VII. Thus from Form I *jama'a*, we find Form VIII *ijtama'a, yajtami'u, ijtimā'*. As with VII, the stress does not recede as far as what has now become the first syllable. While this form may be made from verbs with virtually any first radical sound, certain natural phonetic changes take place (particularly with dentals) as follows: if the first radical is *d, dh* or *z*, the inserted *-t-* itself becomes a *-d-* and tends to assimilate with the radical *d* or *dh*, which are accordingly written with *shadda* (*daraka*: *iddaraka*; *dhakhara*: *iddakhara* or *idhdhakhara*; *zaḥama*: *izdaḥama*.) If the first radical should be *ṣ, ḍ* or *ṭ*, the inserted *-t-* itself becomes a *-ṭ-* (*ṣana'a*: *iṣṭana'a*; *ḍaraba*: *iḍṭaraba*; *ṭala'a*; *iṭṭala'a* (note assimilation here!)) Again, if the first radical is *ẓ*, the *-t-* tends to assimilate to it (*ẓalama*: *iẓẓalama*). Finally, initial *w-* or (rarely) *hamza* assimilate *themselves to the inserted -t-* (*wafaqa*: *ittafaqa*; *akhadha*: *ittakhadha*). This form is extremely difficult to analyse as to meaning, which is unfortunate inasmuch as it is of very common occurrence. It hovers on identification with the "reflexive" sense of V and VII, even sometimes doubling or interchanging with one or other of these, but unlike the latter it commonly takes an object. Sometimes it is identical with Form I in sense. Typical Form VIII verbs are: *ijtama'a*, "to come together, to assemble", where Form I means "to bring together, gather, collect (something)"; *iṭṭala'a* (with *'alà*), "to become aware of, informed about", where Form I means simply "to rise"; *ittakhadha*, "to take for oneself, set aside, cultivate", where Form I carries broad connotations of "taking", as already noted; *istama'a* (with *ilà*), "to listen", where Form I means simply "to hear"; *iḍṭaraba*, "to be disturbed, upset, agitated", where Form I means "to beat, strike". And so on.

141. *Form X: appearance* Since Form IX (like Form XI) is reserved for verbs associated with Colours and Defects, we shall leave them until we treat the adjectives in question. Thus we come to Form X, the last of the forms in common use. The characteristic feature here is the prefixing of *ista-* (*hamzat al-waṣl*) to Form I, with *sukūn* on the first radical and the middle vowel regularised as *-a-* in the *māḍī*. The *hamza* disappears in the *muḍāri'*, which has the vowel-pattern *a-sukūn-a-sukūn-i-u*. The *maṣdar* has, once more, a characteristic long *ā* in the final syllable. Note that while the vowel-pattern echoes VII and VIII, it does not exactly coincide at all points. The stress here recedes, if appropriate, as far as the second syllable of the prefix (-ta-). Here is a typical Form X from KHRJ (note stress!):

Māḍī	*Muḍāri'*	*Maṣdar*
istákhraja	yastákhriju	istikhrā́j

142. *Form X: meanings*. Three connotations are commonly found here, of which only one is peculiar to the form alone:

(*a*) A sense of asking or requesting is introduced. From *adhina*, "to permit", comes *ista'dhana*, "to ask permission"; *ghafara* is "to forgive", *istaghfara* "to seek forgiveness".

(*b*) Another sense is that of doing something for one's own advantage. Thus, the pattern given at the end of para. 141 means "to extract (minerals), to exploit (a mine, resources, people)"; *'amara* is "to inhabit, to people", but *ista'mara* is "to colonise (often in a bad sense), to practise imperialism".

(*c*) With II, Form X shares the estimative sense: *istaqbaḥa* is "to find repulsive, to loathe", and its opposite is *istaḥsana*.

Often, as with the other forms, the shade of meaning in X is difficult to pin down in a given case: *qabila* is "to receive, accept", but *istaqbala* is commonly used only for receiving or welcoming people; *qāma* (Hollow!) is "to rise", *istaqāma* is "to be straight". And so on.

143. *Positive time-indicators*. These are so called in contrast to the negative time-indicators discussed in the last chapter. Concerning three of them, *qad, sa-* or *saufa*, and the *māḍī* of *kāna* followed by the *muḍāri'* of another verb, we have already said what needs to be said. (For the first and third, see the *Vocabulary and remarks* to para. 108, pp. 112, 110f. respectively; for the second, see para.

136.) Leaving aside Conditional Sentences (which we shall treat separately) and isolated cases like *lammā* with *māḍī*, three important instances remain:

(*a*) The *māḍī* of *kāna* followed by the *māḍī* of another verb: *kāna kataba*. This is virtually always to be translated by the English pluperfect, "he had written". Note that, as with the third of the three instances just recapitulated, the two verbs often "enclose" the explicit noun-subject: *kāna rajulun kataba*, "a man had written", rather than *kāna kataba rajulun*. Note, too, that *qad* may be added to this construction (as well as substituting for it): it may precede the first verb or the second, the latter being perhaps more elegant and forceful: *kāna rajulun qad kataba*. Above all, remember (both with this construction and the next) the rules of agreement regarding verbs preceding, and verbs following, their subject respectively.

(*b*) The *muḍāri'* of *kāna* (which is *yakūnu*) followed by the *māḍī* of another verb: *yakūnu kataba*. This is to be translated by the English so-called future-perfect, "he will have written". Once again the verbs commonly "enclose" the subject, and once again *qad* may be added to the construction, but this time only before the second verb.

(*c*) *Qad* preceding the *muḍāri'* is to be rendered by the present or near-future with "perhaps", "...may...", "sometimes": *qad yaktubu*, "he may write" etc.

144. *Practice material*. Work through the material in the separate section, p. 124.

19

Passives; Plurals of four-consonant nouns; Nouns of Time and Place; Nouns of Instrument

145. *Passives in general*. Arabic is one of many languages having a special form of the verb to express the Passive. (Other languages, like English and French, achieve the same result by compounding the verb "to be" with the past-participle of the verb in question: "A kills B" becomes "B *is killed* by A".) The general pattern of the Arabic verb used for the Passive is essentially identical with or similar to the *māḍī* and the *muḍāri'* (including the Subjunctive and Jussive variations) as we have so far encountered them, but the vowel-pattern is characteristically different: basically, it is *u-i-a* in the *māḍī* and *u-sukūn-a-u* in the *muḍāri'*. The 3 m.s. Passive of both Aspects is given in the next paragraph for the Ground and each of the main Derived Forms, using the radicals KTB throughout for demonstration purposes. Perhaps the most important thing to note about the

Arabic Passive is that it is of fairly rare occurrence in any case, and that it is virtually *never used where the agent's identity is stated.* The Arabic name for it is *al-majhūl*, "the not-known", in token of this fact.

146. *Principal Passives in 3 m.s.* Once the following table has been learned, the remaining persons, numbers and so on can be readily made as for the Active *māḍī* and *muḍāri'* in all the relevant positions:

	Māḍī	*Muḍāri'*
I	kutiba	yuktabu (cf. IV)
II	kuttiba	yukattabu
III	kūtiba	yukātabu
IV	uktiba	yuktabu (cf. I)
V	tukuttiba	yutakattabu
VI	tukūtiba	yutakātabu
VII	unkutiba (very rare)	yunkatabu (very rare)
VIII	uktutiba	yuktatabu
X	ustuktiba	yustaktabu

Note that the additional prefixed syllables tend to be made with *u* in the *māḍī*, but with *a* in the *muḍāri'*; also that the "structural" appearance differs from the Active only in III and VI of the *māḍī*, where *ū* replaces *ā*, i.e. *wāw* replaces *alif.*

147. *Plurals of four-consonant nouns.* The plurals we have encountered so far have been those of three-consonant nouns, with one or more short vowels and sometimes with a long vowel also. Many Arabic nouns, however, have four consonants (not just a special pattern of three consonants with a *shadda* as in a trade-form like *fallāḥ*), with two short vowels or one long and one short. These nouns obtain their four consonants in different ways, some because these consonants are all an integral part of the word, some because one consonant has been added to three radicals in the process of making a new pattern: an example of the former is *khinzīr*, "pig" (KHNZR), or *sikkīn*, while the latter pattern is represented by *masjid*, "mosque" (from SJD connoting "prostration"). However, unless they are participles (which, as we saw in para. 100, mostly take Sound Plurals), they should all be treated identically when forming plurals, according to the following rules.

(*a*) If there is a short vowel between the third and fourth consonant, as in *masjid*, the plural is normally of the pattern *masājid(u).*

(*b*) If there is a long vowel between the third and fourth consonant, as in *khinzīr* or *sikkīn*, the plural is normally of the pattern *khanāzīr(u)*, *sakākīn(u).* Even the Passive Participle of I, when used as a noun, commonly behaves thus: *maktūb*, "letter", gives *makātīb(u).*

These rules ease greatly the burden of learning plurals: it will be noted that in general the longer the word, the easier to forecast is the plural.

148. *Nouns of Time and place.* Arabic makes considerable use of special noun-patterns to express the idea of the place (and to some extent the time) of a given action. *In the case of Form I* the pattern is either as for *masjid* or like *maktab*, "mosque" and "office" (or "desk") respectively (literally "a place of prostration" and "a place of writing"). Sometimes, the form will have bound-*t* as a variant, or a substitute, or giving a new shade of meaning: thus, *maktaba(h)* is a "library, bookstore", but *madrasa(h)* is the only form for "school". All of these form their plurals as in para. 147 (*a*). *In the Derived Forms* the Noun of Place is identical with the Passive Participle: since, however, such cases are practically confined to a relatively few Weak Roots, we shall deal with these as we come to them or when we study Weak Verbs at length. These Passive Participle-Place Nouns, relating to the Derived Forms, normally form their plurals in the Sound *Feminine.* Note that you should try to assign a specific meaning to each Noun of Place (and Time): do not content yourself with a general understanding of the literal sense (cf. what has been said above about *majsid* and *maktab*). See also para. 149.

149. *Nouns of Instrument.* Special patterns are likewise often used to designate the instrument by which a given action is performed, but these are confined, practically speaking, to Form I. The two most common patterns in use are exemplified by *miftāḥ*, "key" from FTḤ, and *miknasa*(*h*), "broom", from *kanasa*(*i*), "to sweep". The former makes a plural as in para. 147(*b*), the latter as in 147(*a*). (It may be evident by now that it is not always easy, when meeting the plurals of four-consonant nouns based on three radicals, to re-construct the exact singular involved: theoretically, at least, *makānisu* might come from *miknasa*(*h*) or *maknis*; and *mafātiḥu* might come from *miftāḥ* or *maftūḥ*. As always in Arabic, even more then in most languages, reliable experience must be laboriously built up by constant recourse to a dictionary in the hope of discovering actual occurrences.) Note that the *miftāḥ* pattern sometimes serves as a Noun of Time and Place for initial-W Roots: *walada*, "to bear, beget", makes *mīlād*, "birthday" (*miwlād* undergoes a necessary phonetic change to *miylād, mīlād*).

150. *Practice material.* Read the story and the proverbs in the separate section, p. 125.

20

Conditional and Quasi-Conditional Sentences; Colours and Defects; Elatives

151. *Conditional Sentences in general.* Conditional Sentences are those which cause a particular statement or command to depend on the fulfilment of a given condition: "If you lay by one dollar per week, you will have over $500 at the end of ten years"; "If you see anything strange, shoot first and ask questions afterwards!"; "If I had not known he was a criminal, I should have felt inclined to believe what he was saying." Such sentences can often become complex, with one or more inset clauses dependent on the main ones; they may contain negative and affirmative elements indiscriminately; they may range from likelihood, through mere possibility, to outright hypotheticality and absurdity; they can often express the condition by other words than "if" ("had I known. . . , were it not for the fact that. . . , assuming that. . . ", etc.); and they may place the clause setting the condition (the Protasis) *after* the consequential statement or command (the Apodosis). In many languages, but only to a very limited extent in modern English, Conditional Sentences need special consideration as regards structure, particularly in the matter of tenses.

152. *Conditional Sentences in Arabic.* Most of the foregoing remarks apply to the case of Arabic, with one exception: in Arabic the Protasis (*sharṭ*, lit. "condition") must practically always precede the Apodosis (*jawāb*, lit. "answer, response"). Three special points need attention in Arabic Conditional Sentences: the particle used for "if"; the Aspect of the verb employed; and the introduction of the *jawāb*, by *fa-* or in some other way. Moreover, there are some Arabic Conditionals that would at first sight not appear to be so, and these we call Quasi-Conditionals. Each of these problems will now be dealt with separately. Since they are interdependent, a multi-purpose series of examples will be given in para. 157.

153. *The Conditional Particle in Arabic.* The actual word used for "if" in Arabic has considerable bearing on the time and the probability of the statement. Three cases normally arise: *in* is the commonest particle, denoting simple possibility and usually affecting the verb with a present or near-future timing, whatever the Aspect actually used; *idhā* implies some degree of probability, and is often translated by "when, whenever" (contrast *lammā*), as well as by "if" (the timing is still usually present to near-future); *lau* denotes a hypothetical or impossible condition ("if you did this, he would do that; if you had done this, he would have done that"), and the time-factor is naturally somewhat irrelevant, albeit English uses past tenses here.

154. *The Verbal Aspect of Conditional Sentences.* Save for the occasional Imperative (as in the second English example in para. 151), the Aspect of Arabic verbs in Conditional Sentences is normally always either *māḍī* or Jussive. This has no real bearing on time, which is governed by other considerations, as seen in para. 153. In the same sentence, *māḍī* may be paired with *māḍī*, Jussive with Jussive; or the *sharṭ* may take one, and the *jawāb* the other. The ultimate choice from among these four possibilities often depends on stylistic considerations, euphony, effect and so on. It should be pointed out here that this limitation of Aspect implies a similar limitation of the Negative Particles employed in Conditional Sentences to *mā* and *lam* (cf. para. 134), unless a negative form of the Imperative is demanded, when we use *lā* with the Second Person of the Jussive (cf. para. 137 (*a*)). Compound tenses occasionally occur in Conditional Sentences (i.e. those formed with *kāna* and some other verb), but even here the particular aspect of *kāna* used will fulfil the requirement of *māḍī* or Jussive.

155. *Introduction of* jawāb. The *jawāb* is introduced by *fa-* (not translatable, but corresponding to a breathing-space or the English ". . . well now! . . .") in three situations: where the *jawāb* begins with anything other than a verb; where the *jawāb* begins with a verb in the Imperative; and where the *māḍī* verb of the *jawāb* is intended to have a really past and effective sense. In Conditional Sentences beginning with the particle *lau* (see para. 153 above), these considerations usually lapse in favour of the regular introduction of the *jawāb* by *la-* (also untranslatable in most cases).

156. *Quasi-Conditional Sentences.* These are sentences in which the particles listed in para. 153 are replaced by such others as *man* (here signifying "whoever, he who, those who, the one(s) who, people who. . ." etc.); *mā* or *mah-mā* ("whatever, that which, the things which. . ." etc.); *aina-mā*, "wherever"; *matà* (*-mā*), "whenever" (often equivalent to *idhā* of para. 153); and so on. These may be described as the "-ever particles". It is best to regard them as simple Conditional Particles, with which they can be interchanged: "Whoever commits a crime must pay the penalty" may be equated with "If a man commits a crime he must pay the penalty."

157. *Examples of Arabic Conditionals.* Try to relate the following sentences to as many of the points as relevant between paras. 151 and 156. You should also render them into Arabic characters:

(1) *idhā waṣala fa-adkhil-hu*: When (whenever, if) he arrives, show him in!

(2) *in kataba waṣala al-maktūbu al-yauma*: If he writes the letter will arrive today.

(3) *lau lam yaktub la-katabtu ana nafsī*: If he hadn't written I should have written myself. (NOTE: *lau lam* is preferred to *lau mā*.)

(4) *in wajadta kitāban fa-huwa lī*: If you find a book it belongs to me (is mine).

(5) *in qāla hādhā fa-qad kadhaba*: If he says that he has lied. (NOTE: *fa*-required here on two counts.)

(6) *man 'allama jāhilan (fa)-lam yata'allam shai'an*: Anyone who teaches an ignorant man learns nothing (*or* whoever teaches an ignorant man = if you teach. . ., he learns nothing).

(7) *mā (mah-mā) ṭalabta fa-huwa la-ka*: Whatever you ask for, it is yours.

(8) *kāna idhā naẓara kitāban qara'a-hu min al-fauri*: Whenever he noticed a book he would read it on the spot. (NOTE: By putting *kāna* outside a Conditional Sentence, particularly with *idhā*, the whole time may be transferred to the past. This sentence could be understood as meaning: "He was (the sort of man who): whenever he notices a book he reads it immediately". The *kāna* here is 3 m.s., agreeing with *naẓara* and/or *qara'a*: if the person, gender and number of these vary, that of *kāna* is adjusted accordingly. Cf. next sentence.)

(9) *kānat idhā waṣalat fa-al-bābu maftūḥun*: Whenever she arrived the door was open (she was: whenever she arrives, well now! the door is open).

158. *Colours and Defects*. Arabic has a special pattern of adjective and verb where the ideas of colour or of deficiency are involved. The following are specimens of the adjective patterns:

	Masc. sing.	*Fem. sing.*	*Plural* (masc. and fem. where appropriate)
red	أَحْمَرُ	حَمْرَاءُ	حُمْرٌ
deaf	أَطْرَشُ	طَرْشَاءُ	طُرْشٌ

The verb-forms used are the IX and the XI, the former being the more common. Here are the essential parts of ḤMR IX, "to be(come) red" (you will not be able to handle such a verb in every situation until you have studied the phenomenon of Doubled Verbs at length, i.e. those in which the second radical is repeated, a process closely paralleling what happens in Forms IX and XI):

Māḍī	*Muḍāri'*	*Maṣdar*
iḥmarra	yaḥmarru	iḥmirār

NOTE: Both the first and the third items begin with *hamzat al-waṣl*.

159. *Elatives* (*patterns*). We have met the Elative on a number of occasions. It too has special patterns, liable in the masculine to confusion with the adjectives of Colour and Defect:

	Masc. sing.	*Fem. sing.*	*Plural*
bigger, biggest	أَكْبَرُ	كُبْرَى	several forms, but rarely used

It follows that the Elative of an adjective of Colour or Defect has to be made differently: "redder" might be *ashaddu ḥumratan* (Accusative. bound-*t*), lit. "stronger as to redness" (Accusative adverbially "of respect").

160. *Elatives* (*use*). The Elative corresponds to the English Comparative and Superlative, and *broadly speaking* it may be equated with the former when indefinite and with the latter elsewhere. However, remember (cf. two places in *Vocabulary and remarks* to para. 144, pp. 124, 125) that "the biggest city" in Arabic may be either *akbaru madīnatin* or *al-madīnatu al-kubrà*, i.e. the Elative as Superlative may follow an articled noun in complete agreement, or it may precede as masculine singular an unarticled noun in Construct. As a general rule, always use the Elative in the masculine singular, disregarding number and gender, unless the Arabic construction requires the Elative itself *to have the article* (not simply "to be definite"), when agreement must be observed. It is not enough to differentiate between the Elative as Comparative and the Elative as Superlative. These are non-Arabic concepts, and can be misleading. The word *akbaru* is always used for the Comparative, but also very often for the Superlative; the word *kubrà* is used only for the Superlative, and only then in certain cases as just defined. Note the following specimen instances:

The use of masc. or pl. pronouns and nouns would not affect *akbaru*	*hiya akbaru min-hu*: She is taller than him (he). *hiya akbaru al-nisā'i*: She is the tallest of the women *hiya akbaru-hunna*: She is the tallest of them.
But:	*hiya al-kubrà*: She is the tallest.
as against:	*huwa al-akbaru*: He is the tallest.

161. *Practice material.* Work through the material in the separate section, p. 127.

21

Minor peculiarities in verbs; Peculiar common nouns; Some essential distinctions

162. *Verbs with initial* wāw. We have seen several examples of these in our reading materials, and the essential thing about them has already been said, namely that they lose the initial radical altogether (in the overwhelming majority of cases) in the *muḍāri'*: *wajada, yajidu*. It merely remains here to emphasise certain points. First, this peculiarity applies only to Form I, and not even to the Passive *muḍāri'* of that form. (In all other situations, these verbs are essentially standard, though the *w*, unvocalised, will of course often be sounded as *ū* or *au*: *muslim*, but *mūjid* (for *muwjid*); *maktūb*, but *maujūd* (for *mawjūd*). Special attention should perhaps be drawn to four phonetic phenomena, as exemplified in: *ījāb*, IV *maṣdar*, for the impossible *iwjāb*; the difficulty of making a Form VII from these verbs (see para. 139); their assimilation of the *w* to the *t* in Form VIII (para. 140); and the form *istījāb*, X *maṣdar*, for the impossible *istiwjāb*.) Secondly, that such verbs normally take *i* as the middle vowel of the *muḍāri'* (save with *ḥ* and *'ain* as indicated in para. 92). Thirdly, that this loss of the radical makes it relatively simple to form the Imperative: *yajidu*/*yajid*/*jid* (i.e. no helping *hamza* is needed).

163. *Verbs with* hamza *as a radical*. The basic problem here is the general one of how to write the *hamza* in a given situation, and on that matter all that can be said effectively in an elementary work has been said in para. 53, particularly in subparas. (*b*) and (*c*). However, in a limited number of specific cases (those involving two *hamzas* in succession or *hamza* and a long vowel), the problem has both scriptorial and phonetic factors. Practically speaking, all such cases relate to verbs where the *hamza* is initial, and the main instances may be summarised as follows (taking the root 'LF throughout for uniformity):

Form I:	Imperative	اِيلَفْ (for اِئْلَفْ)[1]
	Active Participle	آلِفٌ (for أَالِفٌ)
	Muḍāri' 1 c.s.	آلَفُ (for أَأْلَفُ)

[1] But remember the common cases of *khudh*, *mur*, and *kul* (see last item in *Vocabulary and remarks* to para. 144, p. 125).

Form III:	Māḍī	آلَفَ	(for أَالَفَ)	
	Imperative	آلِفْ	(for أَالِفْ)	
Form IV:	Māḍī	آلَفَ	(for أَأْلَفَ)	
	Imperative	آلِفْ	(for أَأْلِفْ)	
	Maṣdar	إِيلَافٌ	(for إِئْلَافٌ)	
	Muḍāri‘ 1 c.s.	أُولِفُ	(for أُؤْلِفُ)	i.e. a constant change for this form
Form VI:	Māḍī	تَآلَفَ	(for تَأَالَفَ)	(i.e. a constant change for this form)
	Muḍāri‘	يَتَآلَفُ	(for يَتَأَالَفُ)	(i.e. a constant change for this form)
	Imperative	تَآلَفْ	(for ثَأَالَفْ)	(i.e. a constant change for this form)
	Active/Passive Participles	مُتَآلَفٌ	(for مُتَأَالِفٌ)	(i.e. a constant change for this form)
	Maṣdar	تَآلُفٌ	(for تَأَالُفٌ)	
Form VIII:[2]	Māḍī	اِيتَلَفَ	(for اِئْتَلَفَ)	
	Muḍāri‘ 1 c.s.	آتَلِفُ	(for أَأْتَلِفُ)	
	Maṣdar	اِيتِلَافٌ	(for إِئْتِلَافٌ)	
	Imperative	اِيتَلِفْ	(for اِئْتَلِفْ)	

Some passives are similarly affected, but these are sufficiently rare to make it hardly worth giving them in detail. Indeed, all these instances (and others) could be stated in two simple rules, with a third as footnote:

(*a*) *Hamza* plus a short vowel, followed by the corresponding vowel-lengthener is like any other consonant so placed, save that *hamza* plus *fatḥa* plus *alif* is written as *alif madda* (see para. 54).

(*b*) *Hamza* with a short vowel, followed by *hamza* with *sukūn*, is written and pronounced as though it were *hamza* followed by the corresponding long vowel. (Where *ā* is involved, the written form is with *madda*.)

(*c*) Where the first *hamza* of (*b*) is only *hamzat al-waṣl* (as in the Imperatives of I and VIII listed above, and in the *māḍī* and the *maṣdar* of VIII), every opportunity is taken to "revert" to the normal theoretical form. Thus, if اِيلَفْ is preceded by *fa*-, one should find فَاْئْلَفْ not فَايِلَفْ .

164. *Doubled Verbs*. We have already met one or two examples of these verbs, in which the radicals are not 1-2-3, but 1-2-2. Such verbs have a tendency at all times to unite the second and third radicals under *shadda*, which means that they

[2] But remember that some verbs assimilate the *hamza* to the *t* throughout this form (see para. 140).

are often one vowel short of the standard patterns, or diverge from them in some other way: *ẓanna*, not *ẓanana*; *yaẓunnu*, not *yaẓnunu*. This unification is practically universal in such verbs, save in the following two situations: where 2 and 2 are naturally separated by a long vowel (*maẓnūn*, not *maẓūnn*, in the Passive Participle of I); where the third radical, i.e. the second occurrence of 2, naturally bears *sukūn*, as in the Jussive and the Imperative (*yaẓnun*, not *yaẓunn*; *uẓnun*, not *uẓunn* or *ẓunn*). *However*, so strong is the tendency to unite that the second of these two situations is often circumvented, and one finds forms like *yaẓunn(i)*, *ẓunn(i)*, with "false" vowels appended to satisfy the universal Arabic reluctance to have a syllable both long and closed, or closed twice (see para. 49 (*a*)). Yet even this reluctance is usually overcome, in these Doubled Verbs, throughout much of Forms III and VI, and in the Active Participle of I: typical examples would be *ẓānna*, *taẓānna*; *yuẓānnu*, *yataẓānnu*; and *ẓānn*(*un*) for *ẓānin*(*un*). One final thing needs to be said about these Doubled Verbs: when unification takes place, if radical 1 already has a vowel, it keeps it and 2 loses its own vowel (*dulila* becomes *dulla*); if radical 1 has no vowel, as in several places in the *muḍāri'*, it takes that of 2 (*yudlalu* becomes *yudallu*). It should go without saying that II and V are absolutely regular: *dallala*, not *dallla*, which would violate too many "rules" and susceptibilities to bear enumeration!

165. *The verb* laisa. Once again, we have already met this verb, but it may be useful to tabulate here its peculiarities of form, use and syntactical construction:

(*a*) *Form*. This verb has only one form, corresponding in general *appearance* to the *māḍī* Aspect. Moreover, though we find *laisat*, *laisā*, *laisatā*, and *laisū* regularly formed from the 3 m.s., all the other persons adopt the form *las-* (*lastu*, *lasna*, etc.).

(*b*) *Use*. It is used to negate Nominal Sentences (see para. 135); and it may also be used with the *muḍāri'* of another verb to negate the present near-future, i.e. it may replace *mā* or *lā* in such cases as those given in para. 135: *laisa yaktubu*, "he won't write". (There seems here to be a certain degree of emphasis.) It will be noted that both these uses are in present time.

(*c*) *Construction*. We have already seen that when negating a Nominal Sentence, it commonly takes its predicate in the Accusative (see again para. 135). It may also govern its predicate by *bi-*: "he is not a boy" could therefore be either *laisa waladan* or *laisa bi-waladin*.

166. *Some peculiar common nouns*. Many ordinary nouns, particularly those associated with personal relationships, have miscellaneous peculiarities. Several of these we have already encountered, but it will be convenient to tabulate them here in one paragraph:

ab (pl. *ābā'*): father (see under *ab* in *Vocabulary and remarks* to para. 127 (p. 119))
umm (pl. *ummahāt*): mother (no fem. ending in the singular; special pl. form of Sound Fem.)

ibn (pl. *abnā'*, *banūna*): son, boy (see under *ibn* in *Vocabulary and remarks* to para. 108 (p. 111))
bint (pl. *banāt*): daughter, girl (mutilated fem. ending in sing., special pl. form of Sound Fem.)
akh (pl. *ikhwa(h), ikhwān*): brother (behaves as for *ab* (see *Vocabulary and remarks* to para. 127, p. 119). First pl. denotes real, or natural brothers; second plural refers to figurative "brothers", e.g. members of a league or a club. Root 'KHW)
ukht (pl. *akhawāt*): sister (cf. remarks on *bint* above. Root 'KHW)
dhū (fem. *dhāt*; pls. *dhawū, dhawāt*): having, possessed of (a certain quality)–e.g. *dhū 'aqlin*: possessing intelligence, intelligent ('āqil) (Used to form personal adjectives from abstract nouns, and is always found in Construct. The masc. sing. behaves like construct *abū*, the masc. pl. like a Sound Masc. construct. The fems. resemble *bint* or *ukht*. There is also a Dual, *dhawā, dhawatā*; and other (rare) forms of the plural)
fam (pl. *afwāh*): mouth. Either completely regular in declension, or with a construct form *fū* etc., like *abū*. Root FWH

167. *Some essential distinctions*

(*a*) The prefixes *mu-*, *ma-*, and *mi-* often give great difficulty to beginners in the early days of learning Arabic. While they sometimes occur in *structurally* identical patterns (e.g. *mdrs(h)* could be read as *madrasa(h)*, "school", or *mudarrisa(h)*, "instructress"), they are really quite distinct. The first, *mu-*, is the prefix of *all* Participles in the Derived Forms, and also of one pattern of the Form III *maṣdar*. The prefix *ma-* belongs to the Passive Participle of Form I; the Noun of Place–Time from Form I; and the Broken Plurals of four-consonant nouns beginning with *m* (whatever the vowel of the singular). The prefix *mi-* belongs mainly to Nouns of Instrument in the singular. (Cf. throughout paras. 147–9.)

(*b*) The particles *in*, *inna*, *an* and *anna* give similar trouble, though they are quite distinct in most cases. The first, *in*, is a Conditional Particle normally followed immediately by a Jussive or *māḍī* (para. 153). The second, *inna*, is a statement-starter, often untranslatable, but giving some degree of emphasis to the remark; it must be "neutralised" immediately by a pronominal suffix or a noun in the Accusative, and it is then followed either by the predicate of a Nominal Sentence or by a complete Verbal Sentence; it is often used to introduce verbatim speech after *qāla*. The third particle, *an*, links the verbs of hoping, commanding, wishing etc. to a following Subjunctive; it may be prefixed by prepositions normally associated with certain verbs (*qadara 'alà* etc.); and it itself enters into such combinations as *li-an*, *li-allā* etc. The final particle, *anna*, links verb to verb in situations not calling for *an* (it can usually be translated, unlike *an*, by "the fact that"); after *qāla* it introduces reported statements. In construction and behaviour it resembles *inna*, in function it resembles *an*: like the latter it enters into numerous combinations, such as *li-anna*, *ghaira anna*, and verbs may "govern" it by prepositions. (For the last three cf. particularly Chapters 14 and 15 and *Vocabulary and remarks* to their exercise material, paras. 108, 117, found on pp. 112, 113, and 117.)

168. *Practice material.* Work through the material in the separate section, p. 129.

22

Hollow Roots: Māḍī and muḍāri' of Form I

169. *Hollow Roots in general.* By this point, we have reviewed virtually all the essential features of Arabic grammar; most of what the student now requires for further progress can be gained from prolonged and repeated "exposure" to real Arabic, with occasional reference, on specific problems of language, to any of the accepted grammatical manuals (see Postscript).[1] However, we still need to examine in a minimum of detail the phonetic, and sometimes scriptorial, changes undergone by roots with *w* or *y* in second or third place, when such roots are fitted into the various patterns so far encountered in the Standard Verb. Roots with middle *w* or *y* are called Hollow; those with final *w* or *y* we shall call Weak. The vital key to understanding virtually all the changes involved is a sound grasp of a principle we have already stated more than once since para. 49(*a*): Arabic cannot tolerate a syllable that is both long and closed (nor, incidentally, one that is short but closed twice).

170. *Hollow Roots:* Māḍī *I.* In the *māḍī* of Form I we have to distinguish two broad categories of Hollow Verb (with a third minor category): those with *w* and those with *y*. Both categories, in those situations where the third consonant is vowelled (3 m.s., 3 f.s., 3 m.p. etc.), have a central long *ā* vowel: thus, *qāla*, "to say" (from QWL) or "to take a nap" (from QYL); *kānat*, "she was" (from KWN); *sārū*, "they went" (from SYR); *qālā*, "they (two) said", "they (two) took a nap"; and so on. In all other positions, however (i.e. where the third radical is un-

[1] Non-linguistic problems (references to history, literature, philosophy etc.) need a long apprenticeship in acculturation for their solution. Sometimes they remain intractable. Remember, too, that Arabic is an extremely rich, widespread and long-lived language, with consequent variations of style and vocabulary; and that its script is peculiarly liable to miscopyings, misprints and confusion!

vowelled), the two categories differentiate as: *qultu*, "I said"; *qilta*, "you took a nap"; *kunna*, "they (f., and note *shadda*) were"; *sirtum*, "you (pl. m.) went"; etc. The third, and minor, category to which we have just referred derives mostly from roots with middle *w*: such roots in *māḍī* Form I cannot be distinguished from the other two categories in the "open" position, but when a "closed" syllable arises they always take the vowel *i*. Thus, *nāma* but *nimtu* (from NWM, "sleeping"); *khāfat* but *khiftum* (from KHWF, "fearing"); and *nālū* but *nilnā* (from NWL/ NYL, "obtaining"). If to this short list we add *zāla, ziltu* (from ZWL/ZYL, "ceasing", but usually found in negative in sense of "continuing"!), the list of the third category is virtually complete for all practical purposes.

171. *Hollow Roots:* Muḍāriʿ *I.* The same basic principles obtain here. Roots with middle *w* form their "open" *muḍāriʿ* patterns in long *ū*, and their "closed" ones in short *u*: *yaqūlu, yakūnūna* but *yaqulna, takunna* (the latter with *shadda*). Similarly, we find in the second category: *taqīlu* ('she is taking a nap") and *tasīrīna* ("you (f.) are going"), but *taqilna* and *yasirna.* In the third category, the "open" vowel in *muḍāriʿ* Form I is *ā*, the "closed" vowel *a*: *yanāmu, yanamna*; *takhāfu, takhafna*; and so on. It will be noted that in the *muḍāriʿ* all vowels are shortened uniformly without a change of quality, whereas in the *māḍī* the change is one of quality as well as length.

172. *Hollow Roots: Subjunctive, Jussive and Imperative I.* Once the Indicative pattern of the *muḍāriʿ* is mastered for each person, number and gender, the conversion to the Subjunctive is straightforward, since (as with the parallel situation for the Standard Verb) no new case arises which calls for the non-vowelling of the third radical: *yakūnu* etc. becomes *yakūna* etc.; *takūnīna* etc. becomes *takūnī* etc.; and *yakunna, takunna* remain unchanged. In the Jussive, however, all the final *-u* vowels are replaced by *sukūn*, and consequently the long vowels are shortened: *yakūnu* becomes *yakun, yasīru* becomes *yasir*, and *yakhāfu* becomes *yakhaf.* The Imperative is still formed regularly from the Jussive (see paras. 114 and 115), but *note* (*a*) that no *hamza* is needed *(kun, qul, sir, nam* etc.); and (*b*) that some persons of the Imperative recover the full long vowel, since the third radical is no longer unvowelled (*kūnī, qūlū, sīrā* etc.).

173. *Practice material.* Work through the material in the separate section, p.131.

23

Hollow Roots: Participles and Maṣdar *of Form I; Forms II, III, V and VI*

174. *Hollow Roots: Participles I.* In the First Form, the *Active Participle* of *all* Hollow Roots is identical with that from roots with *hamza* as the second radical. Thus, *sā'il* could normally be taken to be the Active Participle of the common root S'L and translated "asking; a beggar"; but it could occasionally be referred to SYL and accordingly rendered "flowing (of a stream); fluid, liquid". Likewise, *nā'im* would normally be taken as coming from the obvious root NWM and rendered "sleeping, asleep"; but it could in rare instances be referred to N'M, with the sense of "moaning". Until you know Arabic well enough to be reasonably certain as to the most obvious sense, always refer such Active Participles to *all three* roots in the dictionary. The *Passive Participle* of Hollow Roots in Form I is determined by the middle radical: verbs with *w* all behave like *maqūl, makhūf*; those with *y* all have the pattern *mazīd* (from ZYD, which we have met) and *mabī'* (from BY', denoting "selling"). There are, as it happens, fewer middle-*y* Hollow Verbs capable of forming true passives in Form I than is the case for those with middle-*w*.

175. *Hollow Roots*: Maṣdars *I.* It will be remembered (para. 166(*c*)) that there is really no escape from learning by heart the individual *maṣdar* of each verb in Form I. While this is still largely true of the Hollow Roots, it is nevertheless a fact have that a very high proportion of them have at least one of their possible *maṣdar* patterns in 1 a 2 3: *qaul, sair, kaun, khauf, naum* etc. This does not preclude the simultaneous, or the exclusive, occurrence of other patterns (*maqāl, masīr, kiyān* (for *kiwān*), *makhāfa(h)* etc.), often with variant shades of meaning; but it is useful to be able, at least in most cases, to count on knowing automatically one probable *maṣdar* pattern. As with most *maṣdars* (and Participles), many of these often acquire a semi-independent life of their own as common nouns: the series from *qaul* to *naum*, for example, commonly have such virtually non-verbal, fully nominal senses as "statement, trip, existence, fear, sleep" in addition to "(the act of) saying, going, being, fearing, sleeping".

176. *Hollow Roots: Forms II, III, V and VI.* These are *absolutely in accordance with the Standard Verb in every respect*, that is the middle *w* or *y* is treated exactly like any other consonant. It is not therefore proposed, as is usually done in the majority of Arabic grammar-manuals, to set out lengthy tables that serve no purpose other than to obscure this simple basic fact. Remember to introduce some element of "diphthongisation" when you *pronounce* the "repeated" middle radical in II and V: for example, pronounce *sayyara* as *saiyara*, *mukhawwif* as *mukhauwif*, *takawwun* as *takauwun* and so on. However, remember that this has no bearing on the strict regularity of the written forms (and in most cases of the pronounced forms as well).

177. *Practice material.* Work through the material in the separate section, p.134.

24

Hollow Roots: Forms VII and VIII, IV and X; Hollow Passives

178. *Hollow Roots: Forms VII and VIII.* In these forms no distinction is made between roots in *w* and those in *y*, and we shall accordingly use only one verb in each case for purposes of demonstration. Both forms show a somewhat unexpected vowel-quality in the *muḍāri'* and its derivatives: *ā* (*a*) rather than *ī* (*i*); but it will be noted that this vowel (unlike that of Form I *māḍī*) shortens uniformly, without change of quality. (This is also the case in the *māḍī* of VII and VIII, and indeed virtually everywhere outside *māḍī* I.)

	Māḍī	*Muḍāri'*	*Maṣdar*	(Imperative)	(Both Participles)
VII	inqāda	yanqādu	inqiyād	inqad	munqād
VIII	ikhtāra	yakhtāru	ikhtiyār	ikhtar	mukhtār

The first verb means "to be led, guided; to be tractable", and derives from QWD; the second signifies "to choose, elect, select", deriving from the root KHYR, which we have already met in the sense of "good". The patterns in the last two columns derive regularly according to the general rules (paras. 114 and 121 respectively). They are given here partly for completeness of reference, and partly to emphasise the absolute identity (in Hollow Roots, Forms VII and VIII) of the Active and Passive Participle: the word *mukhtār*, for example, commonly used in the sense of "small-town mayor, village headman", could be in theory either Passive, "the elected one", or Active, "the one having freedom of choice". Remember that *all* the initial *hamzas* here are of *waṣl*; and also that the shortened vowel of the Imperative is restored to full length wherever the third radical no longer has *sukūn* (para. 172): *inqādū*, *ikhtārī* etc.

179. *Hollow Roots: Forms IV and X.* Once again, no distinction is made between roots in *w* and those in *y*, so that only one verb will be demonstrated in each case. Vowel-shortening is uniform throughout. The *maṣdar* of both forms deserves special attention.

	Māḍī	*Muḍāriʻ*	*Maṣdar*	(Imperative)	(Active Part.; Passive Part.)
IV	'ajāba	yujību	'ijāba(h)	'ajib	mujīb; mujāb
X	istafāda	yastafīdu	istifāda(h)	istafid	mustafīd; mustafād

The first verb we have met several times already, and its root is known to be JWB; the second means "to take advantage (of: *min*)", deriving from FYD, a derivation of which we have already met as *fā'ida(h)*. Note, once again, that the patterns in the last two columns need not be learned by heart, since they derive quite regularly. (Unlike the cases of VII and VIII, Active and Passive Participles of Hollow Roots can be clearly distinguished in IV and X.) Remember that while all the initial *hamzas* of X are of *waṣl*, those of IV are of *qaṭʻ* (para. 125). Once again, the shortened vowel of the Imperative must be "restored" in appropriate phonetic contexts. *'ajībī*, *istafīdū* etc.

180. *Hollow Roots*: *Passives.* By combining the principles of para. 146 with those enunciated repeatedly from para. 169 to this point, the student should be able to forecast most of the patterns involved. Once again, II, III, V and VI are *absolutely standard*, while VII practically never occurs. The remaining forms are given below for reference: we use QWL, but they apply equally to roots with middle *y*.

	Māḍī	*Muḍāriʻ*
I	qīla	yuqālu
IV	'uqīla	yuqālu
VIII	uqtīla	yuqtālu
X	ustuqīla	yustaqālu

Vowel-shortening is uniform throughout.

181. *Practice material.* Work through the material in the separate section, p.136.

25

Weak Roots: Basic patterns of Form I

182. *Weak Roots in general.* While, in a sense, all roots containing any unstable radical could be described as "weak", we use the term here in the restricted connotation of those roots having *w* or *y* as their third radical. In some ways their behaviour parallels that of Hollow Roots; at times, however, the Weak Roots are considerably more complex and diverse; in at least one respect, namely the lack of any distinction between *w* and *y* roots *in the Derived Forms*, they are rather simpler than the Hollow Roots to learn and remember. Once again, the basic operative principle is that a syllable in Arabic cannot normally be both long and closed. Perhaps the most obvious characteristic of the Weak Roots is a tendency, where the weak radical is retained, to make diphthongs.

183. *Weak Roots:* Māḍī *of I.* As with the Hollow Verbs, there are in Form I two major categories, divided according to the exact nature of the final radical as *w* or *y*; and a third, minor category that may have either radical originally, but displays only *y*, and that with a fixed, deviant vowel-pattern. We give below the three categories set out at length for the three verbs *da'ā* (D'W), "to call" (and many shades of meaning, with different prepositions relating to "invitation", "prayer", "blessing" and "cursing"); *ramà* (RMY), "to throw, aim, pelt"; and *raḍiya* (RḌW), "to accept, be tolerant, indulgent" (of, towards: *bi*, *'an* and other constructions).

I		II		III	
da'ā	دعا	ramà	رمى	raḍiya	رضي
da'at	دعت	ramat	رمت	raḍiyat	رضيت
da'auta	دعوت	ramaita	رميت	raḍīta	"
	etc.		etc.		etc.
da'au	دعوا *	ramau	رموا	raḍū	رضوا
da'auna	دعون	ramaina	رمين	raḍīna	رضين
da'autum	دعوتم	ramaitum	رميتم	raḍītum	رضيتم
da'autunna	دعوتنّ	ramaitunna	رميتنّ	raḍītunna	رضيتنّ
da'aunā	دعونا	ramainā	رمينا	raḍīnā	رضينا

I		II		III	
da'awā	دعوا *	ramayā	رميا	raḍiyā	رضيا
da'atā	دعتا	ramatā	رمتا	raḍiyatā	رضيتا
da'autumā	دعوتما	ramaitumā	رميتما	raḍītumā	رضيتما

*Notice (in this column only) the ambiguous appearance in Arabic when written without vowels.

It will be noted that the weak radical disappears *without any trace* in the following situations only: 3 m.p. (all three columns); 3 f.s. and 3 f.d. (columns I and II only). In most other situations it remains as a diphthong (columns I and II) or a long vowel ī (column III).

In a few instances the third radical retains its consonant function: 3 m.d. (all three columns); and 3 m.s., 3 f.s., 3 f.d. (column III only). The *sound* of long *ā* is found only in 3 m.s., columns I and II; and only in column I is it attained by substituting *alif* for the radical *w*, since column II uses the radical *y* to make *à*.

184. *Weak Roots: muḍāri' of I*

I		II		III	
yad'ū	يدعو	yarmī	يرمى	yarḍà	يرضى
tad'ū	تدعو	tarmī	ترمى	tarḍà	ترضى
"	"	"	"	"	"
tad'īna	تدعين	tarmīna	ترمين	tarḍaina	ترضين
ad'ū	أدعو	armī	أرمى	arḍà	أرضى
yad'ūna	يدعون	yarmūna	يرمون	yarḍauna	يرضون
"	"	yarmīna	يرمين	yarḍaina	يرضين
tad'ūna	تدعون	tarmūna	ترمون	tarḍauna	ترضون
"	"	tarmīna	ترمين	tarḍaina	ترضين
nad'ū	ندعو	narmī	نرمى	narḍà	نرضى
yad'uwāni	يدعوان	yarmiyāni	يرميان	yarḍayāni	يرضيان
tad'uwāni	تدعوان	tarmiyāni	ترميان	tarḍayāni	ترضيان
"	"	"	"	"	"

It will be seen that the position here is rather more complex than for the *māḍī* columns. The third radical now disappears *without any trace* in the following situations: 2 f.s., 3 m.p. and 2 m.p. (all three columns). (It should be particularly noted that while it might also *seem* to disappear in exactly the same way, for 3 f.p. and 2 f.p., in column I, such is not really the case: these persons are regular in formation in all three columns, and the differences they display as between themselves arise from a strictly logical application of the relevant standard pattern to a given final radical-and-vowel formation.) In the *remaining* cases, in columns I and II, the weak radical serves as a long vowel in the singular and plural, and as a consonant in the Dual. In column III, the consonantal function is also present in the Dual; but the plural varies the prevailing long *à* vowel with an *ai* diphthong in 3 f.p. and 2 f.p. (the diphthong in 2 f.s. of this column is accounted for differently under a general analysis just given). Certain special *ambiguities* should be stressed: in column I, as just mentioned, 3 m.p. and 3 f.p., and 2 m.p. and 2 f.p. coincide exactly in sound and appearance (albeit arriving at this identity by different routes); in columns II and III respectively, the same is true of 2 f.s. and 2 f.p.

185. *Weak Roots: Subjunctive, Jussive and Imperative of I*

(*a*) The general rules for making the *Subjunctive* given in para. 105 apply here, but certain features should perhaps be re-emphasised to avoid doubt. In all three columns 3 f.p. and 2 f.p. are *not* affected; in all three columns 2 f.s., 3 m.p., 2 m.p. and all the Duals are "truncated" by having the final consonant and its vowel removed (remember to add the "otiose" *alif* in 3 m.p. and 2 m.p.!); in all other situations, in columns I and II, the weak radical takes an *a* vowel, *but column III remains unchanged* for these latter instances. It may be noted that while the ambiguity in columns II and III between 2 f.s. and 2 f.p. is now removed, a new one is created as between 2 f.s. and 2 m.s./3 f.s. (visual only in column II, but both visual and nearly phonetic in column III).

(*b*) What has been said about the Subjunctive applies in great measure to the *Jussive*, as might be expected from para. 106. However, the basic principle of vowel-shortening comes into play as soon as *sukūn* is imposed in *all three columns*, on any person ending in the Indicative in a long vowel: *yad'u*, *yarmi*, *yarḍa* etc. Putting this in other words, the final radical disappears completely in such cases. Most ambiguities disappear completely in the Jussive, but note two important new cases in column I: 3 m.p. with "otiose" *alif* and 3 m.d.; 2 m.p. with "otiose" *alif* and 3 f./2 c.d.

(*c*) From the Jussive it is not difficult to proceed, in general accord with paras. 114–15, to the *Imperative*. From the three Jussives just given at the end of the last sub-para., we obtain the truncated forms; *uḍ'u*, *irmi*, *irḍa*. The other persons of the Imperative are formed from these in more or less the normal way, but harmonising the final vowels and endings in accordance with the tables in para. 184. Thus we have:

	I		II		III	
f.s.	ud'i	ادعى	irmī	ارمى	irḍai	ارضي
m.p.	ud'ū	ادعوا *	irmū	ارموا	irḍau	ارضوا
f.p.	ud'ūna	ادعون	irmīna	ارمين	irḍaina	ارضين
c.d.	ud'uwā	ادعوا *	irmiyā	ارميا	irḍayā	ارضيا

*Note ambiguous appearance in unvowelled form.

186. *Weak Roots: Active Participles I.* No distinction is made here between the three types of Weak Root, so that one illustration will serve for all three. We will take as a model the Active Participle of the root QḌY, which we have already met in para. 173 in the sense of "judge". It is best set out as a noun-table:

	Indefinite		*Definite* (with article or otherwise)	
Nominative	قاض	qāḍin	القاضي	al-qāḍī
Accusative	قاضيا	qāḍiyan	,,	al-qāḍiya
Genitive	قاض	qāḍin	,,	al-qāḍī

Such participles, when used as ordinary nouns, can still make a Sound Plural (*qāḍūna*/*qāḍīna*), but they often take, additionally or instead, a special Broken Plural of the form قضاة (*quḍāt*). Many very common and useful nouns belong in this class, and it must accordingly be thoroughly well known. The feminine Active Participle is perfectly regular (*dā'iya(h)*, داعية), but see para. 188.

187. *Weak Roots: Passive Participles I.* There is a distinction here between column I and columns II/III. All verbs in the *da'ā* category form their Passive Participles I regularly, as *mad'ūw*, مدعوّ . All verbs in the *ramà*/*raḍiya* categories form their Passive Participles I, with vowel-conversion by the dominant (cf. para. 53 (*c*)), as: *marmīy, marḍīy*, مرميّ / مرضيّ . Note that in none of these cases are we really dealing with a syllable both long and closed, since one or other of the regular declension-endings is understood to be present (cf. towards end of para. 49 (*b*)).

188. *Weak Roots; miscellaneous noun-patterns I.* As usual in Form I, no very helpful rules can be given for the formation of *maṣdars* from Weak Roots. Some are absolutely regular: *ramà* can give *ramy* (consonantal). However, the student should be prepared (in all the forms, as well as I) to find *maṣdars*, as also other nouns, in which the weak radical converts to *hamza*: *da'ā* can give *du'ā'* (of the 1 u 2 ā 3 pattern); or those which assume endings like *quran* (see p. 134, *Vocabulary* *drill* for para. 177): *raḍiya* can give *riḍan*, رضًى . Often the weak radical converts to *alif*, especially before bound-*t*: *marḍāt*, for example, is another possible *maṣdar* of *raḍiya*. In a few nouns, the weak radical assumes an almost totally invariable form in -*à*: *da'wà*, for example, is another possible *maṣdar* from *da'ā*, and the only change this can undergo is that of substituting *alif* for *yā'* in the non-final position, *da'wā-hu*. One Broken Plural pattern from Weak Roots in Form I needs special attention if it is not to be confused with the *qāḍin* pattern. It derives from the otherwise regular feminine of the Active Participle I, and we shall take the pl. of *rāmiya(h)*, "a female marksman", as a model.

Indefinite			*Definite* (with article or otherwise)	
Nominative	روام	rawâmin	الروامى	al-rawâmī
Accusative	روامى	rawâmiya	"	al-rawâmiya
Genitive	روام	rawāmin	"	al-rawāmī

It will be seen that the crucial point of difference from *qāḍin* lies in the Indefinite Accusative. Moreover, since this general pattern of plural is technically Diptote (cf. *qāfila(h)*, *qawāfilu*), the Accusative Indefinite might be expected to influence the Genitive Indefinite, but such is not the case in these Weak Roots.

189. *Practice material.* Work through the material in the separate section, p. 139.

26

Weak Roots: Derived Forms in general; Forms II–IV

190. *The Weak Derived Forms in general.* Once again, there is no need here to burden the memory with lengthy tables, since the majority of the peculiarities are covered by a combination of the fundamental principles set out in Chapters 16–18, with several of the deviant phenomena enumerated in Chapter 25. Certain broad, elementary notions should be clearly understood from the beginning. First, no distinction whatsoever is made in the Derived Forms between roots with the third radical weak in *w* and those in *y*, all being treated as though ending in *y*. Secondly, all the *māḍī* patterns behave like *ramà*. Thirdly, all the *muḍāri'* patterns, with the exception of V and VI, behave like *yarmī*. Fourthly, V and VI *muḍārī'* behave like *yarḍà*. Fifthly, all the Weak Derived Active Participles behave like *qāḍin* (as do also the maṣdars of V and VI). Sixthly, all the Weak

Derived Passive Participles (often used as Nouns of Place, see para. 148) behave like *quran.* Finally, one *maṣdar* of III, and those of IV and VII–X, convert the weak radical into *hamza.*

191. *Weak Roots II: basic patterns.* We use ṢLW II, "to pray" (see p. 138, *Vocabulary and remarks* for para. 181, for a special function of this verb), to demonstrate the three basic patterns (*māḍī, muḍāri'* and *maṣdar*) and their derivatives (Imperative, and Active and Passive Participles), though the three latter are predictable in every case.

Māḍi	*Muḍāri'*	*Maṣdar*
صلّى	يصلّي	تصلية
ṣallà	yuṣallī	taṣliya(h)
(Imperative)	(Active Part.)	(Passive Part.)
صلّ	مصلّ	مصلّى
ṣalli etc.	muṣallin	muṣallan

Note particularly the *maṣdar*: this pattern occasionally occurs with standard roots, e.g. *tajriba(h)*, rather than *tajrīb*, from JRB II, "to test, experiment with; to experience". The Passive Participle as a Noun of Place means "chapel, oratory".

192. *Weak Roots III: basic patterns.* We shall use LQY III, "to meet, have an interview with" (more deliberate in sense than I, *laqiya*).

Māḍī	*Muḍari'*	*Maṣdar*
لاقى	يلاقي	ملاقاة mulāqāt
lāqà	yulāqī	لقاء liqā
(Imperative)	(Active Part.)	(Passive Part.)
لاق	ملاق	ملاقى
lāqi etc.	mulāqin	mulāqan

193. *Weak Roots IV: basic patterns.* We shall use LQY IV, 'to throw, cast".

Māḍī	*Muḍāri'*	*Maṣdar*
ألقى	يلقي	إلقاء
'alqà	yulqī	'ilqā'
(Imperative)	(Active Part.)	(Passive Part.)
ألق	ملق	ملقى
'alqi etc.	mulqin	mulqan

194. *Practice material.* Work through the material in the separate section, pp. 143ff.

27

Weak Roots: Forms V–VIII and X; Weak Passives

195. *Weak Roots V: basic patterns.* We shall use WLY V, "to assume, be invested with (authority)" (and several other meanings).

Māḍī	*Muḍāri'*	*Maṣdar*
تولّى	يتولّى	تولّ
tawallà	yatawallà	tawallin
(Imperative)	(Active Part.)	(Passive Part.)
تولّ	متولّ	متولّى
tawalla	mutawallin	mutawallan

196. *Weak Roots VI: basic patterns.* We shall use 'MY VI, "to feign blindness, turn a blind eye".

Māḍī	*Muḍāri'*	*Maṣdar*
تعامى	يتعامى	تعام
ta'āmà	yata'āmà	ta'āmin
(Imperative)	(Active Part.)	(Passive Part.)
تعام	متعام	متعامى
ta'āma	muta'āmin	muta'āman

197. *Weak Roots VII: basic patterns.* We shall use QḌY VII, "to elapse, come to an end".

Māḍī	*Muḍāri'*	*Maṣdar*
انقضى	ينقضي	انقضاء
inqaḍà	yanqaḍī	inqiḍā
(Imperative)	(Active Part.)	(Passive Part.)
انقض	منقض	منقضى
inqaḍi	munqaḍin	munqaḍan

198. *Weak Roots VIII: basic patterns.* We shall use SHRY VIII, "to buy".

Māḍī	*Muḍāri'*	*Maṣdar*
اشترى	يشتري	اشتراء
ishtarà	yashtarī	ishtirā'[1]
(Imperative)	(Active Part.)	(Passive Part.)
اشتر	مشتر	مشترى
ishtari	mushtarin	mushtaran

199. *Weak Roots X: basic patterns.* We shall use SHFY X, "to recover (from an illness)".

Māḍī	*Muḍāri'*	*Maṣdar*
استشفى	يستشفي	استشفاء
istashfà	yastashfī	istishfā'
(Imperatve)	(Active Part.)	(Passive Part.)
استشف	مستشف	مستشفى
istashfi	mustashfin	mustashfan

200. *Weak Roots: Passive patterns.* By combining the principles of para. 146 with those enunciated from para. 182 to this point, the student should be able to forecast most of the patterns involved. All Weak Roots are treated in the Passive as though the weak radical were *y*, the *māḍī* behaving like *raḍiya* and the *muḍāri'* like *yarḍà*. The following table is given in terms in QḌY, though this root does not necessarily exist in all the Derived Forms:

	Māḍī	*Muḍāri'*
I	quḍiya	yuqḍà (cf. IV)
II	quḍḍiya	yuqaḍḍà
III	qūḍiya	yuqāḍà
IV	uqḍiya	yuqḍà (cf. I)
V	tuquḍḍiya	yutaqaḍḍà
VI	tuqūḍiya	yutaqāḍà

[1] The *maṣdar* of this particular verb is usually taken in practice to be *shirā'*, from I. Such a non-conformity is not uncommon: cf. HBB IV, but *ḥubb*; and SFR III, but (sometimes) *safar*.

VII	unquḍiya	yunqaḍà
VIII	uqtuḍiya	yuqtaḍà
X	ustuqḍiya	yustaqḍà

201. *Practice material.* Work through the material in the separate section, p. 145.

28

Roots with multiple peculiarities; The problem of numerals; A list of basic roots

202. *Multiple peculiar roots in general.* Much is often made of these in the standard manuals, but the position is essentially fairly simple in most cases. One of the multiple peculiarities often relates to *hamza*, particularly in the initial position: the principles explained in paras. 53 and 163 apply here. Where a Hollow Root is also involved paras. 169–80 should be consulted once more. Similarly with para. 162 for initial *wāw*, and paras. 182–200 for Weak Roots. To take a few examples, representative Form I patterns of the two roots connoting "coming" ('TY and JY'), and the roots 'WB and WLY respectively, would appear as follows:

Māḍī	*Muḍāri'*	*Imperative*	*Active Part.*
أتى atà	يأتي ya'tī	ايت īti (for i'ti)	آت ātin
جاء jā'a	يجيئ yajī'u	جئ ji'	جاء jā'in (for jā'i')
آب āba	يؤوب ya'ūbu	أب ub	آئب ā'ib
ولى walà; waliya	يلي yalī	ل li (!)	وال wālin

203. *Multiple peculiar roots: some special cases.* While the unstable consonants can occur in one given root as both second and third radical, no root is normally capable of being treated as simultaneously Hollow and Weak. In such cases, the second radical (normally *w*) is treated as fully consonantal. Thus 'WY gives *'awà*; *ya'wī* etc., and no really extreme complications are found in actual practice. However, two roots deserve special mention: R'Y gives *ra'à*, *yarà* in I, and *'arà*, *yurī* in IV, i.e. the medial *hamza* in these four situations disappears completely in all but the *māḍī* of I (*ra'à* is the ordinary verb for "to see", its Form IV meaning "to show"). Secondly, the root ḤYW/ḤYY is treated sometimes as Doubled and sometimes as Weak, while in Form X one of the unstable radicals often disappears altogether: the *māḍī* of I is *ḥayya* or *ḥayiya* in 3 m.s., but usually regular like *raḍiya* elsewhere, even in 3 f.s. and 3 m.p.; in the *muḍāri'* of I we find *yaḥyā* etc. (not normally written, as one might expect, as *yaḥyà*); Form IV gives *'aḥyā* (note spelling, once more), *yuḥyī*; Form X gives *istaḥaiya* etc. (in those cases where the third radical normally takes a vowel), or *istaḥyā* (note spelling again), or *istaḥà*. Once established, these last two deviants take endings as for SHFY X. (Form I of this root means "to live, be alive"; and Form IV "to revive, bring to life"; while Form X usually means "to be ashamed (of: *min*)".) Even for these two roots, virtually all other possible patterns are regular in their deviations.

204. *The Arabic numerals in general.* The numerals, and particularly the Cardinal Numbers, present difficulties in respect of: their combination with each other, in the teens especially; their various ways of governing the thing numbered; and the principle of Polarity (i.e. opposed gender) in some of the units. There are also a number of minor problems, which are best treated individually. We shall deal briefly with all these problems (some of which we have actually met in reading), and then say a little more about Ordinals and Fractions.

205. *Cardinal Numbers: Combination.* Most of the Cardinal Numbers are simple, full-fledged nouns of various patterns, combining with each other by means of the link "and", *wa-*. Usually, the unit will precede the ten (the number 23 is 3-and-20 rather than 20-and-3), but order is otherwise from highest to lowest. (An older order, from lowest to highest, may explain why Arabic numerals still *seem* to read from left to right, against the whole trend of the script: the date 1964 was originally written and read from right to left as 4-and-60-and-900-and-1000; it is now usually read as 1000-and-900-and-4-and-60, but still preserves the original written order.) The one anomaly in this general principle of combination is that the teens, from 11 to 19, form fixed compounds, undergoing no change except for a partial Accusative-Genitive case-marking in the case of 12.

206. *Cardinal Numbers: Government. The number 1*, if used at all (e.g. for emphasis) with a thing numbered, is a simple adjective following the noun: *kitābun wāḥidun, zaujatan wāḥidatan.* (The forms *aḥad*, fem. *iḥdà* (indecl.), may be regarded as "pronouns", either standing alone or followed by a noun in Construct or a Pronoun Suffix: we have seen examples of all these.) *The number 2*, if used at all (e.g. for emphasis) with a thing numbered, is a Dual noun following a Dual noun in apposition: *kitābāni ithnāni, zaujataini ithnataini.* (Remember that this word takes *hamzat al-waṣl*!) *The numbers from 3 to 10* are in Construct with a Genitive Plural noun (at an earlier stage, Arabic reserved certain Broken Plurals for this use, the so-called "plurals of paucity", but this limitation has long been a dead-letter in practice). *The numbers from 11 to 99* govern the thing numbered in the Accusative singular. *From 100 onwards*, whole hundreds are placed in Construct with a Genitive singular noun; where hundreds (and above) are compounded with tens and units, however, the last item in the compound determines the government. Thus, in the two ways of reading 1964 above, the determinant would be either 1,000 or 60 respectively. When it is necessary to make a Cardinal Number definite ("*the* twenty books" rather than merely "twenty books"), the thing numbered and the numeral are *both* given the article, the numeral following the noun in apposition, and the noun being plural in all cases. However, modern usage increasingly favours appending the article only to the numeral, which preserves its normal order and government, often as an "improper" Construct.

207. *Cardinal Numbers: Polarity.* This is an interesting feature that Arabic shares with certain other languages, and one doubtless holding a number of implications in the areas of both psychology and anthropology. The Cardinal units, from 3 to 10 only, have parallel forms of masculine and feminine appearance: *khams, khamsa(h)*; *sitt, sitta(h)* etc. However, in use it is the masculine form that qualifies feminine nouns, and vice versa! Moreover, the same principle applies to the unit-element of the fixed compounds (see paras. 205 and 209) from 13 to 19, as well as to any unit from 3 to 10 included in higher compounds. However, neither the whole tens, nor 100, nor 1,000, takes any account of the gender of the thing numbered.

208. *Cardinal Numbers: 3 to 10.* Below is given, for easy reference, the bare masculine form; it should be remembered that each one is a normal noun in its own right:

3: *thalāth*
4: *arba'*
5: *khams*
6: *sitt*
7: *sab'*
8: *thamān(in)*: like *qāḍin* (see para. 186)
9: *tis'*
10: *'ashr* (f. *'ashara(h)*)

209. *Cardinal Numbers: 11 to 19.* Most of these are fully predictable but below we give complete lists of the two sets of fixed compounds for easy reference.

NOTE: Particular features to note are: the form of the "ten"-element in both lists as compared with para. 208; 12, which declines the dual unit-element for the Accusative-Genitive; and 18, which has the unit-element, in the right hand list, in the Construct Accusative pattern of *qāḍin.*

	Use with masculine		Use with feminine	
11	aḥada	ʻashara	iḥdà	ʻashrata
12	ithnā	〃	ithnatā	〃
13	thalāthata	〃	thalātha	〃
14	arbaʻata	〃	arbaʻa	〃
15	khamsata	〃	khamsa	〃
16	sittata	〃	sitta	〃
17	sabʻata	〃	sabʻa	〃
18	thamāniyata	〃	thamāniya	〃
19	tisʻata	〃	tisʻa	〃

210. *Cardinal Numbers from 20 upwards.* The whole tens from 30 to 90 are formed as Sound Plurals from the masculine pattern of the units from 3 to 9: *thalāth(un)* gives *thalāthūna, thamān(in)* gives *thamānūna* and so on. Twenty is formed from yet another slightly deviant pattern of 10 as *ʻishrūna.* We have already met 100: *mi'a(h),* written either as مائة or مئة (pl. Sound feminine). 1,000 is *alf* (pl. *ulūf* or *ālāf*). It should be noted that when *alf* is multiplied, the rules enunciated in para. 206 apply strictly, i.e. in particular the relevant unit is followed by the Genitive Plural of *alf* (*ālāf* is usually employed here, *ulūf* being reserved for such phrases as "thousands and thousands"): *sabʻatu ālāfin* etc. However, in similar circumstances, the numerical 100 has the unit combined with its *singular* form: *thalāthu mi'atin, thamānī mi'atin* (not *mi'ātin*); these multiple-hundreds are often written in Arabic as one word. In the last century or so, the number *malyūn* (pl. according to rule!) is freely used for 1,000,000 in place of the old *alf(u) alf(in).*

211. *Ordinal Numerals: general; units and whole tens.* The Ordinal Numerals qualify the thing numbered as adjectives (cf. para. 85): both they and their noun are usually in the nature of things Definite, but agreement is in any event as full as possible. In the *units,* from 1 to 10, agreement is complete: 1st has a special form, which we have met (*auwal(u)*; fem. *ūlà* (indeclin.)), but the Ordinals from 2nd to 10th are formed from the unit Cardinals (directly in most cases) on the pattern of the Active Participle Form I – *thālith, khāmis, thāmin* and so on. All of these make regular feminines. Particular comment should perhaps be made on the appearance of 2nd (*thān(in)* like *qāḍ(in)*), and also that of 6th (*sādis,* not *sātt*). Since these are adjectives, the principle of Polarity no longer applies. These units combine with whole tens from 20 upwards in the same way as for the Cardinals. In the case of the *whole tens* themselves (including the hundreds and thousands), the Cardinal Numerals are used as Ordinals, but (even allowing for what was said about the occasionally Definite Cardinals at the end of para. 206) this normally does not lead to real confusion.

212. *Ordinal Numerals: 11 to 19.* As with the Cardinals, the special unit-forms of the Ordinals enter, more or less regularly, into fixed combinations with a form of the numeral 10 to make the teen-Ordinals. Once again, for easy reference, these fixed forms are given as a table. As with the units themselves, it will be noticed that the principle of maximum adjectival agreement overcomes that of Polarity in the Ordinals:

	Masculine		Feminine	
11th	al-ḥadiya	‘ashara	al-ḥādiyata	‘ashrata
12th	al-thāniya	"	al-thāniyata	"
13th	al-thālitha	"	al-thālithata	"
14th	al-rābi‘a	"	al-rābi‘ata	"
15th	al-khāmisa	"	al-khāmisata	"
16th	al-sādisa	"	al-sādisata	"
17th	al-sābi‘a	"	al-sābi‘ata	"
18th	al-thāmina	"	al-thāminata	"
19th	al-tāsi‘a	"	al-tāsi‘ata	"

213. *Fractions.* These are all, with the exception of "half" (*niṣf*, pl. *anṣāf*), of the pattern 1 u 2 3: *thulth*, *rub‘*, *khums*, *suds* etc. They can be dualised, and they also unite with Cardinal Numerals in the usual way: *thulthāni* is "two-thirds"; *thalāthatu akhmāsin* is "three-fifths"; and so on.

214. *Other numeral problems.* For these, and also for dates, time, days of the week, months of the year and so on, the student should consult the standard manuals and dictionaries (see Postcript).

215. *Basic roots.* The following 130 or so roots provide the essential nucleus of a "fruitful" Arabic vocabulary. They do not include obvious and familiar roots like KTB or F‘L, or those with only limited development to one or two words, however important the latter may be. The student should both fit his own actual word-holdings into them wherever possible, and also follow their development out, group by group, in a standard dictionary.

Group I (24)

hamza	*bā’*	*tā’*	*jīm*
’THR	BḤTH	TB‘	JRY
’KHDH	BD’	TMM	JLS

’KHR	BDL		JM‘
’MR	BSṬ	*thā’*	JML
’MN	B‘D	THBT	JNB
’NS	BQY		JWB
’HL	BLGH		
	BNY		

Group II (17)

ḥā’	*khā’*
ḤBB	KHBR
ḤDD	KHRJ
ḤDTH	KHṢṢ
ḤSN	KHṬB
ḤṢL	KHLṢ
ḤḌR	KHLF
ḤFẒ	
ḤQQ	
ḤKM	
ḤLL	
ḤML	

Group III (25)

dāl	*rā’*	*sīn*	*ḍād*
DKHL	R’Y	S’L	ḌRB
D‘W	RJ‘	SKN	
DF‘	RDD	SLM	*ṭā’*
DLL	RF‘		ṬB‘
DWR	RKB	*ṣād*	ṬLB
		ṢḤḤ	ṬL‘
dhāl	*zā’*	ṢDR	
DHHB	ZYD	ṢDQ	*ẓā’*
		ṢN‘	ẒHR
		ṢWR	

Group IV (29)

‘ain	*fā’*	*qāf*	*kāf*
‘JB	FTḤ	QBL	KRM
‘DD	FRQ	QDR	
‘DL	FṢL	QDM	

‘DW
‘RḌ
‘RF
‘ẒM
‘QD
‘QL
‘LM
‘ML

FḌL
FKR
FHM

QṢR
QḌY
QṬ‘
QLL
QWL
QWM

lām

LZM
LQY

Group V (31)

mīm

MTHL
MDD
MRR
MLK

nūn

NZL
NẒR
NẒM
NFS
NQL
NHY
NWR

hā’

HMM

wāw

WJB
WJD
WJH
WḤD
WRD
WSṬ
WS‘
WṢL
WḌ‘
W‘D
WFQ
WQ‘
WQF
WLD

yā’

YBS
YSR
YQẒ
YQN
YMN

216. *Practice material.* Work through the material in the separate section, p. 147.

POSTSCRIPT

From this point on, the average-to-good student should be encouraged to *read rapidly through* at least one of the several small standard manuals of Arabic grammar, for example by A. S. Tritton (the best, despite eccentricities and grave pedagogical faults); D. Cowan; F. J. Ziadeh and R. B. Winder (good tables); J. A. Haywood and H. M. Nahmad (overburdened with detail and has some rather bad errors); or G. C. Scott (sensible and generally reliable). For the advanced student of Classical Arabic, W. Wright's grammar is of course essential. Again the average-to-good student can get along with J. G. Hava's Dictionary for immediate and general purposes; but for Modern Arabic in particular that of H. Wehr is indispensable (either in the original German or in the English adaptation). Likewise, the monumental (and expensive) works of E. W. Lane and R. Dozy remain essential (though inadequate) for work on the full range of "Classical" Arabic. Various other dictionaries are forthcoming.[1] Several "readers" are obtainable, both in the Classical and the Modern "areas", but they are all subject to faults of varying degrees, and the student will find any attempt to read alone hard work indeed – not least because of the vast extent of unfamiliar, non-linguistic context. (There is no question but that a teacher and guide is virtually essential to the first three or more years of Arabic studies!)

Appended after Texts and Analyses (p. 151) are:

(*a*) Some fifty English type-sentences for putting into Arabic near the end of the course.

(*b*) Typical University of Toronto first-year Arabic Examination Questions of all kinds set during the years 1958–63.

(*c*) A few selected passages of Arabic for further reading without the aid of more than a "small" dictionary as named above.

[1] An inexpensive and very practical distillation of Wehr appeared in 1973: *Arabic–English Dictionary*, by Maan Z. Madina (Pocket Books, New York).

TEXTS AND ANALYSES

NOTE: Paragraph numbers in this section refer back to paragraphs in the main text, unless other page references are given.

89. *Practice sentences.* (New vocabulary and notes follow, in order of occurrence: note Arabic numerals, from which our own derive)

١ قطع الخبز بسكين

٢ وقع الخبز من الرف

٣ وقع / وقعت } الأخباز من الرفوف

٤ أخذت البنت خبزا وأكلت قطعة كبيرة

٥ أخذت البنات أخبازا وأكلن قطعا كبيرة

٦ أخذ الرجل خبزا وأكل قطعة كبيرة

٧ أخذ الرجال أخبازا وأكلوا قطعا كبيرة

٨ الخبز طيب

٩ القطعة كبيرة

١٠ الخبز الطيب هو على الرف

١١ على الرف قطعة كبيرة من الخبز

١٢ وجه البنت حسن

١٣ نظر وجه البنت الحسنة

١٤ نظرت وجه رجل ميت

١٥ الرجل الحسن تاجر

١٦ الرجل الطويل هو التاجر المصرى

VOCABULARY AND REMARKS (in order of item occurrence)

qaṭaʿa: to cut
khubz (pl. *akhbāz*): loaf, bread
bi-: with, by (attached preposition, followed by Genitive case)
sikkīn[1] (pl. to be learned later, on regular pattern): knife

[1] Remember sun-letters: *al-sikkīn* / *as-sikkīn* etc.

waqa'a: to fall
min: from, away from, of (partitive use: piece of; separate preposition, followed by Genitive; takes false vowel *a* before article, but *i* elsewhere)
raff[1] (pl. *rufūf*): shelf
akhadha: to take
bint (pl. *banāt*): girl, daughter (pls. of this type (Sound Feminine) have one peculiarity, to be mentioned later)
akala: to eat
qiṭ'a(h) (pl. *qiṭa'*): piece (remember, no *alif* to mark accusative *tanwīn*)
kabīr (pl. *kibār*): large, big
rajul[1] (pl. *rijāl*): man (as against a woman)
ṭaiyib:[1] good, fresh, nice
huwa: he, it (separator in Nominal Sentences where masc. sing. involved)
'alà: on, upon, over (preposition takes Genitive: long vowel shortens in pronunciation before *waṣl*; see also para. 48(*c*))
maiyit (pl. irregular: to come later): dead, dead man
tājir[1] (pl. *tujjār*): merchant
ṭawīl[1] (pl. *ṭiwāl*): tall, long
miṣrīy (pl. "Sound": to come later): Egyptian

99. *Practice sentences*

١ العرب ملوك الناس
٢ ملوك الناس هم العرب
٣ الانسان أفضل الحيوان
٤ أفضل الحيوان هو الانسان
٥ من هو صاحب القرآن
٦ صاحب القرآن عند أهل الإسلام هو الله نفسه
٧ ما هو اسم صاحب الكتاب العربي الجديد
٨ اسمه توفيق الحكيم وهو كاتب معروف عند العرب
٩ متي تذهب إلى المدرسة
١٠ أذهب إلى المدرسة كل يوم الا في الصيف
١١ ما تفعل هناك
١٢ أدرس هناك الكتابة والقراءة والحساب
١٣ وأين تدرس اللغة العربية
١٤ اللغة العربية أدرسها أيضا في المدرسة
١٥ هل درست اللغة العربية مدة طويلة
١٦ لا درستها سنة فقط

[1] Remember sun-letters: *al-sikkīn* / *as-sikkīn* etc.

١٧ هل تدرس منذ مدة طويلة

١٨ نعم أدرس أنا منذ أعوام وصديقي يدرس منذ السنة الخامسة من عمره

١٩ كيف تكتب أنت

٢٠ أكتب أنا عادة بالقلم وأكثر الناس يكتبون بقلم رصاص

٢١ دخل الأجناد القدس يقتلون سكانها كلهم ويسرقون أموالهم

٢٢ أخذت البنت مني خبزا تأكله على الفور

٢٣ أخذت أنا منها أخبازا كثيرة ولما وصلت إلى بيتي وضعتها على رف

VOCABULARY AND REMARKS

'arab: Arabs (normally with article: collective noun)

malik (pl. *mulūk*): king

nās: mankind, people (normally with article; collective or pl. with no real sing., but see next word; root 'NS or NSW)

NOTE: Sentences 1 and 3 inverted seem to require a "divider" between subject and predicate. Why?

insān: man, human being (often with article; sing. with no real pl., but cf. previous word; root 'NS)

afḍal: more or most excellent, virtuous; best

NOTE: Pattern of last word, 'aKTaB, "more" or "most" plus adjective, is called Elative Form in Arabic. In some situations, not here, it differs from the Standard Noun as regards endings (see later under Diptotes).

ḥayawān: animal, animals (often with article; collective or sing., root ḤYY or ḤYW)

man: who? (Do not confuse with preposition *min*, which must be followed by noun or attached pronoun. *Man* is normally followed by verb, or (as here) a Nominal-Sentence "divider")

ṣāḥib: (here) author; (also) owner, friend, companion etc. (has many pls., but a common one is *aṣḥāb*)

al-qur'ān: Koran (normally with article; root QR', "to read, recite")

'inda: (preposition) according to, in the eyes of; near, by; at the house of; among

ahl: people (connected with), family (usually in construct with another noun; a collective with no sing.)

islām: Islam (the faith or the civilisation, as well as the act of becoming a Muslim; usually with article)

allāh(u): God (Note spelling: Muslim printers usually keep a special type-fount of this sacred name. We have here a sun-letter *l* following what is really the article (hence the *shadda*, the final vowel and also the *hamzat al-waṣl*); and the long vowel *ā* is indicated here, as in a handful of other words, by a vertical *fatḥa*, rather than by *fatḥa* plus *alif*) *nafs* (pl. *nufūs*; *anfus*): soul; self (in latter sense, combined with the appropriate pronoun suffix: *nafsu-hu*, *nafsu-hā*, *nafs-ī* etc. In sentence 6 above, the word bears the same case as *allāh* (i.e. it means "God Himself"), because it is another way of saying the same thing. Where two nouns stand together and refer to the same person or thing, we say they are "in apposition" and give them the same case-ending)

mā: what? (cf. second part of note on *man*, above. Remember to watch out for other important uses of *mā*, some of them quite distinct from this)

ism: name, especially the first, personal name (with *hamzat al-waṣl*; pl. *asmā'*, *not* with *waṣl*; root SMW)

'arabīy (pl. "sound": to come later): Arab, Arabian, Arabic

jadīd: new, recent

Taufiq al-Ḥakīm (b. 1898): prolific and attractive Egyptian writer in practically all genres

ma'rūf: well-known (root 'RF, "to know")

matà: when? (There are many words for "when" in Arabic, most of them with distinct functions; this one is used to ask questions (cf. *lammā*, below))

dhahaba (a): to go

ilà: (preposition) to (of motion), up to, towards (cf. para. 48(*c*))

madrasa (pl. to come later): school (root DRS, "to study")

kull: each, every; all (normally always in Construct); followed by an *indefinite* noun, as here, only the *first two* apply (see further remark under next word; also see under *saraqa*, below)

yaum (pl. *aiyām*): day, complete 24-hour period. (Here *kulla yaumin*, "every day", has the first element in the Accusative (the second is fixed by Construct); this is done adverbially, a very common usage in Arabic. Remember the specific functions of the Nominative and Genitive Cases: any noun not fitting these, even if not the object of a verb, should be put in the Accusative Case)

illā: except (For the present, you may assume that this particle has no governing power, i.e. takes no case.)

fī: (preposition) in, on, at; concerning (the standard Arabic preposition for practically all time relationships – "on Monday", "at Christmas", "in winter" etc.)

ṣaif: summer (usually with article)

fa'ala (a): to do

hunāka: there, in that place

darasa (u): to study

kitāba: writing, calligraphy (usually with article, if not first element of construct)

qirā'a: reading (as for preceding; root QR')

ḥisāb: reckoning, arithmetic; account (as for preceding)

aina: where?

lugha (pl. to come later): language (root LGHW)

aiḍan: also (indefinite accusative!)

hal: an initial word, signalling a question (not always used; an alternative is a prefixed *'a-*, but this can be mistaken for many other things (e.g. 1 c.s. prefix of the *muḍāri'*), so *hal* is preferable. No "signal" is needed with "where?", "when?" etc.)
mudda: period of time, "spell" (here accusative indefinite (see remark on *yaum*, above))
lā: no! (also used as "not" with certain verbal constructions to be studied later)
sana (pl. to come later): year (root usually considered to be SNW)
faqaṭ: only, ... and no more (always placed at end of statement)
mundhu: (preposition) since, ago; for (of a period of time beginning in the past and extending into the present. Note that sentences 15 and 16 above probably refer to an action that is finished ("did you study ... I studied"), whereas 17 and 18 speak of an action continuing into the present ("have you been studying ... I have been studying ... for so and so long"))
na'am: yes (one of many words, perhaps the most generally useful)
'ām (pl. *a'wām*): year (root 'WM; remember, *alif* is not a consonant and so cannot be a radical – only W and Y can so serve)
ṣadīq (pl. to come later): friend
khāmis: fifth (an ordinal adjective, one that places things in order)
min: of (here), i.e. out of, forming part of (the partitive use)
'umr (pl. *a'mār*): life, lifetime
kaifa: how?
'āda (pl. to come later): custom, use, habit (in Indefinite Accusative serves adverbially (see remark on *yaum*, above): "usually"; root 'WD)
akthar: most, the majority (often in Construct; cf. Note following *afḍal*, above)
qalamu raṣāṣin: a pencil (lit. "pen of lead". A type of improper Construct (see para. 87); hence the first element is not necessarily definite in sense. To make such "compound nouns" definite, the article is added to the *second* element; remember that this is *not true of proper Constructs*)
sākin (pl. *sukkān*): inhabitant (see next item for remarks)
saraqa (i): to steal (notice *sukkāna-hā kulla-hum* ("its inhabitants, all of them": apposition, as explained in remark on *nafs* above); *kulla sukkāni-hā* is not incorrect, but considerably less emphatic and idiomatic. Contrast this whole sentence with that in para. 78: here the two actions are much more closely linked, as explained in para. 93)
māl (pl. *amwāl*): property, possessions (root MWL)
faur: normally found only as *fauran* or *'alà/min al-fauri*, "immediately"
lammā: when (followed by *māḍī* and referring to one action in past)
waṣala (i): to arrive, reach (often with *ilà*) (Do not try to put this verb in the *muḍāri'* yet; most verbs beginning with *w* drop it throughout the *muḍāri'*)
waḍa'a (a): to place, put (Do not try to put this verb into the *muḍāri'* yet!)

NOTE: As a supplement to this vocabulary, we give here the *muḍāri'* middle vowel of certain important verbs, and the plural of certain important noun-adjectives, which we have so far not treated fully for one reason or another. أخذ (u) دخل (u) قتل (u) نظر (u) أكل (u) صغير (*ṣighār*) قطع (a) وجه (several pls., most common *wujūh*) وقع (a), (but see warning at end of above vocabulary under *waṣala* and *waḍaʻa*)

NOTE: We shall not normally give the *muḍāriʻ* vowel for verbs with the *māḍī* in *i* or *u*, nor for those with *ḥ* or *ʻain* as second or third radical (cf. para. 92 on these three points).

108. *Practice material*

١ في قديم الزمان كان يسكن في القاهرة رجل اسمه على وكان له ابنان وبنات كثيرات
٢ هل تعلم كم كان له من بنين — نعم اثنان
٣ هل تعلم كم كان له من بنات — لا غير أنهن كثيرات
٤ هل تعلم كم كان له من زوجات — لا
٥ في أى زمان كان الرجل يسكن في القاهرة
٦ هل يسكن في القاهرة اليوم — لا هو ميت منذ مدة طويلة
٧ ما كان اسمه
٨ هل تعلم أسماء ابنيه وبناته (cf. para. 88, Note)
٩ هل كان الرجل يسكن في القاهرة مدة طويلة — الله أعلم لأن الرجل المذكور هو ميت منذ مدة طويلة
١٠ قال رجل لصديق قد أخذ منه مبلغا ما بالدين هل ذكرت أن لى عليك منذ سنة مائة دينار قال المدين كلا يا عزيزى غير أنني أطلب منك أن تتركني شهرا شهرين لكى لا أذكر
١١ صائد الأسود الماهر هو الذى يرجع سالما من الغابة وان لم يأخذ حتي شعرة أسد .

VOCABULARY AND REMARKS

qadīm: ancient, former, olden
zamān: time, era

NOTE: The first word is combined with the second in an "improper" Construct (para. 87). It would be equally possible (but clumsier and less normal here) to make the adjective qualify the noun in the regular way: *fī al-zamāni al-qadīmi*. The whole phrase ("in ancient times", "once upon a time") represents a stock adverbial displacer (para. 78) in a Verbal Sentence.

kāna: 3 m.s. *māḍī* of "Hollow" Verb, i.e. verb with *w* or *y* as middle radical (to be studied at length later). *Sometimes* usefully translated as "he was" or "he became" (but not as "to be", since Nominal Sentences fulfil a large part of the function of the English verb "to be"). (In the present sentence it has two functions: first, it is followed by the *muḍāri'* (same number, person and gender!) to give the sense of *habit* ("used to dwell") or *continuity* ("was dwelling"), i.e. it is used as a time-indicator (para. 62); later, it links its subject to the preposition *li-* to indicate the idea of "having" ("two sons . . . were to him", "he had two sons"). As a general principle, there is really no Arabic verb "to have": in the past it is expressed as here, in the present one uses a Nominal Sentence, often inverted (para. 80(*b*)); "he has a son" is expressed as "to him (is) a son". Other prepositions may be used in such constructions besides *li-*: *ma'a* and *'inda*, for example, both mean much the same here, but the first (and, to some extent, the second) tend to suggest that the thing is actually on one's person, e.g. money in a pocket. Cf. also *'inda* in *Vocabulary and remarks* to para. 99, p. 107)

sakana (u): to inhabit, dwell (with Accusative or *fī*)

al-qāhira: Cairo (originally an adjective attached to the word "city": *al-madīna (t) al-qāhira*, The Victorious City)

rajul (pl. *rijāl*): a man (as contrasted with a woman. The student should realise that, in default of an explicit subject for the verb so far (and since, in a short isolated sentence of this kind, the subject can hardly be implicit within the verb), this noun is almost certainly the subject of the verbal compound *kāna yaskunu*. The normal place for this subject might have been after the first of the two verbs (or even after the second). Why, then, is it "delayed"? In general, for emphasis (cf. para. 78); but particularly, here, because the sentence goes on without delay to say something more about this man. A short Nominal Sentence follows immediately: "his name (is) 'Alīy"; and in Arabic usage this statement is regarded as closely linked to the word "man". We should in fact translate it as though a word like "who, which, that" (a relative pronoun) connected them: "(who) his name is 'Alīy" or, in normal English, "whose name is 'Alīy". *Note particularly* that such "relative clauses", in Arabic, may *not* have a *relative pronoun* when the *antecedent noun* is, as here, *indefinite*. Such loose relative clauses are called in Arabic *ṣifa(h)*, i.e. adjective, and we shall use this term: they are perhaps one of the trickiest and most easily overlooked features of Arabic structure. One further point: notice that this *ṣifa*, being a Nominal Sentence, is in the present, while the general action is in the past. This is an example of Arabic "economy": the word "was" would be superfluous here, since the man's name was, is, and always will be what it was in his lifetime. It is a sort of permanent truth about him!)

'alīy: the personal name "Ali" (easily confused with *'alà* in writing)

ibn (pl. *abnā', banūna*): son (the sing., but not the first pl., is an important instance of *hamzat al-waṣl*. The second pl., in Construct, is commonly used in tribal names: *banū kalb(in)*, the Kalbites (literally The Sons of Kalb). Root BNW) *kathīr*: much (in Sound Pl., masc. or fem., "many")

'alima (a): to know, be aware

kam: how many? how much? (When associated with a noun, this particle may either place the noun in the Indefinite Accusative *singular* (*kam kitāban*: how many books?); or, as here, be linked to it (often in the pl., Definite or Indefinite according to sense) by a partitive *min*: "how many . . . of sons?". Notice that *kam* may best be regarded in sentences 2–4 as the subject of *kāna* ("how many (there) were to him of . . ."))

ithnāni: two (Dual Nominative masculine. Another important instance of *hamzat al-waṣl*; root THNY)

ghaira anna: however, but (originally "except for the fact that . . .". *Note particularly* the word *anna* or any expression containing it must be followed by either an Accusative noun or (as here) an attached pronoun. This has no bearing on function, and the sentence following the *anna* may be either Verbal or (as here) Nominal. Note that Arabic, while having many "but" words ("adversatives"), makes do with *wa-* more often than English would use "and": in other words, Arabic (particularly until the present century) has been pitched in a lower key of emphasis and contrast than English. Remember often to raise the pitch when putting into English: do not become addicted to the Biblical "and"!)

zauj (pl. *azwāj*): husband ("wife" is formed as a regular feminine, with a Feminine Sound Pl.)

aiy (regular fem.): which? what? (normally found in Construct with a following noun: *fī aiyi zamān(in)*, "at what time?" In negative sentences, and in sentences already interrogative on some other score, this word should be rendered "any, some")

yaum: in the Definite Accusative, "today" (adverbial use of Accusative, an extremely common Arabic phenomenon, as already noted)

a'lamu: most knowing, one who knows best (a special *indefinite* nominative ending, to be discussed in the next chapter; cf. remark on *afḍal*, in *Vocabulary and remarks* to para. 99, p. 107. The short Nominal Sentence, "God is most knowing (knows best)", is used to counter a question difficult or impossible to answer; root 'LM)

li-anna: because (re-read Note on *ghaira anna* above! The phrase immediately following is a Nominal Absolute (see para. 81); then comes a Nominal Sentence)

madhkūr: (afore)mentioned, under discussion (root DKHR; see *dhakara*, below)

qāla: 3 m.s. *māḍī* of "Hollow" Verb (see *kāna* entry, above), "to say" (root QWL)

qad: a somewhat vague time-indicator (a particle having no simple equivalent in English, but serving to emphasise the *reality* or the *pastness* of an action. Its force can sometimes be conveyed in English by stress: "he *did* (do) it" or "he *has done* it"; sometimes, again (as here), the emphasis is on the pastness relative to another verb, so that the appropriate rendering in English is by the so-called pluperfect tense: "he *had done* it". Avoid translating this particle by quasi-Biblical "indeeds" or "verilys": try to understand its *function* in a given context, and then give it appropriate weight (sometimes little or none) in your rendering. NOTE: the clause here beginning with *qad* happens to be a *ṣifa* (see explanation under *rajul*, above); it is, moreover, a parenthetical *ṣifa*, one inserted to give you certain necessary but additional information about the "friend", but which delays the man's actual remark until the interrogative particle *hal*)

mablagh (pl. to be learned later by rule): sum, amount (root BLGH; the *mā* following this, as is usually the case when it follows Indefinite nouns, gives the sense of "a *certain* sum", "*some* sum *or other*")

dain (pl. *duyūn*): debt (The whole expression *akhadha* ... *bi-al-dain* (lit. "to take ... in debt") should really be viewed as meaning "to borrow"; cf. *madīn*, below)

dhakara (u): to remember, recollect; to recall (silently or aloud), to relate, mention (cf. *madhkūr*, above)

anna: that, the fact that (cf. remarks on *ghaira anna* and *li-anna*, above. This particle should be distinguished from *an* (see para. 104), albeit it looks much like it and is often rendered identically in English: by and large, *an* is limited to Subjunctive relationships as there described, whereas *anna* provides a similar clause-link in most other situations. Explanation continues over next two entries!)

lī 'alai-ka plus subject: "to me against you (is) such-and-such", i.e. "you owe me ..." (a good example of the inverted Nominal Sentence (see para. 80(*b*). *Full explanation continues into next entry*!)

mi'a(h): 100 (notice pronunciation, the *alif* being redundant. This word is technically a noun in Arabic; and, according to one of the several complicated rules for the use of numerals, is in Construct (sing.) with the thing numbered (*dīnār*, a coin of widely discrepant values in different parts of the Arab world at various times): *mi'a(tu) dīnār(in)*, 100 dinars. At the same time, *mi'a* is the *grammatical* subject of the inverted Nominal Sentence referred to in the previous entry, though the *logical* subject is clearly the whole expression *mi'a dīnār*. *Yet again*, the *anna* with which this sentence is introduced still demands its Accusative noun, and *mi'a* is the only available candidate. Hence *mi'a* is read *mi'ata*, in the Accusative, while still playing its part as the subject of a Nominal Sentence!)

madīn (pl. Sound Masc.): debtor (root DYN; cf. *dain*, above)

kallā: not at all, by no means, absolutely not! (an emphatic form of *lā*)

yā: a "vocative" particle, used to address someone, as with archaic English "O!" in expressions like "O King!" (However, it is not necessarily archaic in Arabic, so do not render it in English in most cases. Usually followed by an

Indefinite noun without *tanwīn*: *yā malik(u)*; here following noun has attached pronoun 1 c.s., which "swallows up" ending. Note Accusative Vocative where Construct involved. *yā malik(a) al-'irāq(i)*, but Nominative otherwise)

'azīz (pl. *a'izza(h)*): dear, beloved (also "mighty"; *yā 'azīzī* corresponds to something like "my dear chap!", "old man!", "my friend!" etc.)

ṭalaba (u): to ask, request, *min* someone *an* plus Subjunctive: to ask someone to do something (translate the *muḍāri'* here by "I would (must) ask you to . . .")

taraka (u): to leave, leave alone; to desert

shahran shahrain: a month or two, literally "for one month, for two months" (in both cases adverbial Accusative of time duration)

li-kai: in order that, so that (followed by Subjunctive. A similar use is made of *li-an* (do not confuse with *li-anna* above!) and *li-* (do not confuse with *li-*, meaning "to, for, for the sake of", which is a preposition attached to nouns!). The word *lā* serves here as the general negative "not")

ṣā'id (pl. Sound Masc.): hunter (root ṢYD)

asad (pl. *usūd* and others): lion

māhir (pl. Sound Masc.): clever, skilful

NOTE: Carefully examine the relationship of the above three words in the light of paras. 85–8. Assign the right function to the following *huwa* in accordance with para. 80(*a*).

alladhī: the one who (masc. sing. This shade of meaning is more often conveyed by *man* (which you already know as the interrogative "who?"); and *alladhī* more commonly serves as a relative pronoun, "who, which, that", where the antecedent noun is masc. sing. *Definite*, i.e. where a *ṣifa* is not involved. Another important instance of *hamzat al-waṣl*)

sālim (pl. Sound Masc.): safe (notice adverbial Accusative "safely")

ghāba (pl. Sound Fem.): forest, jungle, thicket (root GHYB)

wa-in: even though, even if (lit. "and if". Demands verb in Jussive (see para. 104) or *māḍī*: situation complicated here by presence of negative (see next entry!))

lam: not (negative particle, to be followed by Jussive; usually a time-indicator for the past, but not necessarily so in a Conditional Sentence, as here. Translate either "even though he doesn't catch" or "even though he hasn't caught" (*akhadha* has a wide range of application: take, receive, get, seize, catch etc.))

ḥattà: even, so much as (In this sense, it is a non-governing particle, having no effect on verb–object relationships. Equally often, however, it is a preposition, meaning "as far as, up to, until" (of distance or time); or a conjunction ("until") requiring a *māḍī* verb when something actually occurs, and a Subjunctive when its occurrence is only presumed or expected or intended (in the latter case, where purpose enters, the sense is often "so that, in order that"))

sha'ra: a single hair ("Hair", in general, as a substance, is *sha'r*, and one of the uses of the bound-*t* is to give a sense of "singularity" (the *unit form*). This is especially common in speaking of fruits, vegetables, birds, insects etc., i.e. of things that come in clusters, and are less commonly thought of as units)

117. *Practice material*

في يوم من الأيّام رأى تاجر ولدا يلعب أمام أحد البيوت فسأله قائلا هل والدك في البيت يا بنيّ ولمّا أجابه هذا الولد بالإيجاب قرع البائع باب البيت المذكور فلم يفتح له أحد فصرخ في وجه الولد قائلا كيف تكذب عليّ هكذا كيف تقول أنّ والدك في البيت فأجابه الولد إنّه في البيت حقّا يا سيّدي غير أنّ هذا البيت ليس بيتنا نحن .

VOCABULARY AND REMARKS

fī yaum(in) min al-aiyām(i): one day, on a certain day (You should have no difficulty in identifying and understanding the individual words or the literal meaning of the phrase. This phrase is more emphatic than *yauman* (adverbial Accusative))

ra'à: to see (a weak verb, with several special peculiarities of its own, to be noted in due course)

la'iba (a): to play (Note that this verb introduces what may here be conveniently regarded as a *ṣifa* and also serves as a prolonger of the past time established by *ra'à*. While it is perfectly possible in Arabic to make absolutely clear that the boy *was* playing (see para. 108, remark under *kāna* on use of perfect of *kāna* before *muḍāri'* of other verbs), it would not normally be judged necessary to do so in cases of this kind. After you have grasped that this is a *ṣifa*, remember that you do not always need the "who" in English either: "saw a boy (who was) playing")

amāma: before, in front of (preposition)

ahad: one (It is often, even usually, found in Construct with a following plural, but you do not always need to translate e.g. "one of the houses": "a certain house" would be better here. Standing alone (cf. a few lines further on) as a noun or pronoun, it can often mean "someone, anyone". Its fem. is *iḥdà*, which has no cases. The more common form of the numeral "one" is *wāḥid* (fem. in bound-*t*), which is usually found as an adjective following the noun: *bait(un) wāḥid(un)*, "one house", i.e. one and one only, not two)

sa'ala (a): to ask

qā'ilan: Active Participle (formed according to a standard deviation yet to be learned, i.e. replacement of middle *w* or *y* by *hamza*) from *qāla*, which we have already met as a Hollow Verb meaning "to say" (The word is here in the adverbial Accusative; it could obviously not be put for any good reason in the Genitive, and if it were Nominative it would be treated as the subject of the verb ("a speaker asked"). However, it might seem so obvious that the manner of asking would be by utterance that one would wonder why the word is needed at all. "Saying" would here certainly be strange and superfluous in English. The fact is that the word really performs the function of our colon and quotation marks, and thoroughly modern Arabic would probably replace it by a version of these (but cf. the warning in para. 19))

wālid (pl. "Sound", if used; Dual more common in sense of "parents"): father (a polite word. This is really another Active Participle from the verb *walada*(*i*), "to beget, give birth to")

fī al-bait: at home (as well as "in the house". The point of the story turns on a misunderstanding over these two shades of sense)

bunaiya: my son (Taken together with the preceding vocative particle (already explained under para. 108, p. 113), it here equates with English "sonny", "my boy!", "lad". Note that this apparent single word breaks down into *bunai* ("diminutive" form of *ibn*) and *-ya* (for which see para. 98). In fact, this combination is here the normal form of this expression as used)

ajāba-hu: (he) answered him (This is the 3 m.s. *māḍī* of a "Hollow" Verb in the so-called Fourth Derived Form (we shall be considering these forms in the next few chapters)

bi-al-ījāb: in the affirmative (The noun is technically a *maṣdar* of the Fourth Form of the root WJB, but this does not matter here)

qara'a: to knock at, to bang on (a door)

bā'i': (usual pl. *bā'a(h)*): seller, salesman (Once again (cf. *qā'ilan*, above), we are dealing with the Active Participle of a Hollow Verb, *bā'a* (root BY'), "to sell")

fa-: but, and, so (This is a more radical conjunction than *wa-*, often indicating a change in the subject of the verb, an unexpected development or a contrast (all of which applies here). In dealing with such particles in general, remember what was said under *ghaira anna*, in para. 108, p. 112)

fataḥa: to open; (also) to conquer (Remember, when pronouncing this verb in the text, that its *muḍāri'* middle vowel is governed by its third radical (cf. para. 92), and also that it here follows the negative particle *lam* (see explanation under *lam* in para. 108, p. 114)

ṣarakha(*u*): to shout, cry

fī wajh(i) al-walad(i): the literal meaning should be clear, but translate "at the boy"

kadhaba (i): to lie, tell lies (to someone, it will be seen, is conveyed by *'alà* here, not *li*: this is a use that might be referred to as the "unfavourable" or "disadvantageous" sense of *'alà*, whatever the actual rendering may be in English. For *'alaiya* see para. 98. Note, too, that the normal English rendering of the whole expression would be "how *can* you lie. . . ?"; once again, the principle of economy is involved: it would seem somewhat ridiculous in Arabic actually to employ one of the many Arabic expressions for "can, be able", since the question of ability is not really involved here. The man is making an emphatic protest, not asking if the boy is capable of telling a lie!)

hā-kadhā: thus, in this way (note vertical *fatḥa* in *hā*-, as with the Demonstratives)
taqūlu: 2 m.s. *muḍāri'* of *qāla* (a typical *muḍāri'* of Hollow Verbs having middle radical *w*)
inna: an initial "statement-marker", which can be used to introduce both Nominal and Verbal Sentences (the latter by way of a Nominal Absolute) in some degree of emphasis: thus, in the present case, one might translate "he *is* at home" (In general, try to avoid translating *inna* by pseudo-Biblical "verily", "indeed", etc! Remember that *inna*, like *anna*, requires a pronoun suffix or a noun in the Accusative after it, and that this has nothing to do with the *function* of the noun or pronoun in the sentence. In one situation, i.e. after the verb *qāla*, *inna* and *anna* are more or less interchangeable, and can both be translated as "that" ("he said that (such was the case) . . ."). But cf. para. 167(*b*))
ḥaqqan: truly, really (adverbial Accusative of *ḥaqq*, "truth", "reality")
saiyid (usual pl. *sāda(h)*): gentleman, master, lord (The expression *yā saiyidī* might correspond to "sir", in addressing someone respectfully; cf. previous vocative expressions we have had. Root SWD)
laisa: is not (3 m.s. of an "incomplete" verb, used to negate the present, but having no real *māḍī* or *muḍāri'* as such. Its full conjugation will be given later. It should be noted that its predicate is put in the Accusative, unlike the predicate of a Nominal Sentence (of which it may be regarded as the negative opposite))
naḥnu: this word here performs the emphatic function of the independent pronouns (cf. para. 94): i.e. translate here "this house is not *our* house (or "*ours*")" (Remember that emphasis in Arabic is commonly achieved by position or by the use of extra words, not simply by stress of voice)

118. *Translation into Arabic*. Translate the following sentences into Arabic (where necessary, extra vocabulary is given below).

(1) *Open the door!* (Remember variations of number and gender)
(2) *Do not open* (*lā* plus Jussive) *the door!* (Remember that, though you are addressing the Second Person, "you", there can still be variations of number and gender)
(3) *I did not open the door.*
(4) *I have not opened the door.* (Is there any difference in Arabic between (3) and (4)?)
(5) *I will open the door.*
(6) *When he arrived, I was opening the door.* (In the second clause use *kāna* plus *muḍāri'*, as explained under *kāna* in para. 108, p. 110; 1 c.s. *māḍī* of *kāna* is *kuntu*)
(7) *He fell onto the road because the car-door* (the door of the car) *was* (*kāna*, with predicative in the Accusative, as for *laisa*) *open.*
(8) *All lessons are difficult* (two constructions: see explanation under *saraqa* in para. 99, p. 109), *but this lesson is more difficult than any* (translate *any lesson*,

using *aiy*; remember that a *ṣifa* must follow) *which I have studied* (add *it*) *so far*. (9) *The letter was written in Arabic.*

ADDITIONAL VOCABULARY

door: *bāb* (pl. *abwāb*; root BWB)
road: *ṭarīq* (common pl. *ṭuruq*)
car: *saiyāra(h)* (pl. Sound; root SYR)
lesson: *dars* (pl. *durūs*)
difficult: *ṣa'b* (fem. regular)
than: *min* (following elative on pattern *'aKTaB*)
so far: *ḥattà al-ān(i)* (literally "until the present"; root 'WN. Accusative of noun also possible – adverbially and not governed by *ḥattà*. Cf. *yaum* and *ḥattà* under para. 108, pp. 112, 114)
Arabic: the Arabic language (an expression already encountered)

127. *Practice material*

١ قال طفل لأمّه هل أقدر على أخذ التفاحة الموجودة في الخزانة وأجابت الأمّ بقول نعم يا عزيزى ثمّ أجاب الطفل إنّني أشكركِ لقولكِ نعم فسألت الأم ألهذا الحدّ أنت جائع يا بنىّ — قال الطفل لا يا أمّى غير أنّني قد أكلتها من قبل .

٢ قال طفل لوالده انظر يا أبي هذا الرجل لا يوجد في رأسه شعر فأجاب الأب اسكت لألّا يسمعك ثمّ صرخ الطفل سائلا ولماذا وجب علىّ أن أسكت يا أبي أتظنّ أنّه لا يعلم هو ذلك .

٣ قال الأوّل إنّ أبي يقدر على التكلّم في أىّ موضوع تذكره فأجاب الثاني قائلا وما وجه العجب في ذلك إنّ أبي يقدر على التكلّم دون أى موضوع من المواضيع .

VOCABULARY AND REMARKS

ṭifl (pl. *aṭfāl*): infant, child
umm (pl. *ummahāt*!): mother
qadara (i): to be able, to "can" (usually followed by *'alà*, which is in turn followed either by the *maṣdar* of the appropriate verb (as here) or by *an* and the Subjunctive. With the latter construction, *'alà* is often omitted. One of many such verbs; cf. *wajaba*, below)
akhdh: *maṣdar* of 'KHDH I (Re-read para. 116(*c*). The *maṣdar* is here linked to the noun it governs by a genitival construction. This is the most convenient of all, but as will be seen below is not always possible or desirable, especially when the *maṣdar* needs to be made definite for some reason, either by the article or by a pronoun suffix)

maujūd: existent, available, to be found; it could well be omitted in translation here (While here used as an adjective, it is technically a Passive Part. of *wajada* (*i*), "to find". Cf. also *yūjadu*, below)

khizāna (pl. Sound or *khazā'inu*): storage-room, vault, treasury; (here) cupboard, pantry

qaul: *maṣdar* of *qāla*, here in Construct with the indeclinable word *na'am*; thus the literal translation would be "The mother answered (by the saying of) yes" (Modern Arabic tends increasingly, especially as it uses punctuation, to elide the words here rendered in parentheses; cf. also next entry)

shakara (u): to thank someone (Accusative) for something (*li*, followed by abstract noun or *maṣdar*. Note that the *maṣdar* here shows verbal force, governing the indeclinable word *na'am* in a theoretical Accusative: it cannot be joined with it in Construct, being already so articulated with the suffix *-ki*. Cf. last entry)

hadd (pl. *ḥudūd*): limit, extent, edge (and many important ramifications of meaning; explanation continues into next entry!)

jā'i' (pl. *jiyā'*, *juwwa'*: root JW'): hungry (The whole sentence is an interrogative Nominal Sentence, with an adverbial phrase *prefixed* for reasons of style and emphasis. The literal rendering is: "Question? to this extent you hungry . . ."; the normal version would be: "Are you *so* hungry. . . ?" Purists might prefer *ilà* to *li-* here)

min qablu: previously, earlier, already (Note the ending: this is a "frozen" adverbial phrase. Different translators would give *qad* varying force here: "I had already eaten it" or "I've already *eaten* it")

ab (pl. *ābā'*): father (The plural is commonly used in the sense of "ancestors, forefathers"; the Dual, *abawāni*, in the sense of "parents". It will be noted that this word seems to lack a radical. However, this deficiency does not affect its declension as an otherwise Standard Noun, whether with or without the article; but when it appears as the first element in a Construct, or carries a pronoun suffix, the following forms are used for the respective cases: *abū*, *abā*, *abī*. The form *abī* in the text is an example of the usual all-purpose, all-consuming ending of the 1 c.s. attached suffix (see para. 98). A number of other words behave either exactly like *ab* (e.g. *akh*, "brother") in this respect or in a roughly similar manner. We shall note them as they appear (and in para. 166). Root 'BW)

yūjadu: is found (This is an example of the Passive 3 m.s. *muḍāri'* (we shall study the Passive systematically after completing the Derived Forms). It is here used, as the *muḍāri'* commonly is, with *lā*, to indicate general or present–near-future negation: "is not found". Assuming that *hādhā al-rajul* is not the object of *unẓur* (which is possible), one must take it to be a Nominal Absolute (para. 81). In either case, we have a following sentence meaning literally: "is not found upon his head hair" (the subject following the adverbial phrase, rather than immediately upon the verb, for purposes of emphasis (see towards the end of para. 78)). Finally, note what was said above under *maujūd*, the Passive Part.

of the same verb: i.e. the present sentence could be rendered "Hair does not exist (is not found) on his head", or, more idiomatically, "There's no *hair* on his head")

ra's (pl. *ru'ūs*): head (familiar from maps as "Ras", i.e. cape of land. Notice preposition used: *'alà* would probably suggest "on top of" rather than simply "on")

sakata (u): to be silent, hold one's tongue

li-allā: lest, in case (followed by Subjunctive. It is probably a contraction of *li-an lā*, "in order that ... not" (cf. para. 108, under *li-kai*, p. 114))

samiʻa: to hear

sā'ilan: asking (Active Part., adverbial Accusative, of *sa'ala*; cf. use of *qā'ilan*, and do not insist on translating!)

wa-li-mā-dhā: (and) why, then...? (A particularly emphatic, but quite normal, way of asking the reason for something. The word for "why?" in Arabic can be traced through the following scale of rising emphasis: *lima...limā...limā-dhā*. As usual with such linguistic processes, the "inflated currency" becomes the ordinary small coin of intercourse, and the less emphatic forms tend to go out of use.)

wajaba (i): to be necessary, obligatory, incumbent (This is one of the normal ways of rendering "must" or "ought" in Arabic. But note that the verb is impersonal, i.e. it is always found in the 3 m.s. without a person for subject. Thus, "I must do this" is expressed in Arabic in one of two ways: "It is incumbent upon (*'alà*) me that (*an*) I (should) do (Subjunctive) this"; or "The doing (*maṣdar*) of this is incumbent upon me". In the first case, the technical subject of the verb is the whole subjunctive clause, in the second it is the *maṣdar*: this pair of alternatives recurs constantly in Arabic constructions (see *qadara*, above). Note, finally, that *wajaba* is in the *māḍī*, though we could also use the *muḍāriʻ*, and we should probably render by the English present in either event. The Arabic "thinking" here might be that all verbs are of "action" rather than "state", i.e. that *wajaba* really means "to have *become* necessary" at a certain time in the past and hence, by implication, to *be* so at the present time. This is becoming something of an indicator for distinguishing older stages of the language from the more modern, where usage tends to follow English or French in many ways)

ẓanna (yaẓunnu): to suppose, think (usually with an implication of error. The root is ẒNN, and this is a so-called Double Verb (1–2–2 instead of 1–2–3), about which we shall have more to say later (para. 164))

al-auwal: the first, i.e. "the first speaker" (This word is to be constrasted with *al-thāni*, "the second", which comes later. Both words have various morphological peculiarities: for the moment, however, you may consider the former as regular, while noting simply that *al-thānī* does not here take the normal Nominative case-ending *-u*)

takallum: (the act of) speaking (*maṣdar* of Form V KLM, to which we have not yet come. Refer back to *qadara*, p. 118, for the full construction. Notice *fī* here means "about, concerning, on")

aiy: any (see *Vocabulary and remarks* to para. 108 (p. 112) for construction)

mauḍū' (pl. *mawāḍī'u* or Sound Fem.): topic, subject, matter (Though here used simply as a noun, the pattern is that of the Passive Part. I of *waḍa'a*, which we have already met in the sense of "to put, to lay down", i.e. we have here "something laid down (for the sake of argument), a postulation". Note that since the word here occurs indefinitely, it is followed by a *ṣifa* construction with a pronoun-suffix referring back: ". . . on any subject (which) you mention (it)". An idiomatic rendering would be: ". . . on any subject you (care to) mention")

wajh: reason, cause ("for" is expressed by Construct. We have already met the word in the common meaning of "face"; it has many others)

'ajab: wonder, astonishment, surprise (often tinged with admiration)

dūna: without (preposition. Note other prepositional phrases *bi-dūni* and *bi-lā* in same sense. Translate the following phrase with appropriate emphasis: ". . . without any topic from among the topics" is an Arabic way of saying ". . . without any topic whatsoever")

138. *Practice material*

TRANSLATION INTO ARABIC

(1) When he had drunk the water, he began to eat some bread.
(2) The secretary's broken pen fell from his hand after he had written only two words.
(3) The women went out of the house but did not enter the street.
(4) The minister's wife stole her husband's seal and issued false papers.
(5) He came by a car which stopped twice en route.
(6) Why did you not travel with the caravan which left yesterday?
(7) When his friends came he was not in his house.
(8) They wanted to write their names, but they had not yet learned to write.
(9) A woman teacher opened a school in that city, in which she taught reading, writing and arithmetic.
(10) He used to eat a great deal when he was a child.
(11) "The king will not leave his palace, nor will he eat or drink with his ministers." This is the text of a proclamation which the Queen issued yesterday.

ARABIC PASSAGES

١ ضربتها بشيء كان في يدى على رأسها
٢ مات الشاعر المشهور في السن الّتي مات فيها معاصره الوزير يحيى
٣ نظرت عجوز بنتا صغيرة فسألتها عن أبيها فقالت البنت إنّه مريض فأجابت العجوز إنّه بخير هو

يظنّ نفسه مريضا فقط ، وبعد أسبوعين رأت العجوز البنت الّتي قد رأتها من قبل فسألتها مرةً
ثانيةً عن والدها فأجابت هى هو يظنّ نفسه ميتا فقط .

VOCABULARY AND REMARKS

water: *mā'* (pl. *miyāh, amwāh*; root usually considered to be MWH)

to begin: several possibilities, but use *akhadha* (which you know as "to take" etc.) in combination with the *muḍāri'* of the other verb

some: say "a piece of" or use the partitive *min*, giving the noun the definite article generically: *min al-khubz(i)* (cf. French 'du pain')

secretary: *kātib* (pl. *kuttāb*. A very common pl. where the Active Participle of Form I is used with a professional sense; cf. *tājir* and contrast *khātim*, below)

hand: *yad* (pl. to come later; root YDY)

after he had. . . : *wāw* of Preceding Circumstance!

word: *kalima(h)* (pl. Sound Fem.)

to go out of: *kharaja (u) min*

to enter: *dakhala* can be used here with Accusative or *fī* (and other constructions are possible), latter having stronger idea of "penetration"

minister (of state): *wazīr* (pl. *wuzarā'u*. Note common Diptote pl. for personal noun-adjectives of this pattern. This word has been Europeanised as "Vizier". Cf. *marīḍ*, below)

seal: *khātim* (several pls., e.g. *khawātimu*. A common type of Diptote pl. for Active Participle patterns of I, especially if they are fem. with bound-*t*. Cf. "caravan", below)

to issue: ṢDR IV

false: *bāṭil*

paper: *waraq* (pl. *aurāq*. Unit form is used for "sheet of paper", and this can take Sound Fem. Pl. Basic connotation is that of "leaves", "foliage", but the words are used in both senses)

to come: *jā'a*, *atà* (Both of these common verbs belong to classes we have yet to study (Hollow and Weak, respectively). Either can be used in sentences 5 and 7, without special adaptation, since only 3 m.s. of *māḍī* is involved. Roots JY' and 'TY)

by: *bi-*

which: do not translate in *ṣifa* clause (elsewhere, *alladhī* (m.) and *allatī* (f.), both with *hamzat al-waṣl*)

twice: transl. "two times" (Dual. In this sense, of occasion or repetition, "time" is *marra(h)*. Remember adverbial Accusative!)

en route: transl. "in the way", "in the road"

to travel: SFR III

caravan: *qāfila(h)* (pl. *qawāfilu*. cf. "seal", above)

to leave, to depart: *sāra* (Hollow Verbs form 3 f.s. of *māḍī* by regular addition of -*t*; root SYR)

yesterday: *amsi* (Note fixed ending!)
was not: do not attempt *lam* with Jussive of *kāna* yet!
to want: *arāda* (IV Form of Hollow RWD. 3 m.p. of *māḍī* is formed from this by appending regular ending. This verb governs a *maṣdar* or *an* followed by Subjunctive: "they desired the writing of their names", "they desired that they write (Subjunctive)". After "to learn", only *maṣdar* is possible (with article))
woman-teacher: Active Participle II fem. (takes Sound Pl. Fem.) of 'LM
city: *madīna(h)* (pl. usually *mudun*)
in which she taught: remember to translate: "... which (*ṣifa* or not?) she taught in *it* ..."
a great deal: transl. "much"
when he was: *wāw* of Accompanying Circumstance!
palace: *qaṣr* (pl. *quṣūr*)
text: *naṣṣ* (pl. *nuṣūṣ*)
proclamation: *maṣdar* of ẒHR IV (Note how a *maṣdar* often goes off on a non-verbal, or only semi-verbal, life of its own as an abstract noun. The same is often true of Participles, though their extension is usually concrete)
which the Queen issued: remember to translate: "... which (*ṣifa* or not?) the Queen issued *it* ..."
ḍaraba (i): to hit, strike
shai' (pl. *ashyā'u*): thing; something, anything; a little, a small part (of = *min*) (Note Diptote pl., but triptote sing.)
māta: to die (Hollow Verb; root MWT)
shā'ir (pl. *shu'arā'u*): poet (Note pl. is irregularly like that of *wazīr* pattern. Same applies to 'ālim ('ulamā'u), "learned man", "scholar", "theologian". The latter, in the spelling *ulema* or even *ulemas*, has become accepted in English as a technical term of reference for a body of religious influence formerly very powerful in the Islamic world)
mashhūr: famous (What pattern is this?)
sinn (*asnān*): age (of a person); tooth (usually considered fem.)
mu'āṣir (pl. Sound Masc.): contemporary (What pattern?)
yaḥyà: a proper name, "John"
'ajūz (pl. *'ajā'izu*): old person (usually female)
'an: about, concerning
marīḍ (pl. *marḍà*): ill, sick (The pl., which is indeclinable, is common for this pattern of sing. in "unpleasant" senses: e.g. for *asīr* ("a captive") and *qatīl* ("a murdered man"). Cf. "minister", above)
bi-khair: in (a state of) well-being, well, all right
ba'da: after (preposition. Opposite is *qabla* (cf. with *min qablu*, an adverbial phrase you have already met))
usbū' (pl. *asābī'u*): week (Note that the form here used is *not* pl. Root SB')
ra'at: she saw (This is 3 f.s. *māḍī* of *ra'à*, "to see", one of the few Arabic verbs not susceptible of strict classification morphologically. Root R'Y)

marratan thāniyatan: once more, again (lit. "a second time". Cf. "twice", above, and *al-thānī* in *Vocabulary* and *remarks* to para. 127, p. 120)

Notice, in last line, how *hiya* and *huwa* happen to come together: relate each to its own sub-construction.

144. *Practice material*

١ ما هى أوّل جريدة عربيّة صدرت في العالم العربيّ — الحوادث اليوميّة
٢ في عصر من صدرت هذه الجريدة — في عصر نابوليون بونابرت
٣ وما اسم المدينة التي صدرت فيها — القاهرة وهى عاصمة مصر
٤ أوجب الله الصوم على المسلمين والمسلمات في كلّ يوم من أيّام شهر رمضان .
٥ قال ولد لولد آخر أنا وأبي نعرف نحن كلّ شيء في الدنيا فقال صديقه وأين إذاً أكبر مدينة في الدنيا فأجاب الولد الأوّل بعد شيء من التأمّل هذا من الأشياء التي يعرفها والدى فسلني عن شيء أعرفه أنا .

VOCABULARY AND REMARKS

jarīda(h) (pl. *jarā'idu*): journal, newspaper (Note how *auwal* (in m.s.) is placed in Construct with this. Almost equally well, but less elegantly and forcefully, it could follow it with complete agreement: *al-jarīdatu al-ūlà* (fem. indeclinable). This optional construction is common with Elatives such as *afḍalu*, i.e. all the "more and most" adjectives)

ṣadara (*i, u*): to come out, appear, be issued (We have already had Form IV of this. Note that this verb begins a *ṣifa*: "the first newspaper" is Definite in English, but the word *jarīdatin* in this construction is Indefinite in Arabic. Think in Arabic terms only!)

'ālam (pl. *'awālimu*): world (cf. *dunyā*, below)

ḥāditha(h) (pl. *ḥawādithu*): event, incident, happening (Note, despite lack of punctuation, capitals or italics, that this is part of a title)

yaumīy: daily (*nisba* form, i.e. "related" adjective like *miṣrīy*)

'aṣr (pl. any of the three in para. 76): age, era, epoch

NOTE: In the answer to question 2, there occurs a famous European proper-name: note the difficulty of rendering this positively into Arabic script, even if full vocalisation is used. Common names tend to crystallise, but variations are common. Often, in modern publications, the name will be repeated parenthetically in Latin characters after its Arabic version, or some identifying phrase like "the American President" or "the famous French general" will be added. Such phrases do not always merit translation.

'āṣima(h) (pl. *'awāṣimu*): capital, chief city

aujaba ('alà): to impose (something in Accusative: on somebody), make obligatory (for). (Form IV of *wajaba*, which we have already met)

ṣaum: fasting, going without nourishment (*maṣdar* of ṢWM I)

muslim (fem. reg.; pls. Sound): Muslim (Form IV Active Participle)

ramaḍān(u): Ramadan (the ninth month of the Islamic lunar year)

ākhar(u) (fem. *ukhrà*, indeclinable): other (Do not confuse with *ākhir* (*ākhira(h)*), "last", which is triptote)

'arafa (i): to know, be acquainted with; to recognise (Often this refers to concrete objects or persons, as against *'alima*, which covers ideas and facts. But there are many borderline cases. A classical distinction, in mediaeval times, was between mystical apprehension and intuition (for 'RF) and scientific learning (for 'LM), but this is certainly no longer valid)

dunyā: (usually with article) the world, the universe, this earthly existence (The word is of more limited application than *'ālam* above, which refers to any conceivable type of world, and hence takes a plural. *Dunyā* is fem. and indeclinable. It is technically an Elative fem., meaning "nearest, lowest, here-belowest")

idhan: in that case (Note that it is in appearance an Accusative noun, and distinguish it from the *idhā* you will meet in Conditional Sentences)

akbaru madīnatin: see remark under *jarīda(h)* at beginning of this section

ta'ammul: reflection, consideration (*masdar* of 'ML Form V. For this use of *shai'*, see *Vocabulary and remarks* to para. 138, p. 123. Translate "after a little reflection")

hādhā min al-ashyā'i: this (*or* that) is one of the things . . . (the partitive use of *min*)

fa-sal-nī: *sal* is the m.s. Imperative (*irregular*) of *sa'ala* (Similar (but not identical) cases are: *kul* (from *akala*); *khudh* (from *akhadha*); and *mur* (from *amara (u)*, "to command"))

150. *Practice material*

١ قال شاعر لصديقه هل تعتقد بأنّي وجب عليّ أن أضع بعض النار في شعرى لأزيده حرارة فأجاب الصديق قائلا الأفضل أن تضع كلّ شعرك في النار لتزيدنا راحة .

٢ قال الحكماء علّم علمك من يجهل وتعلّم ممّن يعلم فإنّك إذًا حفظت ما علمت وعلمت ما جهلت .

٣ إنّك لا تعرف أغلاط معلّمك حتّى تجلس عند غيره .

٤ خذ الخير من أهله ودع الشر لأهله .

VOCABULARY AND REMARKS

'QD VIII: to think, believe (This verb is usually followed by the preposition *bi-*. Note how the latter can even attach itself to a "conjunction" like *anna* when a new clause (rather than a noun) is introduced. Note, too, that the *-nī* attached to *anna* serves here as a Nominal Absolute: "Do you believe (in the fact) that I: it has become incumbent upon me that I should . . . ?", "Do you think I should. . . ?")

waḍa'a (a): to put (Verbs beginning with *w* commonly lose it in the *muḍāri'*: *waḍa'a, yaḍa'u* (hence *'aḍa'u*, 1 c.s.). They also commonly take *i* as middle vowel in the *muḍāri'*, but the third radical *'ain* prevents that here. Cf. *wada'a*$_1$ below)

ba'ḍ: some, a little (Nearly always in Construct with another noun)

nār (pl. *nīrān*): fire (fem.; root NWR)

shi'r (pl. *ash'ār*): poetry (contrast with *sha'r*, hair)

li-: see under *li-kai* in *Vocabulary and remarks* to para. 108, p. 114

zāda, yazīdu: to increase (here, transitive; Hollow: ZYD. See next item)

ḥarāra(h): heat, warmth (Note that in Arabic you do not "increase the heat of something, give it more heat", but rather "increase it (in respect of: adverbial Accusative) heat")

al-afḍalu an plus subj.: the best thing is that you (I, he, etc.) should . . . , the best thing is for you to . . . (cf. *afḍal* as used here, with para. 99, p. 106, sentences 3 and 4)

rāḥa(h): comfort, ease, well-being (for construction, see *ḥarāra(h)*, above. The Arabs love puns on words with similar radicals and patterns. Root RWḤ or RYḤ)

ḥakīm (pl. *ḥukamā'u*): wise-man, doctor, philosopher (Notice the use of *qāla* in the *māḍī* for a general truth: "Shakespeare said, says, has said . . .")

'ilm (pl. *'ulūm*): knowledge, science (This is the first object of "teach!", the second being *man*, "the one who, the man who" etc.)

jahila: to be ignorant, not to know; to be crude and barbaric (The pre-Islamic age is known as *al-jāhilīya(h)*, the Times of Barbarism)

mimman: *min man*, "from the one who".

fa-inna: for, since, because (Sometimes, however, it is simply *fa* combined with *inna*)

ḥafiẓa: to keep, preserve (Sometimes it means "to learn by heart" (esp. the Koran), but this does not apply here)

mā: that which, the thing which, what, whatever (the impersonal equivalent of *man*)

ghalaṭ (pl. *aghlāṭ*): blunder, error

ḥattà: until, before (As a conjunction, it often takes the Subjunctive where the consequence is hypothetical)

jalasa 'inda: to sit at the feet of, study under

ghairu-hu, ghairi-hi: someone else, someone other than he (The pronominal suf-

fix is varied according to the situation: *ghairī*, *ghairu-ka* etc.)
khair: good, goodness, good things, benefit
ahlu-hu: those concerned with it, those who have it (lit. "the people of it"; cf. *Vocabulary and remarks* to para. 99, p. 107)
wa-da': *wada'a*, *yada'u* means "to leave (alone)" (cf. *waḍa'a*, above. The 2 m.s. Jussive is *tada'*, giving merely *da'* for the Imperative m.s.)
sharr: evil, badness, evil things, harm

161. *Practice material*

١ الكلمة إذا خرجت من القلب وقعت في القلب وإذا خرجت من اللسان فلم تجاوز الأذنين .

٢ نشأت مكّة أوّل ما نشأت عند بئر زمزم يشرب سكّانها من مائه وأمّا حيواناتهم فهى أيضا
كانت تشرب من ماء هذا البئر الواحد فلمّا كثر سكّانها بسبب وصول الحجّاج عرفوا الاحتياج
إلى وجود آبار أخرى .

٣ كان للمأمون عبد كان صاحب غسله فبينما هو يصبّ الماء على يديه إذ سقط الإبريق من يده
فغضب المأمون عليه فقال يا أمير المؤمنين إنّ الله يقول إنّ الكاظمين للغضب لهم السلامة قال
قد كظمت غضبي عنك فأجاب العبد وقال الله أيضا إنّ السلامة لمن عفا عن الناس قال قد فعلت
فأجاب وقال الله ثالثا إنّه يحبّ المحسنين فضحك الخليفة قائلا اذهب لعنك الله فأنت حرّ .

VOCABULARY AND REMARKS

qalb (pl. *qulūb*): heart (Notice how this Conditional Sentence has a Nominal Absolute (para. 81) placed outside the whole construction)
waqa'a(yaqa'u) fī: to make an impression on (What is the literal meaning?)
lisān (pl. *alsina(h)*): tongue; *also* language
JWZ III: to pass, go beyond
udhn, udhun (pl. *ādhān*): ear (Usually found in Dual. Remember that parts of the body in pairs are fem.)
nasha'a (a): to spring up, grow up (See next entry but one)
makka(h), makkatu: Mecca (place-names are nearly all fem.)
auwala mā nasha'at: when it first sprang up, i.e. in its early days (One might regard the compound *auwala-mā* (adverbial Accusative in Construct with an indeclinable pronoun) as meaning "when first (something happened)". This is a case where the Arabic and English usages are far apart. Note that *nasha'at* must be fem. this time, though previously it could have been masc.)
bi'r (pl. *ābār*): well, spring, source (fem. or masc.)
zamzamu: Zamzam, name of Mecca's holy well

ammā . . . fa: as for . . . (well) (A device to gain emphasis, a sort of super-Nominal Absolute: often not translated)
kathura: to grow, become numerous
bi-sababi plus Genitive: on account of, because of (The word *sabab* (pl. *asbāb*) denotes "cause" primarily, but has many shades of meaning)
wuṣūl: *maṣdar* I of WṢL
ḥājj (pl. *ḥujjāj*): pilgrim
iḥtiyāj ilà: necessity for (*maṣdar* VIII of ḤWJ)
wujūd: *maṣdar* I of WJD (also commonly means (but not here) "existence")
al-ma'mūn: Al-Ma'mūn, son of Hārūn al-Rashīd, Caliph from AD 813 to 833 (Note how preposition *li-* completely obliterates the *alif* of the article. Pattern is Passive Part. I)
'abd (pl. *'abīd*): (black) slave (with pl. *'ibād* it often refers to men generally, but not here)
ṣāḥibu ghasli-hi: the master of his washing, in charge of his toilet, his valet (The word *ghasl* is *maṣdar* of *ghasala (i)*, "to wash")
baina-mā . . . idh: while (something was happening) . . . lo and behold! (this happened) (The first word is usually followed by a noun-pronoun plus *muḍāri'* or Active Participle, the second by a *māḍī*)
ṣabba (yaṣubbu): to pour (Doubled Verb)
yadai-hi: note Dual Construct form (see also *udhn*, above)
saqaṭa (u): to fall
ibrīq (pl. see para. 147): jug
ghaḍiba 'alà (*maṣdar* is *ghaḍab*): to become angry with
amīru[1] *al-mu'minīna*: Prince of Believers, Commander of the Faithful (the standard address to Caliphs. The pl. of *amīr* is as for *wazīr*. The second word should be recognised as an Active Participle Form IV of 'MN, Gen. Sound Pl. The following phrase, "God says . . .", indicates a Koranic quotation or paraphrase)
kaẓama (i): to suppress, restrain (Note here that we have the Active Participle, Sound Masc. Pl. (Accusative after *inna*), which, being Definite already, is unable to govern *ghaḍab* by the Construct; again, it is difficult for it to govern accusatively, because *ghaḍab* itself is Definite and an Accusative ending would not "show up". Accordingly, it does the equivalent of the second alternative and governs through *li-*. Translate "those who suppress (their) rage", and remember that the whole phrase is a Nominal Absolute)
salāma(h): (with article) salvation
'an-ka: (away) from you
li-man: (belongs) to those who . . . (always, *man* is followed by sing. verb)
'afā 'an: to pardon (Weak Verb; root 'FW.)
qad fa'altu: I *have* done (so)

[1] Here *amīra*: see *Vocabulary and remarks* to para. 108 (p. 113), under *yā*.

thālithan: thirdly, in third place (adverbial Accusative. Most unit ordinals have the Active Participle I pattern)
aḥabba (yuḥibbu): to love (Doubled Verb in Form IV)
muḥsin: beneficent (Active Participle Form IV, hence Sound Pl.)
ḍaḥika: to laugh
la'ana: to curse (The phrase *la'ana-ka allāhu*, "God curse you!" (i.e. "Confound you!", "Blast your eyes!") is an example of the *māḍī* used optatively (to express a wish or prayer) with the name of God)
ḥurr (pl. *aḥrār*): free, emancipated (Arabic is full of stories of slaves gaining their freedom by skill in repartee: in the present case, what is admired is this negro underling's apposite quotations from the Koran to God's "Shadow on Earth")

168. *Practice material*

١ قال معلّم لمتعلّم اذكر أربعة أشياء فيها حليب فأجاب التلميذ العاقل هى الزبدة والجبن وبقرتان .

٢ كثيرا ما نسمع أو نقرأ في الجرائد خبر نزول صاعقة في منزل من المنازل وهدمها له أو إحراقها له .

٣ الجمل من أنفع الحيوان للإنسان يستعمله في حمل الأثقال وخصوصا في الصحارى والبلاد التي ليس فيها ماء ولا تصل إليها السكك الحديديّة ، ويقدر الجمل على السير أيّاما كثيرة دون أن يأكل أو يشرب وليس في هذا كجميع الحيوانات الحمل الأخرى أعني الحمار والفرس ، انظر إلى جسمه تر على ظهره شيئا مرتفعا يقال له سنام ومن سنامه هذا يأخذ أكله وشربه في مسافراته الطويلة .

VOCABULARY AND REMARKS

arba'a(h): four (Though fem. in form, it is associated with noun of opposite gender (principle of Polarity, covering numbers 3–10). Like all units 3–10, it also governs a noun in the Genitive pl., i.e. is itself in Construct. Root RB')
ḥalīb: milk
tilmīdh (pl. as in para. 147): pupil
'āqil: intelligent, bright
zubda(h): butter, cream
jubn: cheese (also "cowardice"!)
baqar: cattle (takes unit ending ("cow"), which in turn can take pl. or Dual)
kathīran mā (pronounced *kathīrammā*): often, frequently (the opposite is *qalīlan mā*)
au: or (used in Arabic only of real alternatives, i.e. not for negatives where we mean "and not": "Don't move or speak!")

khabar (pl. *akhbār*): news (Notice that this noun initiates a double Construct; see also *hadm* and *iḥrāq*, below)
nazala (i) (maṣdar is *nuzūl*): to descend, come down, alight; often used of "putting up" at an inn (but not here. See next item but one)
ṣā'iqa(h) (pl. *ṣawā'iqu*): thunderbolt, lightning-strike
manzil (pl. as in para. 147): house, dwelling (Originally, a "temporary halting place, stage, inn". Noun of Place from NZL, cf. *nazala*, above)
hadm: *maṣdar* of *hadama (i)*, "to destroy" (Notice how this *maṣdar* governs: cf. under *kaẓama* in *Vocabulary and remarks* to para. 161, p. 128. This *maṣdar* should probably also be read as a remote second element in Construct with *khabar* ("the news . . . of its destruction of it". See also next item)
iḥrāq: Form IV *maṣdar* of ḤRQ, to set fire to (the construction here is as for the preceding item in every respect)
jamal (pl. *jimāl*): camel (the most general term)
anfa'u: most useful (note preceding *min* is partitive, and following *ḥayawān* is in Construct)
'ML X: to use, employ (the Ground Form, *'amila*, is "to do, make")
ḥaml: *maṣdar* of *ḥamala (i)*, "to carry" (see below, under *ḥayawānāt*)
thiql (pl. *athqāl*): load, weight
khuṣūṣan: especially (adverbial Accusative)
ṣaḥrā'u (pl. *ṣaḥārà*, indeclinable): desert (now you really know what "Sahara" means!)
balad (pl. *bilād*): land (Sometimes, especially in older Arabic, the same word means a "town"; and its pl. is used for "land", with a new pl. *buldān*)
waṣala ilà: to reach
sikka(h) (pl. *sikak*): road; coin (essentially, "something beaten flat")
ḥadīd: iron (as substance) (Its adjective is formed with *nisba* ending *-īy*. The normal translation of *al-sikaku al-ḥadīdīyatu* is "railways")
sair: *maṣdar* from *sāra*, to go (Hollow Verb)
dūna an: without (as conjunction: takes Subjunctive)
fī hādhā: in this (respect)
ka-: like (preposition: takes Genitive)
jamī': all (followed by Genitive)
al-ḥayawānātu al-ḥamli: beasts of burden (an obviously modern, quasi-compound, improper Construct: hence article, cf. para. 87)
a'nī: I mean, "i.e." (*muḍāri'* 1 c.s. of a Weak Verb)
ḥimār (pl. *ḥamīr*): donkey (in Accus. after preceding word!)
faras (*afrās*): horse, mare (" " " " ")
naẓara ilà: to look at
jism (three pls.): body
tara: (and) you will see (This is 2 m.s. Jussive of *ra'à* (the most difficult Weak Verb). The Jussive is used because the sentence is considered Conditional in Imperative form: (if you) look . . . you see)

ẓahr (pl. *ẓuhūr*): back
murtafiʻ: raised, elevated (Active Part. VIII of RFʻ)
yuqālu la-hu sanām(un): "hump" is said to it, (which is) called a "hump" (This passive use of *qāla* is a common idiom; notice that this clause is a *ṣifa*, and that "hump" is the subject)
akl: food (really a *maṣdar*)
shurb: drink (" " ")
musāfara(h) (pl. Sound): journey (really a *maṣdar*)

173. *Practice material*

ARABIC PASSAGES

١ لو سئل أحدنا ما هو القفل وما فائدته لأجاب قائلا انه تلك الأداة التي تقدر بسببها على الجلوس آمنا في بيتك ليلا ونهارا .

٢ ليس في العالم شيء أحسن من الماء المتحرّك ولذلك يقول الناس إنّ ثلاثة تخرج الحزن وهى الماء والشجر والوجه الحسن .

٣ يذكرون أنّ سبب موت الجاحظ هو الكتب يعني تلك الكتب التي أحبّها حبّا أكثر من حبّه لأىّ شيء آخر فبينما كان جالسا وهى على رفوف موضوعة بعضها على بعض إذ وقعت عليه تقطع حياته وكان ذلك في نصف القرن الثالث للهجرة .

TRANSLATION INTO ARABIC

(1.) Horses cannot go for more than two days without water: in this respect they differ from the camel.
(2.) Look in the cupboard and you will find something to delight you.
(3.) When the famous Arab traveller arrived in North-West Africa, he found a people called the Berbers. He was unable to learn their language, nor could they speak Arabic.
(4.) The Koran says that all believers must fast during the month of Ramaḍān, but this obligation is removed at night.
(5.) Those who keep their anger in check are beloved of God, and salvation will be theirs.
(6.) If I teach what I know to the ignorant they will learn nothing from me, but those who know something can learn more.

ARABIC SAYING

إنّ القاضي إذا اجتهد في قضيّة فما جاز لغيره أن يبطلها وإن كانت عنده خطأ .

VOCABULARY AND REMARKS

qufl (pl. *aqfāl*): lock
fā'ida(h) (pl. *fawā'idu*): benefit, advantage, "point" (root FYD)
adāt (pl. *adawāt*): instrument (root 'DW)
julūs: *maṣdar* of JLS I
āmin: Active Part. of *amina*, to be safe, to feel secure
lailan wa nahāran: night and day (the noun *lail* (pl. to follow) often has a unit-form; *nahār* is the day*time*, as against *yaum*, the 24-hour period)
ḤRK V: to be in motion, to move (intransitive)
li-dhālika: therefore, for that reason
thalātha(h): three (fem. form in Construct with masc. pl. nouns! Here stands for *thalāthatu ashyā'a*, "three things". Remember that *inna* precedes, so case is?)
ḥazina (maṣdar: ḥuzn): to grieve, be sad
shajar (pl. *ashjār*): tree(s) (commonly has unit-form)
maut (pl. *amwāt*): death
al-jāḥiẓ: Al-Jāḥiẓ, d. AD 869 (Perhaps the most prolific and highly esteemed writer of Classical Arabic prose. His name, or nickname, is Active Part. I, meaning "the goggle-eyed", "Popeye")
ya'nī (cf. *a'nī*, *Vocabulary and remarks* to para. 168, p. 130): "He means", "i.e." (takes object)
ḥubb: love (commonly used as though it were the *maṣdar* of the IV Form (the form of this verb normally employed). Translate the Accusative in such cases as this by e.g. ". . . *with* a love (greater than)". Notice how the second *ḥubb* is linked to its "object" by *li-*).
ba'ḍ . . . *ba'ḍ*: one another (translate "placed one upon the other". *Mauḍū'a* agrees *in case* with *rufūf* by "attraction" (though it should not do so logically); and the first *ba'ḍ* is Nominative, being in effect the subject of an inverted Nominal Sentence, which relates to *hiya* or *rufūf* as a sort of *ṣifa*, "(they being) placed . . .")
ḥayāt (bound *-t*): life, being alive
kāna: (here) "to take place"
niṣf (pl. *anṣāf*): half, middle
qarn (pl. *qurūn*): century
hijra(h): Hegira, the migration of Muḥammad from Mecca to Medina, July 16, AD 622, from which date the Islamic calendar is reckoned (notice *li*, where we should say "*of* the Hegira")
to delight, please: 'JB IV
traveller: (here) *raḥḥāla(h)* (fem.; i.e. "globe-trotter", rather than the simple Active Part. III SFR)
North-West Africa: *al-maghrib*
people: here *qaum* (i.e. "community")

Berbers: *al-barbar* (collective)
obligation: WJB IV *maṣdar*
to remove: *rafa'a*
beloved of: *maḥbūb ilà*
qāḍī (pl. *quḍāt*, with bound *-t*): judge (We shall use this noun as a type of Active Part. I in Weak Verbs; here, after *inna*, it is regular *al-qāḍiya*)
JHD VIII: to act conscientiously and for the best in giving a legal interpretation; to strive, take trouble
qaḍiya(h): judgement
jāza: to be permissible (Hollow: root JWZ)
BṬL IV: to annul, render void
khaṭa' (pl. *akhṭā'*): error

FORM DRILL

Give the Imper. masc. sing. of JRB II
" " " " ṢLḤ III
maṣdar of KHRJ IV
Active Part. of KHRJ X
" " " ṢRF VII

VOCABULARY DRILL

You should make sure you know the Arabic for the following (together with pls., *muḍāri'*, *maṣdar*, construction etc. as relevant):

to come (two verbs: *māḍī* only)
to go (two verbs)
to enter (consult dictionary for Accusative, *fī*, *ilà* and *'alà*)
to go out (consult dictionary for *min* and *'alà*)
to sit
to stand (QWM I)
to eat
to drink
to lift, remove (*rafa'a*)
to ask (about = *'an*)
to answer (*māḍī* only)
to stop (I, II, IV, V)
man
woman (sing. *imra'a(h)* with *waṣl*; Definite *al-mar'a(h)*)
boy
girl
book
house
good, fair, nice

bad, ugly, nasty
big
small
near (*qarīb*)
far (*ba'īd*)

177. *Practice material*

FORM DRILL

Give the *maṣdar* of: KHRB II; DKHL III; WQF IV; ḤRM IV and II; KHLṢ V; MRN II; DRK IV; KSHF VIII
Give the Active Part. of: SLM V; FRS VIII; QTL III; DRS II; FṢL VII

VOCABULARY DRILL (cf. para. 173, p. 133):

to dwell, live in, inhabit (with Accusative or *fī*)
to steal
to have (with *li-*, *ma'a*, *'inda*)
to travel (SFR only in III)
to do, make (compare and contrast F'L, 'ML and ṢN')
inhabitant (pl. often means "population")
peasant, farmer, agricultural worker
railway
train (*qiṭār*, pl. as for similar pattern *kitāb*)
town
village (*qarya(h)*; pl. *quran* (قُرًى) , which is indeclinable but loses *tanwīn* when Definite and changes *y* to *alif* when a pronoun suffix is added: القُرَى *al-qurà*; قُرَاهُ *qurā-hu*
market (*sūq*; pl. *aswāq*; this noun is usually fem. Known in West in French form *souk*)

ARABIC PASSAGES

١ كان أحد رجال الدين يعظ جماعة من الناس فقال لهم من أراد أن يدخل الجنّة فليرفع إصبعه من الفور ورفع جميع المستمعين أصابعهم بسرعة إلّا رجلا واحدا فسأله الواعظ ما لك يا عزيزى لا تريد دخول الجنّة فأجاب الرجل الذى لم يرفع إصبعه قائلا من المعلوم أنّى أريد دخولها ولكن لا لزوم للعجلة .

٢ ما هو الشىء الذى له عين ولا يرى (الابرة)

٣ ما هو الشىء الذى تأكله كلّ يوم وهو ليس حيوانا ولا نباتا (الملح) .

٤ ما اسم الملاح المعروف الذى اكتشف طريق الهند عن افريقيا الجنوبيّة

٥ من هو عند أكثر الناس مكتشف أمريكا
٦ قال المسلمون أنّ الاسلام يجمع بين الملك والفقير
٧ كن ممّن إذا قال فعل

TRANSLATION INTO ARABIC

(1.) I was my father's son, then I became my son's father.
(2.) The Bedouin were selling the arms they had stolen.
(3.) The army will have returned to the city before sunset.
(4.) If he does not hear what I say, he must ask about it.

VOCABULARY AND REMARKS

dīn: faith, religion (usually def. and connoting Islam. *rijāl al-dīn*: "clergy" (*rijāl* makes many such compounds))
wa'aẓa (ya'iẓu): to exhort, preach to
jamā'a(h): group, assembly, company
al-janna(h): the garden (of Paradise)
fa-l-yarfa': let him (etc.) raise, he should raise. (A common use of the Jussive 3rd Person preceded by *fa-l-*. Note that the *fa-* is required here, in any case, to introduce the *jawāb* (para. 155), since the particle *l-* precedes the verb)
iṣba' (pl. according to rule, see para. 147): finger
mustami' (pl. Sound Masc.): Active Part. of SM' VIII
bi-sur'atin: speedily, quickly (Lit. "with speed": many equivalents of adverbs are made with *bi-* and an abstract noun)
illā: you have met this before (Note that when it follows a positive statement it governs the Accusative)
mā la-ka: what is the matter with you? (Note that the following negative should be rendered ". . . *that* you do not . . .")
turīdu: *muḍāri'* 2 m.s. of *arāda* (Hollow Verb IV)
dukhūl: *masdar* of DKHL I (Similar *maṣdars* for I of KHRJ, JLS, WQF, NZL and several other verbs of "movement and rest")
min al-ma'lūmi anna: it is obvious that . . . (Lit. "it is (part) of that-which-is-known that . . .". Translate, with following words: "of course I want . . .")
wa-lākin (vertical *fatḥa*): however (Another form, *wa-lākinna*, behaves like *inna, anna*. Both usually have *wa-* as prefix)
lā: here of absolute negation (see para. 137(*b*))
luzūm: necessity (*maṣdar* of *lazima*, "to be necessary")
'ajala(h): haste
'ain (pl. *'uyūn, a'yun*): eye (fem.; and several other meanings, e.g. "spring, source; essence". With pl. *a'yān*, commonly means "notables, prominent men")
yarà: *muḍāri'* 3 m.s. of *ra'à*

ibra(h) (pl. *ibar*): needle
nabāt: plants, vegetation (collective)
milḥ: salt (cf. next item)
mallāḥ: sailor (cf. last item)
KSHF VIII: to discover
al-hind: India (Notice "the way of . . ." in Arabic for our "the way to . . .")
'an: here means "by way of, via"
ifrīqiyā: Africa (fem., indeclinable. In "classical"times usually denoted central North of Africa, i.e. present-day Tunisia and part of Libya)
janūb: south (adj. is in *nisba* (i.e. relative) form)
amrīkā: America (fem., indeclinable)
jama'a baina: to bring together, unite (The word *baina* alone is a preposition meaning "between, among")
faqīr (pl. as *wazīr*): poor, poor man; (sometimes) pious mendicant
to become: *ṣāra (yaṣīru)* (Takes Accusative predicate like *kāna*)
Bedouin: *badw* (collective; the English or French "Bedouin" is an attempt at a Sound Pl. from the unit noun *badawīy*, "nomad(ic)")
arms: asliḥa(h), pl. of *silāḥ*
army: *jaish* (pl. *juyūsh*) (There are several other words for "army", some with specialised significance)
sunset: *ghurūb* (use article!)

181. *Practice material*

VOCABULARY DRILL

to become (remember predicate)
to approach (QRB V, with *min*)
to stand up, rise, get up
to stop (all relevant forms)
to order, command (the person as direct object; the action introduced by *bi-*, with *an* and Subjunctive or *maṣdar*)
to reach, arrive (Accusative or *ilà*)
to collect (trans. and intrans.)
to love, like

earth (*arḍ*; usually fem.; pl. to come later)
sky (*samā'*) (root SMW)
hand
eye
money (*fulūs*, pl. of *fils*;[1] *darāhim(u)*, pl. of *dirham*)
horse
head
people (as many nouns with diff. senses as you know)

[1] *Fils* is (or was) a small copper coin; *dirham* is (or was) a standard silver coin; the great gold coin of Mediaeval Islam was the *dīnār*, pl. *danānīr(u)*. All three words are non-Arabic in origin, and come from the Graeco-Roman world.

to speak (ḤDTH V; KLM V)
to speak to, to address (same verbs in II)

news
speech (*maṣdars* of ḤDTH V and KLM V for "act of speaking"; *qaul* (pl. *aqwāl*) often means "utterance, words", but *qāla* is normally only "to say"; *nuṭq* is a "formal address")
edge, limit, boundary, extent
truth (*ḥaqīqa(h)* is "objective reality, the facts"; *ṣidq* is "sincerity of utterance"; *ḥaqq* has something of both senses, and many others besides)
face

ARABIC PASSAGES

١ أكثر سكّان السودان يتكلّمون باللغة العربيّة وينتسبون إلى الأمّة العربيّة التي تستوطن جزيرة العرب المشهورة بآسمهم والتي من أشهر مدنها مكّة ومدينة النبىّ ، ويوجد أيضا في السودان أجناس أخرى يتكلّمون بلغات مختلفة ، والعرب ليسوا من سكّان هذه البلاد الأصليّين وإنّما جاءوا إليها بعد ظهور النبىّ صلّى الله عليه وسلم بمدّة لأنّ العرب بعد الإسلام فتحوا بلادا كثيرة مثل الشأم ومصر والعراق وإفريقيا الشمالية والمغرب والأندلس ، وبعد ذلك خرج كثير منهم من أوطانهم يأخذون لهم مساكن جديدة في البلاد التي فتحوها ، وقد هاجر بعض القبائل منهم منذ الف سنة إلى بلاد السودان يجدونها صالحة لحاجاتهم وبنى بعض القبائل منهم القرى واستوطنها وبقي بعضهم على حالهم البدويّة يختلطون بالسكّان الأصليّين ويتعلّمون لغتهم وعاداتهم .

٢ التاريخ هو معرفة الحال التي كان عليها آباءنا في قديم الزمان وأخيره ومعرفة الحوادث الحادثة في البلاد التي نسكن فيها وفي الدنيا كلّها أيضا ، وأمّا الإنسان الذى ليس له معرفة التاريخ فهو كالشجر ليس له من عرق ولا فروع يعني ليس عقله بحىّ بل هو ميّت مثل الخشب .

VOCABULARY AND REMARKS

al-sūdān: the Sudan (supposedly related to root SWD, "blackness")
NSB VIII *ilà*: to trace one's descent from (an important Arab concern!)
umma(h): people, nation, community

WṬN X: to live in, make one's home in (to choose for one's own *waṭan* (pl. *auṭān*), "homeland")
jazīra(h) (pl. *jazā'iru, juzur*): island (but *jazīrat al-'arab*, the Arabian Peninsula; "famous by their name" = named after them)
ashhar(u): Elative of *mashūr* (Do not confuse with *ashhur*. Note partitive *min* introducing an "inverted" Nominal Sentence)
nabīy (pl. *anbiyā'u*): prophet (Root NB'! The City of the Prophet is usually known simply as *al-madīna*)
jins (pl. *ajnās*): (here) race of people (Often means "kind, class, species, sex" etc.)
mukhtalif: various (This VIII Form is common as a verb and a *maṣdar*, and often signifies violent "difference", but not necessarily here)
aṣlīy: original (The noun *aṣl* (pl. *uṣūl*) means "root, origin, fundamental principle")
inna-mā: only, merely, simply (Qualifies not the word or phrase immediately following it, but the one beyond that: "they came to it *only* after ...")
ẓuhūr: emergence, appearance (*maṣdar* of I, not to be confused with pl. of *ẓahr!*)
ṣallà allāhu 'alaihi wa-sallam(a): God bless him and give him peace! (The standard formula after the Prophet's name, often abbreviated in writing as صلعم . Both verbs are *māḍī* of Form II (*ṣallà* is Weak, ṢLW), used "Optatively", i.e. to express a wish in reference to God)
bi-muddatin: this refers back to the phrase beginning with *ba'da*: "after the Prophet's emergence ... by a period of time", "some time after ..."
mithl (pl. *amthāl*): like, such as (is really a noun, always in Construct and in apposition to the noun or noun-phrase preceding it: here it is Accusative after *bilādan*)
al-sha'm (or *al-shām*): Syria (a vague, general term, not the modern state)
shamāl (or *shimāl*): north (With relative ending, "northern, north-")
al-andalus: Moorish Spain, not simply "Andalusia" in its modern sense
akhadha la-hu: he took for himself, made himself (something), chose for himself
maskan, maskin (pl. regular): home, dwelling, habitation
HJR III: to (e)migrate (Note use of *qad* here: "they *actually did in fact* do this ...")
qabīla(h) (pl. *qabā'ilu*): tribe
alf: 1,000 (In Construct with Genitive sing., as all numerals from 100 onwards)
ṣāliḥ: suitable, convenient, proper (for: *li*. Accusative as second obj. of *wajada* (or as adverbial Accusative))
ḥāja(h) (pl. Sound): need, requirement
banà (*yabnī*): to build (Weak! Root BNY)
baqiya (*yabqà*): to remain (Weak! Root BQY. Often, like *kāna* etc., has Predicate in Accusative. Here *'alà* to be translated as "in" (as also lower down): the *'alà* of "state")

ḥāl (pl. *aḥwāl*): condition, state (often fem.)
KHLṬ VIII plus *bi*: to mix, mingle, with
ta'rīkh (pl. *tawārīkhu*): history; date, chronology (In the first-sense the *hamza* is often dropped: *tārikh*. What pattern is this, and what would a "historian" be? Root 'RKH)
ma'rifa(h): knowledge, understanding, realisation
akhīr: recent (Note here how *qadīm* precedes in Construct, but, to avoid "breaking" the Construct (see para. 88 and footnote), this word follows, being related back by a pronominal suffix)
ḥāditha(h): note that this is here merely an Active Part. fem. of Form I, qualifying an inanimate pl. noun as an adj. Translate "the events taking place" (*ḥadatha(u)*, "to happen"). (cf. *Vocabulary and remarks* to para. 144 (p. 124), under same word)
min: translate "any vestige of" or some such emphatic phrase (Notice that *laisa* here introduces a sort of "improper" *ṣifa*: the noun to which it relates is Definite, but only as referring to a class of things (generic use). Even so, most Classical grammarians would disapprove)
'irq (pl. *'urūq*): root
far' (pl. *furū'*): branch (Remember that *lā* merely *carries on* the negative force (see para. 137(*c*)): the case of this noun remains Genitive, as for the preceding one)
ḥaiy: alive (root ḤYW. Remember how *laisa* sometimes governs; see para. 165(*c*))
bal: on the contrary
khashab: wood

189. *Practice material*

FORM DRILL

(*a*) Give the Broken Pls. of the following nouns:

mandīl (a kerchief: cf. Spanish "mantilla")	amīn (confidant)
	zauj
miknasa(h)	saiyida(h), (lady)
kātib	

(*b*) Disregarding sense where you do not know it, give the Imperative masc. sing.; Active Part.; 2 f.s. *muḍāri'*; and 1 c.p. *māḍī* of

farra (i) I and II	KHWF II
marra (u) I and IV	ṬWL IV
dalla (u) I and II	KHYR VIII
akhadha	sa'ala
bada'a (a)	'adda (u)
qāla (QWL/QYL)	bā'a

VOCABULARY DRILL (to be used repeatedly)

dismount, get down, put up for the night
to fear (Accusative or *min*; also *'alà* in sense of "for")
to hurry (SR' IV)
to be able, "can" (revise construction)
to have to, "must" (revise construction)
to sleep
to go (two verbs)
to weep (*bakà*)
to remain, stay
to teach
to learn
to open
to think (FKR: about: *fī*) (consult dictionary for varying intensity from I through II and V to VIII)
to fall
to stop (all relevant forms)
to take; to begin (using same verb)
to see (limited knowledge of this verb so far)
to hear
to know (two verbs)
to come back, return
to send back; reject, retort; reflect (*radda* (*u*))
to mount, ride, embark (*rakiba*: *'alà*)
yesterday
today
tomorrow (*ghadan*: adverbial Accusative Root GHDW)
wife
road (two words)
street (pl. *shawāri'u*)
caravan
in front of, before
behind, to the rear of (*khalfa*)
teacher
pupil, learner, student (two words)
line; track; handwriting (*khaṭṭ*: pl. *khuṭūṭ*)
intelligent
crude, stupid, ignorant
head
foot, leg (*rijl*: pl. *arjul*)
hand, arm (pl. *aidin*, *ayādin*, like *rawāmin*; see para. 188)
morning (*ṣubḥ*, *ṣabāḥ*)
day (two senses)
night (pl. *layālin*, cf. "hand" above; remember unit form)
week
month
year (two words)
long, tall
short (*qaṣīr*)
dead (pl. *mautà*, indeclinable)
alive
enemy (*'adūw*: pl. *a'dā'*)
friend
voice, sound, noise, melody (*ṣaut*: pl. *aṣwāt*)
tooth
space of time
door, gate, portal
leaf, sheet (of paper)
party, council, meeting (*majlis*)
abode, residence (from NZL)
ship (*safīna(h)*)
servant (*khādim*: often of either sex)
mountain (*jabal*: pl. *jibāl*)
wind (*rīḥ*: pl. *riyāḥ*; usually fem.)
water
land, earth
fire

sea (*baḥr*: common pl. *biḥār*)
sun (*shams*: fem.)
ready, present (*ḥāḍir*)

ARABIC PASSAGES

١ اعلم يا إنسان أنّ أمّك حملتك في بطنها أشهرا ثم حملتك على يديها سنوات وهى تحملك في قلبها طول حياتها .

٢ جلسنا بقرب النهر ربع ساعة لنستريح قليلا بعد غروب الشمس ثم تمددنا على الأرض ونمنا الليل كله فقمنا الغد قبل طلوع الشمس نذهب إلى شغلنا اليومى .

٣ إذا دخل أبوك وأنت موجود فقم على الفور فإنّ الأب أحقّ بالإكرام من ملوك الأرض كلّهم .

٤ لا تنزلوا قبل توقف القطار لألّا تقعوا تكسرون أرجلكم .

٥ جاء رجل إلى رسول الله صلّعم يريد الاسلام فأسلم ونطق بالشهادتين وعلم أن السارق تُقْطَعُ يده وأن الكاذب يلعنه الله ويعذّبه يوم الدين يدخله النار آلخ ، وكان هذا الرجل قبل إسلامه يفعل جميع ذلك فقال يا رسول الله إنّى لا أقدر على ترك كل هذه الأعمال فاختر أنت منها واحدا أتركه لك فقال النبىّ هل تعدني بترك الكذب قال نعم ثم قَبِلَ عهده وخرج إلى شأنه ، فلمّا أراد الرجل أن يسرق قال في نفسه إن سرقت وسألني عن هذا رسول الله فما أقول له جوابا إذا قلت نعم قطع يدى وإن قلت لا خنت العهد بالكذب فترك السرقة وهكذا صار كلّما أراد أن يعمل ذنبا تذكّر العهد فتركه خوفا من العقاب ووفاءً بالعهد حتى ترك جميع ذنوبه وصار من المسلمين الصالحين رحمه الله .

VOCABULARY AND REMARKS

baṭn (pl. *buṭūn*): belly; womb
sanawāt: pl. of *sana(h)* (Another pl. is *sinūna* or *sanūna* (Masc. Sound Pl.). The form *sanawāt* tends to be used, as here, in expressions like "years on end", while the other is commonly used after numerals)
ṭūla: for the length of, throughout (Adverbial Accusative in Construct)
bi-qurbi: in the proximity of, near
nahr (pl. *anhur*, *anhār*): river
rub' (pl. *arbā'*): quarter (1 u 2 3 is the standard fraction pattern. Once again, this noun is here an Adverbial Accusative in Construct)

sā'a(h) (pl. *sā'āt*): hour; clock, watch (Note: *al-sā'atu kam (hiya)*, the hour is how many?, the hour: how many is it?, what's the time? Root SW')
RWḤ/RYḤ X: to rest
qalīlan: (for) a little (while)
MDD V: to stretch oneself, to lie at full length
al-ghada: on the morrow, the next day (Adverbial Accusative)
ṭulū'; maṣdar of *ṭala'a(u)*, "to rise (of sun)"
shughl (pl. *ashghāl*): occupation, work, job
maujūd: see *Vocabulary and remarks* to para. 127, (p. 119); translate here as "present"
aḥaqqu bi: more deserving of, having a greater right to
KRM IV: to show respect to, to honour (Note here how *maṣdar* simply translates as "respect", at least in normal English)
rasūl (pl. *rusul*): apostle, messenger (The compound phrase used here always refers to Muḥammad)
al-islām: note verbal force of *maṣdar* returns here!
naṭaqa (i) bi: to pronounce, utter
al-shahādatāni: the two attestations: *lā ilāha illā allāhu* (see para. 137 (*b*)) *muḥammadun rasūlu allāhi* (The sincere utterance of these two formulas constitutes the central rite of becoming a Muslim)
'DHB II: to punish, inflict suffering upon
yaum al-dīn: the literal meaning you know (The idiomatic sense is "Doomsday, Resurrection Day". Remember Adverbial Accusative!)
ilà ākhiri-hi: lit. "to the end of it" (the common formula for "etc.", abbreviated as *alif-lām-khā'*)
tark: *maṣdar* (Do not confuse with *turk*!)
'amal (pl. *a'māl*): action, act, activity; work (but not here)
wa'ada(i): to promise (someone: Accusative; something: *bi*)
kidhb, kadhib: *maṣdar*
'ahd (pl. *'uhūd*): pledge, contract (and many other senses!)
sha'n (pl. *shu'ūn*): business, affair
khāna (w): to betray
saraqa(h): *maṣdar* (can also be one of the pls. of sāriq!)
ṣāra: the literal meaning you know (It here serves to give the following quasi-conditional clause a continuous or repetitive past sense (cf. para. 157, example 8) beginning at this particular point in time. Translate: "And so, henceforth whenever he . . . he would . . .")
kulla-mā: whenever (Stronger, more definitely repetitive than *idhā*)
dhanb (pl. *dhunūb*): a sin
DHKR V: to recall
khaufan min: for fear of
'iqāb: punishment
wafā'an bi: out of loyalty to (root WFY, *wafà (yafī)*)

ṣāra min: to become one of (Henceforth we shall not indicate the partitive *min*)
ṣāliḥ: (here) "pious, righteous" (cf. *Vocabulary and remarks* to para. 181 (p. 138) under same word)
raḥima-hu allāhu: May God have mercy on him! (A common "optative" utterance on behalf of deceased Muslims; cf. *Vocabulary and remarks* to para. 181, under *ṣallà*)

194. *Practice material*

TRANSLATION INTO ARABIC

(1) The Queen did not invite (transl. "call") me to the palace, so my father thought up (FKR VIII) a trick (*ḥila(h)*: pl. *ḥiyal*; root ḤWL) by which we were able to get in.
(2) Ask those women what (transl. "concerning what") they want.
(3) If he succeeds (*najaḥa*) in the examination (MḤN VIII *maṣdar*) his parents will give (QWM IV) a party (*walīma(h)*: pl. *walā'imu*).
(4) Take two apples, cut them in pieces, put them in a bowl (*ẓarf*: pl. *ẓurūf*), and leave them for two weeks.
(5) If you want to know the time ask anyone you meet. (Transl. "If you want to know what is the time, then ask about it any person (*shakhṣ*: pl. *ashkhāṣ*) (who) you meet him").

ARABIC PROVERBS AND SAYINGS

١ ارمه في البحر يخرج وفي فمه سمكة
٢ بيت تأكل منه لا تدع عليه بالخراب
٣ بئر تشرب منه لا ترم فيه حجرا
٤ نامت جائعة وزوجها خباز
٥ حبيبك هو من تحبّه ولو كان قردا
٦ لا تأخذ الكتاب من عنوانه
٧ خذ السارق قبل أن يأخذك
٨ يقدّم رِجلا يؤخّر أخرى
٩ يرى الحاضر ما لا يرى الغائب
١٠ من أحبّ شيئا أكثر ذكره
١١ الناس بزمانهم أشبه منهم بآبائهم
١٢ فرّ من الموت وفي الموت وقع
١٣ كل ما تريده نفسك والبس ما يلبس الناس
١٤ كل واشرب ودع الدنيا تخرب
١٥ إن كنت كذوبا فكن ذكورا

١٦ ضربني وبكى وسبقني وشكا

١٧ طبيب يداوى الناس وهو مريض

١٨ عين لا ترى قلب لا يحزن

١٩ إذا حضر الماء بطل التيمّم

VOCABULARY AND REMARKS

samak (pl. *asmāk*; here unit form): fish (What sort of sentence is this?)
kharāb: ruin, ruination (a *maṣdar* of I, *khariba*, which occurs later)
ḥajar (pl. *aḥjār*): stone, rock (has unit form)
khabbāz: *khubz* you know (What must this pattern be?)
ḥabīb (pl. *aḥibbā'u*): friend, beloved
wa-lau: even though (cf. *Vocabulary and remarks* to para. 108 (p. 114) under *wa-in*)
qird (pl. *qurūd*, etc.): monkey, ape
'inwān / *'unwān* (pl. predictable): title (of book); address (of person) (root, theoretically, 'NW)
qabla an (plus Subjunctive): before (as Conjunction; *qabla* is a preposition only)
QDM II, to put forward, advance (something)
'KHR II: to take back, withdraw
ghā'ib: absent (root GHYB)
KTHR IV: to do something a great deal (followed by *maṣdar* of the action)
dhikr: *maṣdar* of *dhakara*
ashbahu: more similar, more like (to: *bi*. Notice how the following "than" (*min*) needs to be completed by a noun or pronoun. You cannot say in Arabic "more similar to X *than to* Y", but "more similar to X *than it (is) to* Y")
farra (i): to flee, run away
wada'a: with following *muḍāri'*, "to let (an object) do (something)"
kadhūb: a great liar, much given to lying (one of several emphatic patterns)
dhakūr: having a retentive memory (see preceding item)
sabaqa (i,u): to precede, outstrip, get ahead of
shakā: to complain
ṭabīb (pl. *aṭibbā'u*): physician, doctor
DWY III: to treat, prescribe for
ḥaḍara (u): to be present, available
batala (u): to be invalid, worthless
YMM V: to perform ritual Islamic ablutions with some dry substitute for water; to take a dust or sand-bath.

PATTERN DRILL

(*a*) Give the Broken Pl. of: *safīna*, *kalb*, *qalb*, *ra's*, *wazīr*, *'ibrīq*, *maskan*, *shahr*, *'usbū'*, *'isba'* (*b*) Give the Active Participle, the fem. sing. Imperative and 3 m.p. Subjunctive of:

KHRJ I and IV	BKY I and IV	KHWF I and II
SYR	SFR III	KHYR VIII
QWL X	'KHDH I and VIII	'LF I and VIII

201. *Practice material*

ARABIC PASSAGES

١ رضي الخصمان وأبى القاضي

٢ شجرة تستظلّ تحتها لا تدع بقطعها

٣ ضيّف البدوىّ يسرقْ البستك

٤ طار طيرك وأخذه غيرك

٥ فقراء ويمشون مشي الأمراء

٦ ليس الخبر كالعيان

٧ يقول للسارق اسرق ولصاحب المنزل احفظ

٨ لا تؤخّر إلى الغد عمل اليوم

٩ ما يعرف حرّ الحمّام إلا من دخلها

١٠ من تكلم فيما لا يعنيه سمع ما لا يُرضِيه

١١ من لم يرض بحكم موسى رضي بحكم فرعون

١٢ أتى رجل من المغرب الأقصى إلى مصر يريد الحجّ وأودع عند رجل من التجّار أحسن الظنّ به ألف دينار فلمّا رجع من حجّه وسأل الرّجل عن ماله أنكره فشكا المغربيّ سرّا إلى السلطان فقال هذا له ايت إلى السوق واجلس بقرب الكاذب فإذا مررت انا عليك فأظهر أنّى أعرفك فإنّني سأقف معك ثم فعل المغربي ما قد أمره به السلطان فجاء هو اليه يطيل السؤال عنه وعن حاله وينصرف عنه فجاء الرجل الخائن وألقى نفسه بين يدى المغربي يقبلها ويسأله العفو عنه ثم أحضر له الذهب المفقود فبالغ السلطان مع هذا في عقابه لألّا يفعل غيره مثل هذا

VOCABULARY AND REMARKS

khaṣm (pl. *khuṣūm*): antagonist, party to a dispute
abà: to refuse; to be adamant (Note: *muḍāri'* is usually *ya'bà* rather than *ya'bi*!)
ẒLL X: to take shade, shelter
taḥta: under, beneath (opposite is *fauqa*)
qaṭ': *maṣdar* of *qaṭa'a*
DYF II: to entertain, show hospitality to

albisa(h): pl. of *libās* (cf. *lisān* and its pl.)
ṭāra (y): to fly (away)
ṭair: bird(s) (sing. or collective)
mashà: to walk (The *maṣdar*, i.e. *mashy*, is here used in the so-called cognate Accusative, "in the manner of the walking off", "as . . . walk")
'iyān: ocular evidence, seeing with one's own eyes (This is a *maṣdar* of 'YN III)
ḥarr: heat (Do not confuse with *ḥurr*)
ḥammām (pl. Sound Fem.): bath (particularly of the "steam" or Turkish sort)
'anà: to concern, be the business of (You have already met this verb in the sense of "to mean")
RḌW IV: to give satisfaction to
ḥukm (pl. *aḥkām*): judgment, rule, authority
mūsà: Moses (indeclinable)
fir'aunu: Pharaoh
aqṣà: remote, extreme (a typical indeclinable Elative from a Weak Root, here QṢW)
ḥajj: pilgrimage (specifically to Mecca and Medina)
WD' IV: to deposit, leave in trust
ḤSN IV: *aḥsana al-ẓanna bi*, "to have a good opinion of" (probably erroneously, cf. *ẓanna*)
NKR IV: to deny (all knowledge of): to refuse (to have anything to do with)
sirr (pl. *asrār*): secret (here Adverbial Accusative!)
sulṭān (pl. by rule!): ruler, authority (Like so many words in Arabic this one is "loaded". To translate it properly one needs to know the time and place of usage. Root SLṬ)
īti: regular Imperative of *'atà* (Weak Verb with initial hamza)
marra (u): to pass (by = *'alà*, *bi*, *min* etc.)
ẒHR IV: to make it appear (as if, as though, that = *anna*)
sa-aqifu: WQF I (also means "to stand")
ṬWL IV: to protract, carry on at length (usually followed by a *maṣdar*)
su'āl (pl. *as'ila(h)*): question(ing), i.e. abstract noun and *maṣdar*
ṢRF VII: to go away (from = *'an*)
khā'in (pl. *khūwān*): treacherous, disloyal (The verb, from KHWN, you have already met)
baina yadai . . . : between the hands of i.e. in front of (someone) (Here the word "hand" has to be brought out explicitly in the following passage)
QBL II: to kiss
'afw: pardon; abstract noun and *maṣdar* (Notice how the *maṣdar* continues to carry the appropriate preposition)
ḤḌR IV: to bring out, produce
dhahab: gold
mafqūd: lost, missing

BLGH III: to go to great lengths (in = *fī* plus *maṣdar*); sometimes "to exaggerate"
ma'a hādhā: despite this, nevertheless (The word *ma'a* is often so used)

TRANSLATION INTO ARABIC

(1) Man is born and must die.
(2) Do not fear for me, but for yourself.
(3) Every mother thinks well of (*Note*: this phrase occurs in Arabic passage No. 12 above) her own child.
(4) Go on your way (walk, proceed) until you come to a village.
(5) We went on our way till we came to a village.
(6) My need is greater than yours.
(7) His need is the greatest.
(8) Whatever he says you must not speak.

FORM DRILL

(*a*) Give the Jussive 2 m.s., 2 f.s., 3 m.p. of:
da'ā; bakà; ṣāma (w); ṣāra; MYL IV; KHYR VIII; SHFY X; ṬW' IV; JRY III; MRR III; KHWF I and II
(*b*) Give the Imperative m.s. and f.s. of:
ḤWL II and III; KHRJ IV; RḌW IV; 'MN IV; WFQ VIII; *ṣāma(w); waṣala*; 'MR I and IV; *māla* (*y*); MRR III; KHWF I and II
(*c*) Give the Broken Pls. of the following nouns (hazard a guess where you do not know which of several possibles actually does apply!):
ẓarf; *wajh*; *qarīb*; *nā'ib*; *zamīl*; *ẓālim*; *kalb*; *qalb*; *faras*; *kitāb*; *kātib*; *maktab*; *maktūb*; *uqnūm*

216. *Practice material*

TRANSLATION INTO ARABIC

(1) He came running, with his brother riding beside him.
(2) He looked at the illustrated books, but was unable to read them.
(3) When he comes stop him immediately.
(4) After the revolution the Prime Minister was expelled from the country, and it was demanded of him that he should not return.
(5) The city was conquered by the Turks, and many of its inhabitants were massacred.
(6) Write what I tell you: don't be afraid (masc. and fem. sing.).
(7) He ordered them to get out of the car.

(8) If anyone had told me that the Arabic language was so difficult, I should not have started to learn it.
(9) Do not forget that a man who steals has no fear of lying.
(10) When he reached the sea he found that the ship had left two hours before sunrise.
(11) Despite his age he works all day, every day: sometimes he thinks himself younger than he really is.
(12) If you want me to read your exercises, you will have to write in a nicer hand than you have done until now.

VOCABULARY AND REMARKS

to run: *jarà*, *sa'à* (*yas'à*! The latter also means "to try, strive (to, for – *li* or *ilà*, followed by *maṣdar* or *an* and subjunctive)")
with: remember the uses of *wāw*!
beside: *'inda* will suffice
to illustrate (to picture, to photograph): ṢWR II
revolution: QLB VII *maṣdar*
Prime Minister: the Minister of the Ministers
so: transl. "to this extent"
to start (doing something) use here *bada'a(a) fī* with *maṣdar*
to forget: *nasiya*
a man who: transl. either literally or as a quasi-conditional
he found that the ship had left: transl. "he found the ship: it had gone"
two hours before sunrise: transl. "before sunrise by two hours"
despite: use *ma'a*
to work: use *'amila*
sometimes: remember *qad* with *muḍāri'*!
to think: remember that he is wrong in his ideas: what verb expresses this?
younger: transl. "smaller as regards age" (Adverbial Accusative)
than he is: *minhu* or *mimmā huwa* (cf. the example three entries further on)
exercise: MRN II *maṣdar* (Pl. Sound Fem. or by rule for 4-consonant nouns)
hand: remember this means "handwriting"!
than you have done: *mimmā fa'alta* (cf. three entries further back)

ARABIC PASSAGES

١ قال حكيم من الحكماء قال لو قيل لى أىّ شىء عندك أعجب لقلت إنه قلب قد عرف الله ثم خالفه .

٢ كلّ سبعة أيّام تسمّى أسبوعا ويقال لها عند العامّة جمعة وأمّا يوم الجمعة فهو العيد الأسبوعىّ للمسلمين يجتمعون به في المساجد لأداء فريضة الجمعة ولا يتركون فيه أشغالهم كالنصارى واليهود إلّا ساعة ساعتين .

٣ زاد عدد سكّان مصر في السنوات الأخيرة زيادة كبيرة ولذلك صارت الحاجة إلى المساكن شديدة وهذا لا يزال مشكلة مع كثرة البيوت التي تبنى في كل جهة من جهات البلاد .

٤ أليس هذا الشخص هو الرجل الذى كلّمتني عنه أمس تقول أنّه قد قضى مدّة طويلة في أمريكا وأنّه سيرجع هناك في السنة الآتية .

٥ دعوت أصدقائي كلّهم إلى وليمة أقيمها في دار أبوىّ فلم يحضر إلّا شخصان ما كدت أعرفهما .

٦ يجب عليك وأنت مارّ بقوم تعرفهم أن تقول السلام عليكم فإذا قال أحد أولا لك أنت السلام عليك فردّ عليه بقولك وعليك السلام ورحمة الله وبركاته .

٧ اشترى رجل سيّارة مستعملة كثيرا ما تخرب وبعد أن أنفق عليها فلوسا كثيرة قرّر أن يبيعها يشترى بدلا منها جملا فما وجد في القاهرة كافّة جملا واحدا يصلح لحاجته .

VOCABULARY AND REMARKS

a'jabu: Elative of a root whose basic sense you know

KHLF III: to oppose, go against, thwart

SMW II: to name, call (can take two objects or be, as here, in passive with one object)

al-'āmma(h): the common people, the generality of men (sometimes contemptuous)

al-jum'a(h): week; Friday (in latter sense often follows *yaum* in Construct)

'īd (pl. *a'yād*): festival, holiday, feast-day

bi-hi: used here instead of *fī-hi*, for time, because another *fī* closely follows

adā' (Root 'DW): performance, discharge, carrying out (e.g. of a debt, duty etc. This is a sort of *maṣdar* I, but the normal *verb* forms in this sense are II or IV)

farīda(h) (pl. *farā'iḍu*): obligation, duty (esp. religious)

naṣārà: indeclinable pl. of *naṣrānīy*.

al-yahūd: the Jews (collective: an individual is in the relative pattern *yahūdīy*)

'adad: number

ziyāda(h): maṣdar of *zāda*, here used as "Cognate Accusative" (cf. *Vocabulary and remarks* to para. 173, p. 132, under *ḥubb*. Transl. *ziyādatan kabīratan* simply as "greatly" in this context)

shadīd: severe, extreme (often of violence, but not here)

lā yazālu: see para. 170 (Note that this verb behaves like a "sister" of *kāna*, taking its predicate in the Accusative)

mushkila(h) (pl. by rule!): problem, difficulty (What pattern is this?)

kathra(h): *maṣdar* of I; abundance, plenty

jiha(h) (pl. Sound Fem.): part, area; direction, compass point (root WJH)

qaḍà: (here) to spend, pass (time)
ātiya(h): fem. Active Part I. of 'TY (The whole phrase here simply means "next year")
dār (pl. *dūr*, *diyār*): abode, residence (usually fem.; a "grander" word than *bait*!)
illā: note that, as we have seen, if the main statement is positive the noun following this particle is Accusative; if the main statement is negative, as here, such a noun is usually Nominative. If prepositions are involved, their effect must of course be allowed for. Translate a negative followed by *illā*, in most cases, by the one English word "only"
kāda (like *nāma*): when positive and combined with a following *muḍāri'*, translate as "almost"; when negative, in similar circumstances, render by "hardly, scarcely"
al-salāmu 'alai-kum: a standard greeting, corresponding to "How do you do?", "Good morning!" etc. (lit. "Peace upon you!". The pronoun suffix can, of course, vary for sex and number. The standard reply is given in the same passage, in a somewhat elaborate form)
auwalan: first (adverb), firstly, in first place (This pattern is probably irregular, since the Accusative of *auwalu* should properly be *auwala*)
radda (*u*): we have seen this word already (Its sense here (with *'alà* of the person addressed and *bi* of the thing said) is "to reply, retort, return, rejoin". Notice the Imperative of a Doubled Verb in I)
raḥma(*h*): mercy
baraka(*h*) (pl. Sound Fem.): blessing
khariba: we have already met this verb in the sense of "to go to ruin"; here, "to break down"
ba'da an: after (as a conjunction); also *ba'da mā* (one of the few cases where *an* can be followed by the *māḍī* (if the thing has actually happened))
NFQ IV (plus *'alà*): to spend (money) on
QRR II: to resolve, decide (with *'alà* followed by *maṣdar*, or with or without *'alà* followed by *an* and Subjunctive)
badal: exchange; *badalan min*, "in exchange for, instead of"
mā wajada: transl. "he *could* not find" (We have commented before on the economy of Arabic, particularly in its omission *wherever possible* of the Modal Auxiliaries (can, could, may, might, shall, will, should, would, ought, must etc.); but the sense of most of them can be expressed exactly in Arabic if necessary, as e.g. in philosophical texts or in legal documents)
kāffatan: one of many words meaning "all, entire, total" (It normally follows a given noun and takes the (adverbially) Accusative Case fem., as here. Transl. "in all Cairo")

FORM DRILL

(*a*) Distinguish the sense of the following expressions:

عشرون ولدا : الولد العشرون : الأولاد العشرون : العشرون ولدا

(*b*) Put the following figures into Arabic words:
52; 365; 1870; 1914; 1939; 1066

(*c*) Add to the numbers in (*b*) the numbered things "boys"; "years"; "days"; "nights"

(*d*) Turn the numbers in (*b*) into Ordinals and add the qualified nouns "day" and "night"

(*e*) Give Broken Plurals of the Arabic nouns for: hand; head; face; eye; mouth; ear; foot; finger; ship; desert; mountain

(*f*) What are the commonly found "*maṣdars*" of ḤBB IV; SHRY VIII; SFR III? What would you expect in each case?

(*g*) Illustrate four ways in which a *maṣdar* or an Active Participle may govern a noun.

TRANSLATION INTO ARABIC

(1) If she arrives, do not admit her.
(2) When she arrived they evicted her.
(3) If they arrive before noon, say I am sick.
(4) The price of this bread is more than it was yesterday.
(5) My price is one today and yesterday.
(6) Do not lie: those who lie go to Hell.
(7) Write your name on this sheet of paper.
(8) I cannot write my name.
(9) He cannot write his name.
(10) Can you write more than a word or two? If she studies she will be able to write great books.
(11) My father has ordered me to return.
(12) He is only a child: do not be cruel to him.
(13) If he had not done it himself, I would not have believed it.
(14) I have never seen a woman more beautiful than she was at that time.
(15) Who gives twice gives quickly.
(16) Anyone who believes what he reads in the papers is a fool.
(17) I happened to be ill yesterday, so I was unable to visit my parents.
(18) If I had not seen it myself, I would never have believed it.
(19) The more I think about it the more I am astonished at it.
(20) The police have been ordered to stop all cars because they have been informed that a prisoner is trying to escape.
(21) I have promised to do it: I can't get out of it now.
(22) All who can walk should leave the building immediately.
(23) As soon as I saw him I recognised him as my brother.
(24) There is no man capable of undertaking this task.
(25) They all came except 'Amr; if he had not been ill, he too would have come.

(26) When he was seven years old, his father sent him to a school, where he learned arithmetic, geometry and other subjects.
(27) It is obvious that a man who will betray his country cannot be trusted.
(28) As you walk along the streets of the town you will be amazed at the many tall buildings and beautiful trees.
(29) Anyone who has lived a long time in the East needs heavy clothing when he returns home, whether it be winter or summer.
(30) How many people are in this room? About four hundred.
(31) Why do you not travel with the caravan which leaves tomorrow?
(32) I came by a car which broke down twice en route.
(33) In this tribe the women are taller than the men.
(34) Don't forget his name and address; they are written on the paper I gave you last night.
(35) When I bought my newspaper I forgot to ask its price.
(36) If you wish to speak to me, you must wait until I have finished my work.
(37) My father has ordered me to return.
(38) I go to the baths every Friday and spend the whole day there.
(39) I met many Egyptians when I was residing in the city of Baghdad.
(40) You will meet many Persians while you are staying in the Nile Hotel.
(41) She did not meet a single person while she was travelling from one town to another.
(42) The ambassadors did not burn the papers in their offices.
(43) Do not burn my house.
(44) Why have you not corresponded with your mother?
(45) The planes took off one hour before noon.
(46) The officials destroyed all my documents.
(47) Do not destroy what your father has made.
(48) When he had drunk the water he began to eat some bread.
(49) He ordered him to dismount.
(50) He was travelling to the airport at that time, but he had not yet arrived.
(51) I wrote to him, but he refused to correspond with me.

UNIVERSITY OF TORONTO
Department of Islamic Studies

First-year Arabic examination questions, 1958–63

1. Translation into fully vocalised Arabic:

(*a*) Honour (fem.) thy father and thy mother.

(*b*) Do not cut off the hand that feeds you.
(*c*) He who cannot obey should not command.
(*d*) Do not go out without a guide (*dalīl*).
(*e*) If you send a letter today, it will arrive on Friday.
(*f*) If you had sent a letter yesterday, it would have arrived today.
(*g*) Anyone who cannot walk will not eat.
(*h*) Those who exert themselves (JHD) will perhaps (*rubbamā*) prosper (FLḤ IV).
(*i*) If you had tried hard you would certainly have prospered.
(*j*) The Governor of the City of Baghdad ordered all officers to wear their uniforms (*zīy*).
(*k*) Can I travel from Damascus to Cairo without stopping (WQFV *maṣdar*)?
(*l*) He who cannot write cannot correspond with (KTB III) his distant (*ba'īd*) friends without an intermediary (*wasīṭ*).
(*m*) If you order me to do it I will obey (ṬW' IV) you.
(*n*) When the Minister arrived in the city he ordered the inhabitants (SKN Act. Part. pl.) to open their houses for inspection (FTSH II *maṣdar*).
(*o*) When you hear a noise, raise your hand.
(*p*) If I had seen anything, I would have called you.
(*q*) These women are handsomer than their husbands, but the most beautiful of them (trans. *also* "the most beautiful") cannot be present today. (to be present: *ḥaḍara* (*u*)).
(*r*) The doctor ordered the sick man to drink his medicine (*dawā'*) every day.
(*s*) Those who walk on the grass (*ḥashīsh*) will be arrested by order of the judge (to arrest: WQF II or IV).
(*t*) Anyone who stops must sit down until I return.
(*u*) If I had known his name I would have called him.
(*v*) I was ordered by the Turks (*atrāk*) to come out of the house with my hands (Dual) on my head (construct last phrase with *wāw* of Circumstance).
(*w*) She was bigger than her brothers: she was the tallest woman in the city.
(*x*) Do not eat that food (*ṭa'ām*) before washing (*ghasala* (*i*), *ghasl*) your hands (Dual).
(*y*) He who seeks (*ṭalaba*) will find.
(*z*) Had he sought he would have found.
(*aa*) Girls are taller than boys, but boys eat more than their sisters.
(*bb*) He was beaten by his parents and left on the road (beat: *ḍaraba*; leave: *taraka*).
(*cc*) What must I do in order to become a Muslim? First, you must say: "There is no god but God, and Muḥammad is His Apostle".
(*dd*) He likes to travel in distant lands, but he has no money.
(*ee*) He was asked by the judge to look at the weapon with which the woman had been killed by the thief.

(*ff*) She was cleverer than her brother; if she had studied more, she could have become the cleverest woman in Egypt.

2. Give the Broken Plurals (more than one where possible) of the following words: *ukht*; *akh*; *iṣba'*; *usbū'*; *ḥakīm*; *ḥākim*; *wazīr*; *ḍābiṭ*; *masjid*; *finjān*; *yad*; *qalam*; *kalb*; *majlis*; *sharīf*; *'āmil*; *amr*; *safīr*; *wajh*; *kātib*; *fann*; *ṣaut*; *miftāḥ*; *gharīb*; *tājir*; *ab*; *maktab*; *sinn*; *marīḍ*; *bayt*; *amīr*; *maṣrif*; *maṣrūf*; *madīna*; *makhraj*; *shahr*; *qāfila*

3. Give the masculine singular Imperative of:

ḤRB III; 'ṬW IV; D'W I; WD' I; 'KHDH I; JY' I; QWL I; SLM II; WṢL I; RMY I; 'KL I; KLM V; BY' VIII; QTL V; LQY III; SYR II; KHYL VIII; KHRJ IV; FTSH II; 'MR I; KHYR VIII; ḤWL II; ḤWL III; ṢYR I; KHLW II; DKHL IV; WQF V; DLL I; MḌY I; QYD VIII; MYZ II and V; 'DHN X; WFQ III; QWM II and IV; ḌRR IV; MSHY I; WRD IV; QLL X; BKY I; HWL VIII; WFQ IV; KHWF II; MRR IV; QWM X

4. Grammar

(*a*) What are the principal modifications of sense usually associated with the IInd and the Xth Derived Forms of the verb? Give one or more examples of each category.

(*b*) List six ways by which the time of an action may be more closely defined in Arabic; not more than three of your examples should be based on negative particles.

(*c*) List the patterns of the Derived Forms of the strong verb, perfect and imperfect. What are the modifications of sense sometimes associated with Forms III and IV?

(*d*) List the main negative particles in Arabic, indicating their respective uses. Illustrate with simple examples.

(*e*) List the main peculiarities of construction associated with the use of Conditional Sentences.

5. Arabic passages to be translated into normal English, making use of the vocabulary given:

١ حدثنا شيخ من موالى المنصور قال قدم علينا غلمان من موالى بني أمية يريدون مكة فلما قدموا
مكة سألوا عن ابن سريج فوجدوه مريضا فأتوا صديقا لهم فسألوه أن يسمعهم غناءه فخرج
معهم حتى دخلوا عليه فقالوا نحن غلمان من قريش أتيناك مسلمين عليك وأحببنا أن نسمع
منك فقال أنا مريض كما ترون فقالوا إن الذى نريده قليل فقال ابن سريج يا جارية هاتي
عودى فأتته به ثم أخذ العود فغناهم وانصرفوا يتعجبون مما سمعوا .

٢ الجواب للاحمق هو السكوت

٣ رأس الحكمة مخافة الله

٤ العقل هو الخط الفاصل بين الانسان والحيوان

٥ حب الوطن من الايمان

٦ لا يشرب المسلمون خمرا ولا يأكلون لحم الخنزير

٧ أين الجرائد التي اشتريتها قبل الظهر

٨ وصل إلى القدس يوم أمس أحد الباحثين المحققين في شؤون التعليم في جامعة بيروت الامريكية ويقوم بدرس أحوال التعليم في الشرق الأوسط .

٩ عقد عمال دائرة البرق والبريد اجتماعا في قاعة جمعية العمال العربية في القدس سمعوا فيه تقريرا عن الطلبات التي قدمها عمال البرق والبريد إلى السلطات .

١٠ قرأت اليوم في الجريدة العربية اعلانا يعلن فيه أبوك بأنه يبيع بيته الجديد الذى في شارع الملك فيصل .

١١ سوف يزور جلالة الملك فاروق الأول غدا دار مصلحة التلفونات لافتتاح الخط التلفوني بين مصر والسودان .

١٢ ينظر المجلس الوطني التركى الآن في مشروع توزيع الأراضي .

١٣ وجه عدد كبير من النواب انتقادا شديدا إلى الحاكم .

١٤ كنت في مصر فزرت صديقا لى قبيل المغرب فجاء ولده يسلم على وهو مصفر الوجه فقلت هل هو مريض .

١٥ إذا كنت كذوبا فكن ذكورا .

١٦ لا تأمن الأمير إذا غشك الوزير .

Vocabulary

1 *'ūd*: lute; *hāti*: āti

6–10 SH'N pl.: affairs; QWM I plus *bi*: to undertake; *dā'irat al-barq wa-al-barīd*: Department of Posts and Telegraphs; QRR II v.n.: report: *qā'ah*: hall; 'LN IV: to announce

11–16 *maṣlaḥa*: (here) Department; WZ' II *maṣd.*: distribution; *al-arāḍī*: pl. of *arḍ*; nā'*ib*: Deputy, M.P.; NQD VIII *maṣd.*: criticism; *qubaila*: diminutive *qabla*; *muṣfarr*: sallow; GHSHSH I: to swindle

Arabic passages

١٧ كان الفلاحون يرجعون إلى البيت قبل غروب الشمس .

١٨ سيكون الخادم حاضرا كل يوم في الصباح .

١٩ كنت يوما جالسا في مطعم في بيروت وكان على قرب مني جماعة من المصريين يأكلون ويشربون ويتحدثون .

٢٠ بعد أن يكتب مكتوبا يضعه في ظرف ويبعث به إلى صديقه .

٢١ خذ اللص قبل أن يأخذك .

٢٢ ان ضيفت البدوى يأخذ كل ما تملكه .

٢٣ قد دخل سارق بيت أخى الكبير وسرق ساعة اشتراها أخى أمس ولما يجده البوليس .

٢٤ لا تأكل هذا الخبز فانه قد صنع منذ أسبوع .

٢٥ لا تصدق كلما تقرأه في الجرائد .

٢٦ كان فلاح يذهب يوما مع ابنه إلى السوق ليبيع حمارا له فيشترى آخر بدلا منه .

٢٧ أريد أن تذهبي إلى السوق فتشترى لى خبزا وبيضا تضعينها في سلة .

٢٨ ان أردت التوفيق فلا تقل ما لا يقوله غيرك .

٢٩ طلب مني أن أقرأ ورقتين من مكتوبه فما قدرت على ذلك لأنه لم يحسن الكتابة .

٣٠ كنت أزور أبوى مرتين في الاسبوع وهم يرون أختي مرة في السنة .

٣١ الانسان حيوان وليس كل حيوان انسانيا .

٣٢ الأم التي أطعمتك وأنت طفل وجب عليك أن تطعمها وأنت كبير .

٣٣ ان أمرتك بأن تفعلى ذلك فلا بد لك من فعل ما قلت .

٣٤ لما رأيته لا يقدر على فهم اللغة العربية سألته عن وطنه أين هو .

٣٥ التلميذ الذى يدرس كل النهار في المدرسة وجب عليه أن يلعب بعد الدرس لألّا يصير مريضا .

٣٦ كنت وأنا طفل أنام كل يوم بعد الظهر .

٣٧ لو وجدت كتابا آخر مثل هذا لبعتها بأكثر مما اشتريتها به .

٣٨ من قرأ القرآن لا يلتفت إلى ما يقرأه فقد دعا على نفسه بغضب الله .

٣٩ أعطاني أبي ساعة لم أر مثلها من قبل .

٤٠ من تحبه وجب عليك أن تحسن ذكره ولو غضبت عليه من حين إلى آخر .

٤١ كانت هؤلاء النساء يأكلن شيئا من الخبز واللحم كل ليلة من ليالى أعمارهن قبل أن ينمن .

٤٢ أما ما تعلمه الانسان وهو طفل فبقي راسخا في ذاكرته وهو شيخ أبيض الشعر .

Vocabulary

KHDM Act. Part. I: servant; Ṭ‘M: (idea of) eating, consuming; *qurb*: proximity; ḤDTH V: to talk; *ẓarf*: envelope, container; *liṣṣ*: thief; ḌYF II: to entertain, show hospitality to; *salla*: basket; WFQ II *maṣdar*: success; ḤSN IV (followed by *maṣdar*): to do something well; *nisba* from "man" – human; *waṭan*: native-land; *la'iba*: to play; *li'allā*: a contraction of *li-an-lā*; LFT VIII: to pay attention; *ḥīn*: time, moment; *laḥm*: meat; RSKH: (idea of) firm fixation; *dhākira*: memory

Arabic passages

يقال إن المأمون لما جاء مصر كان يقيم في كل قرية مر بها يوما وليلة فمر بقريه طاء النمل دون أن ينزل بها لحقارتها فلما تجاوزها خرجت اليه عجوز قبطية وهى تصيح فظنها متظلمة فوقف لها وكان لا يمشي أبدا الا والتراجمة بين يديه فذكروا له أنها تقول نزلت في كل ضيعة وتجاوزت ضيعتي وأنا أسالك أن تشرفني بحلولك عندى فنزل وأحضرت له من فاخر الطعام ولذيذه شيئا استعظمه ولما أصبح حضرت اليه ومعها عشر خادمات تحمل كل واحدة منهن طبقا فيه كيس من ذهب هدية للخليفة فشكرها وأمرها باعادتها فقالت لا أفعل فتأمل الذهب فاذا به كله ضرب عام واحد فقال لمن معه هذا والله أعجب ربما يعجز بيت مالنا عن مثله ثم التفت اليها وقال إنا لا نحب أن نحملك ما لا تستطيعينه كفانا ما رأيناه من كرمك ردّى مالك بارك الله لك فيه قالت يا أمير المؤمنين لا تكسر قلوبنا ولا تحتقر بنا فعندنا بفضل عدلك من الذهب شىء كثير فقبل هديتها وأقطعها أرضا من قريتها بغير خراج وانصرف وهو يتعجّب من سعة كرمها وكثرة مالها .

حكاية اللص مع الصيرفي

حُكى ان رجلا من الصيارف كان معه كيس ملآن ذهبا وقد مرّ على اللصوص فقال واحد من الشطار : أنا أقدر على أخذ الكيس . فقالوا له : كيف تصنع .

فقال : انظروا . ثم تبعه إلى منزله .

(الليلة السادسة والثلاثون بعد الثلثمائة)[1] . فدخل الصيرفي ورمى الكيس على الصفة وكان مزمعا على الصلاة . فقال للجارية هاتي ابريق ماء . فأخذت الجاريه الابريق وتبعته وتركت الباب مفتوحا فدخل اللص وأخذ الكيس وذهب إلى اصحابه وأعلمهم بما جرى له مع الصيرفي والجارية . فقالوا له : والله ان الذى عملته شطارة وما كل انسان يقدر عليه ولكن في هذا الوقت يرجع الصيرفي فلا يجد الكيس فيضرب الجارية ويعذبها عذابا اليما فكأنك ما عملت شيئا تُشكر عليه . فان كنت شاطرا فخلص الجارية من الضرب والعذاب . فقال لهم : ان شاء الله تعالى اخلص الجاريه والكيس . ثم ان اللص رجع إلى دار الصيرفي فوجده يعاقب الجارية لأجل الكيس فدقّ عليه الباب . فقال له : من هذا . قال له : أنا غلام جارك الذى في القيسرية . فخرج اليه وقال له : ما

[1] This story and the following one are from the *Arabian (1001) Nights*: hence the references to the 336th and the 385th nights respectively.

شأنك . فقال له : ان سيدى يسلم عليك ويقول لك : تغيرت أحوالك كلها كيف ترمى بمثل هذا الكيس على باب الدكان وتروح وتخليه . ولو لقيه أحد غريب كان أخذه وراح ولولا ان سيدى رآه وحفظه لكان ضاع عليك . ثم أخرج الكيس وأراه اياه . فلما رآه الصيرفي قال : هذا كيسي بعينه . ومدّ يده ليأخذه منه . فقال له والله ما اعطيك اياه حتى تكتب ورقة لسيدى انك تسلمت الكيس مني فاني اخاف ان لا يصدقني في انك أخذت الكيس وتسلمته حتى تكتب لى ورقة له وتختمها . فدخل الصيرفي ليكتب له ورقة بوصول الكيس كما ذكر . فذهب اللص بالكيس إلى حال سبيله وخلصت الجارية من العذاب .

حكاية الرجل الطحان مع زوجته

حُكى ان رجلا كان عنده طاحون وله حمار يطحن عليه . وكان له زوجة سوء وهو يحبها وهى تكرهه . وكانت تحب جارا لها وهو يبغضها . فرأى زوجها في النوم قائلا يقول له : احفر في الموضع الفلاني من مدار الحمار بالطاحون تجد كنزا . فلما انتبه من منامه حدّث زوجته برؤياه وأمرها بكتمان السرّ فأخبرت بذلك جارها لأجل أن تقرّب اليه . فعاهدها ان يأتيها ليلا . فأتاها ليلا وحفر في مدار الطاحون فوجدا الكنز فاستخرجاه . فقال لها الجار : كيف نصنع بهذا . فقالت : نقسمه نصفين بالسوية وتفارق أنت زوجتك وأنا احتال في فراق زوجى ثم تتزوج بي . فاذا اجتمعنا جمعنا المال كله على بعضه فيصير بأيدينا . فقال لها جارها : أنا أخاف ان يطغيك الشيطان فتأخذى غيرى فان الذهب في المنزل كالشمس في الدنيا .

والرأى السديد أن يكون المال كله عندى لتحرصي أنت على الخلاص من زوجك والاتيان الىّ . فقالت له : اني أيضا أخاف مثل ما تخاف أنت ولا اسلم اليك نصيبي من هذا المال فاني أنا التي قد دللتك عليه . فلما سمع منها هذا الكلام دعاه البغى إلى قتلها فقتلها وألقاها في موضع الكنز . ثم ادركه النهار فعوقه عن مداراتها فحمل المال وخرج . فاستيقظ الطحان من النوم فلم يجد زوجته فدخل الطاحون وعلق حماره في الطاحون وصاح عليه فمشى ووقف . فضربه الطحان ضربا شديدا . وكلما ضربه يتأخر لأنه قد جفل من المرأة الميتة وصار لا يمكنه التقدم . كل ذلك والطحان لا يدرى ما سبب توقف الحمار . فأخذ سكينا ونخسه نخسا كثيرا فلم ينتقل من موضعه . فغضب منه وطعنه بها في خاصرتيه فسقط الحمار ميتا .

(الليلة الخامسة والثمانون بعد الثلثمائة) فلما طلع النهار رأى الطحان الحمار ميتا وزوجته ميتة ووجدها في موضع الكنز . فاشتدّ غيظه على ذهاب الكنز وهلاك زوجته والحمار وحصل له هم عظيم . فهذا كله من اظهار سره لزوجته وعدم كتمانه لها .

Muqaddasī by the Sea

وبينما أنا يوما جالس مع أبي على بن حازم أنظر في البحر ونحن بساحل عدن اذ قال لى ما لى أراك متفكرا قلت أيّد الله الشيخ قد حار عقلى في هذا البحر لكثرة الاختلاف فيه والشيخ اليوم من أعلم الناس به لأنه امام التجار ومراكبه أبدا تسافر إلى أقاصيه فإن رأى أن يصفه لى صفةً أعتمد عليها وأرجع من الشك اليها فعل قال[1] فقال على الخبير بها سقطتَ ثم مسح الرمل بكفّه ورسم البحر عليه لا طيلسان ولا طير وجعل له معارج متلسنة وشعبا عدةً ثم قال هذه صفة هذا البحر لا صورة له غيرها .

NOTE: Muqaddasī (*alias* Maqdisī), perhaps the greatest Arabic writer on geographical matters, finished his book in AD 985, after years of researches and wanderings. The present passage comes from a discussion of what we should now call the "Indian Ocean". He is worried at the discrepancies among his predecessors, some of whom likened its shape to a Persian cloak (*ṭailasān*) and others to a bird (*ṭair*). Characteristically, he takes the advice of a practical ship-owner.

'Abbasid Baghdad in the Time of Ibn al-Rūmī

وقد قضى ابن الرومى حياته في بغداد ولم يفارقها الا قليلا وعلى الرغم من كل المتناقضات التي كدّرت الحياة في عاصمة العبّاسيّين في أيّام ابن الرومى فقد كانت بغداد المدينة الأولى في العالم فيها الثراء وفيها القصور والمباني ودور العلم وقد اشتهر في زمن الشاعر عدد كبير من رجال الدين واللغة والعلم والفلسفة كما اشتهر فيه عدد من الشعراء أشهرهم البحترى .

NOTE: A piece of modern prose in Semi-Classical style. Ibn al-Rūmī was a poet of considerable originality (d. AD 896). Al-Buḥturī (d. AD 897) was the author of one of the most famous collections of poetry in Arabic (one of two, both entitled *Al-Ḥamāsa* (= "Valour"), the other, more famous one being by his teacher, Abū Tammām).

[1] This word is inserted by the editor to mark the end of one quotation and the beginning of another. The conditional clause preceding it makes a polite request.

VOCABULARY

Reference is generally to *page numbers*. Order is alphabetical, by roots; or, where the root is fictional and/or the occurrence is unique, by the word itself. (The first two items are good examples of the latter.) Initial *alif* and initial *hamza* are treated as identical.

إبرة ibra (pl. ibar): 134
إبريق ibrīq (pl. para. 147): 128
ءبو ab (pl. ābā'): 119
ءبي abà (ya'bà): 145
ءتي atà: 122
ātiya(h): 150
ءحد aḥad, iḥdà: 115, 98
ءخذ akhadha: 106, 110, 113, 122, 138
akhdh: 118
khudh: 125
ittakhadha (VIII Form): para. 140
ءخر ākhar (ukhrà), ākhir (reg. fem.): 125
akhīr: 139
ilà ākhiri-hi and abbrev.: 142
II Form: 144
ءخو akh (pl. ikhwa, ikhwān), ukht (pl. akhawāt): 83
ءدو adāt (pl. adawāt): 132
adā': 149
Forms II/IV: 149
إذ idhan: 125
idhā: 76
idh: 128 (with baina-mā)
ءذن Forms I/X: 72
udhn (pl. udhun and dual): 127
ءرخ ta'rīkh, tārīkh (pl. tawārīkh(u)): 139
ءرض arḍ (pl. arāḍin/ī): 136
ءسد asad (pl. usūd, etc.): 114
ءسر asīr (pl. asrà): 123
إصبع iṣba' (pl. aṣābi'(u)): 135
ءصل aṣl (pl. uṣūl), aṣlīy: 138
إفريقيا ifrīqiyā: 136
ءكل akala: 106, 110
akkāl (sound pl.): 55
kul: 125
akl (food): 131
إلا illā: 108, 135, 150
الذى alladhī: 114, 122
ءلف alf: 138, 100
ءله allāh(u): 107, 141, 142, 143
ilāh: 70
إلى ilà: 108
ءمر amara, mur: 125; gramm. construction: 136
amīr (umarā'(u)), amīr al-mu'minīn: 128
أمريكا amrīkā: 136
أمس amsi: 123
ءمل ta'ammul: 125
ءمم amāma: 115
umm (pl. ummahāt!): 118
ammā... fa: 128
umma(h): 138
ءمن ma'mūn: 128
amīr al-mù'minīn: 128

āmin: 132
amīn: 139
أن an: 57, 83
anna: 112, 126, 83
إن in: 76, 83
wa-in: 114
inna: 117, 83
fa-inna: 126
inna-mā: 138
أنا anā: 53
أنت anta, anti: 53
أنتم antum: 53
أنتما antumā: 53
أنتن antunna: 53
أندلس al-andalus: 138
ءنس nās: 107
insān: 107
ءهل ahl: 107
ahlu-hu: 127
أو au: 129
ءول auwal(u): 120, 124
fem. ūlà: 124
auwala-mā: 127
auwalan: 150
ءون (ḥattà) al-ān: 118
أى aiy: 112
أيضا aiḍan: 108
أين aina: 108
aina-mā: 77
بـ--- bi-: 105, 122
بئر bi'r (pl. ābār): 127
بحر baḥr (pl. biḥār etc.): 141
بدء bada'a (and fī and maṣdar): 148
بدل badal / badalan min : 150
بدو badw / badawīy : 136
بدون bi-dūni: 121
بربر al-barbar: 133
برك baraka(h) (pl. Sound Fem.): 150
بطل baṭala: 144
bāṭil: 122
IV Form: 133

بطن baṭn (pl. buṭūn): 141
بعد ba'da: 123
ba'da an / ba'da mā : 150
ba'īd: 134
بعض ba'ḍ: 126
ba'ḍ . . . ba'ḍ: 132
بقر baqar (unit-form type): 129
بقي baqiya (yabqà): 138
بكى bakà (yabkī): 140
بل bal: 139
بلا bi-lā: (under *dūna*) 121
بلد balad (pl. bilād) / bilād (pl. buldān) : 130
بلغ mablagh: 113
III and fī and maṣdar: 147
بنو bint (pl. banāt): 106
ibn (pl. banūna, abnā'): 111
bunaiya: 116
بني banā (yabnī): 138
بوب bāb (pl. abwāb): 118
بيت bait (pl. buyūt, abyāt): 43
fī al-bait: 116
بيع bā'i': (pl. bā'a(h)): 116
bā'a: 116
mabī': 86
بين baina (yadai): 146
بينما baina-mā (. . . idh): 128
تجر tājir (pl. tujjār): 106
تحت taḥta: 145
ترك taraka (u): 114
tark: 142
تفح tuffāḥa: 47
تلفون tilifūn (pl. Sound Fem.): 55
تلميذ tilmīdh (pl. talāmīdh(u)): 129
ثقل thiql (pl. athqāl): 130
ثلث thālith: 129 (in acc.), 100, 101
thalāth(ah): 132, 99
ثم thumma: 44
ثني ithnāni: 112, 99
al-thānī: 120, 100–1
marratan thāniyatan: 124

جبل jabal (pl. jibāl): 140
جبن jubn (two senses): 129
جحظ al-jāḥiẓ (proper name): 132
جدد jadīd: 108
جرد jarīda (pl. jarā'id(u)): 124
جرى jarà (yajrī): 148
جزر jazīra(h) (pls. jazā'ir(u), juzur) } : 138
jazīrat al-'arab }
جسم jism (3 basic pl. forms): 130
جلد jild }
jalida, jalada } : 66
II (denom. and trans.) }
جلس jalasa (i): 67, 126
majlis: 140
Form IV: 67
جمع jama'a: 71–2, 136
jamī': 130
jamā'a: 135
jum'a(h): 149
Form VIII: 71
جمل jamal (pl. jimāl): 130
جنب janūb(īy): 136
جند jund (pl. ajnād): 44
جنس jins (pl. ajnās): 138
جنن al-janna(h): 135
جهد VIII: 133
جهل jahila: 126
majhūl: 74
al-jāhilīya(h): 126
جوب IV ajāba: 116, 88
jawāb (pl. ajwiba(h)): 76
جوز jāza: 133
III Form: 127
جوع jā'i' (pl. jiyā', juwwa'): 119
جيء jā'a: 122, 97
جيش jaish (pl. juyūsh): 136
حبب Form IV: 129
ḥubb: 132
maḥbūb ilà: 133
ḥabīb (pl. aḥibbā'u): 144
حتى ḥattà: 114, 118, 126
حجج ḥajj: 146
ḥājj (pl. ḥujjāj): 128
حجر ḥajar (pl. aḥjār; has unit form): 144
حدث ḥadatha (u): 139
ḥāditha(h) (pl. ḥawādithu): 124
Forms II / V: 137
حدد ḥadd (pl. ḥudūd): 119
ḥadīd (-īy): 130
حرر ḥarr: 146
ḥurr (pl. aḥrār): 129
ḥarāra: 126
حرق IV Form: 130
حرك V act. part.: 132
حزن ḥazina (maṣdar – ḥuzn): 132
حسب ḥisāb: 108
حسن ḥasan: 49
IV Form: 146; Active Part.: 129
X Form: 72
حضر ḥaḍara (u): 144
IV Form: 146
حفظ ḥafiẓa: 126
حقق ḥaqq: 137
ḥaqqan: 117
ḥaqīqa(h): 137
aḥaqqu bi: 142
حكم ḥukm (pl. aḥkām): 146
ḥakīm (pl. ḥukamā'u): 126
حلب ḥalīb: 129
حمر aḥmar (fem. and pl.): 78
ḥimār (pl. ḥamīr): 130
IX Form: 78
حمل ḥamala (i) (maṣdar – ḥaml): 130
حمم ḥammām (pl. Sound Fem.): 146
حوج ḥāja(h) (pl. sound): 138
iḥtiyāj (ilà): 128
حول ḥāl (pl. aḥwāl): 139
ḥīla(h) (pl. ḥiyal): 143
حيو ḥayya (or ḥayiya: yaḥyā): 98
ḥayawān (pl. Sound Fem.): 107, 55, 130
ḥayā(h): 132
ḥaiy: 139
Forms IV / X: 98
خبر khabar (pl. akhbār): 130

all basic patterns of Form I: 89–93
Form IV: 146
رفع rafa‘a: 133
murtafi‘: 131
رفف raff (pl. rufūf): 106
ركب rakiba: 140
رمض ramaḍān: 125
رمى ramà: Full treatment of all basic patterns of Form I: 89–93
روح / ريح rāḥa(h): 126
rīḥ (pl. riyāḥ): 140
Form X: 142
رود Form IV: 123, 135
زبد zubda(h): 129
زمزم zamzam: 127
زمن zamān: 110
زوج zauj (pl. azwāj): 112
zauja(h)(pl. Sound Fem.): 112
زيد zāda (yazīdu): 126
ziyāda(h): 149
زيل / زول zāla (yazālu): 85, 149
س sa-: 70
سءل sa’ala (a): 115, 120, 125
su’āl (pl. as’ila(h)): 146
سبب sabab (pl. asbāb): 128
سبع sab‘(ah) : 99
sābi‘: 100, 101
usbū‘ (pl. asābī‘u): 123
سبق sabaqa (i, u): 144
سجد masjid (pl. masājidu): 74
سجل sijill (pl. Sound Fem.): 55
سرر sirr (pl. asrār): 146
سرع sur‘a(h): 135
Form IV: 140
سرق saraqa (i): 109, 142
سعى sa‘à (yas‘à): 148
سفر safar: 96
Form III: 122
musāfir: 132
musāfara(h) (pl. Sound Fem.): 131
سفن safīna(h) (pl. sufun): 140
سقط saqaṭa (u): 128
سكت sakata (u): 120
سكك sikka(h) (pl. sikak): 130
سكن sakana (u): 111
sākin (pl. sukkān): 109
maskan (pl. masakinu): 138
سكين sikkīn (pl. sakākīnu); 105, 74
سلح silāḥ (pl. asliḥa(h)): 136
سلط sulṭān (pl. salāṭīnu): 146
سلم sālim (pl. Sound Masc.): 114
salām: 150
salāma(h): 128
Form II: 138
Form IV: 69
Islām: 107
muslim(ah) (pls. Sound): 125
سمع sami‘a (a): 120
Form VIII: 72
سمك samak (unit form: pl. asmāk): 144
سمو ism (pl. asmā’): 108
samā’: 136
Form II: 149
سنم sanām: 131
سنن sinn (pl. asnān): 123
سنو sana(h) (pls. sanawāt, sinūna, sanūna) : 44, 109, 141
سود saiyid (pl. sāda(h)): 117; fem. 139
al-sūdān: 137
سوع sā‘a(h) (pl. Sound Fem.): 142
سوف saufa: 70
سوق sūq (pl. aswāq): 134
سير sāra: 122, 85
sair: 130
saiyāra(h) (pl. Sound Fem.): 118
شأم al-sha’m (shām): 138
شءن sha’n (pl. shu’ūn): 142
شبه ashbahu: 144
شجر shajar (unit form: pl. ashjār): 132
شخص shakhṣ (pl. ashkhāṣ): 143

شدد	shadīd: 149
شرب	shariba: 40
	shurb: 131
	Form IV: 67
شرر	sharr: 127
شرط	sharṭ (pl. shurūṭ): 76
شرع	shāri‘ (pl. shawāri‘u): 44, 140
شرى	shirā’: 96
	Form VIII: 96
شعر	shi‘r (pl. ash‘ār): 126
	sha‘r (unit form: pl. rare): 114
	shā‘ir (pl. shu‘arā’u): 123
شغل	shughl (pl. ashghāl): 142
	Form VI: 68
شفي	Form X: 96
شكر	shakara (u): 119
شكل	mushkila(h) (pl. mashākilu): 149
شكو	shakā: 144
شمس	shams: 141
شمل	shimāl, shamāl } (-īy): 138
شهد	al-shahādatāni: 142
شهر	shahr (pl. shuhūr, ashhur): 43, 114
	ashharu: 138
	mashhūr: 123
شيء	shai’ (pl. ashyā’u): 123
صبب	ṣabba (u): 128
صبح	ṣubḥ, ṣabāḥ: 140
صحب	ṣāḥib (pl. aṣḥāb): 107, 128
صحر	ṣaḥrā’u (pl. ṣaḥārà): 130
صدر	ṣadara (i, u): 124
	Form IV: 122
صدق	ṣidq: 137
	ṣadīq (pl. aṣdiqā’u): 109, 60
صرخ	ṣarakha (u): 116
صرف	Form VII: 146
صعب	ṣa‘b: 118
صعق	ṣā‘iqa(h) (pl. ṣawā‘iqu): 130
صغر	ṣaghīr (pl. ṣighār): 44, 110
صلح	ṣāliḥ: 138, 143
صلو	Form II: 138, 94
صنع	ṣana‘a: 134
صوت	ṣaut (pl. aṣwāt): 140
صور	Form II: 148
صوف	ṣūf: 69
صوم	ṣaum: 125
صيد	ṣā’id (pl. Sound Masc.): 114
صير	ṣāra: 136, 142, 143
صيف	ṣaif: 108
ضحك	ḍaḥika: 129
ضرب	ḍaraba (i): 72, 123
	Form VIII: 72
ضيف	Form II: 145
طبب	ṭabīb (pl. aṭibbā’u): 144
طرش	aṭrashu (and other forms): 78
طرق	ṭarīq (pl. ṭuruq): 118
طفل	ṭifl (pl. aṭfāl): 118
طلب	ṭalaba (u): 114
طلع	ṭala‘a (u): 72, 142
	ṭulū‘: 142
	Form VIII: 72
طول	ṭūl: 141
	ṭawīl (pl. ṭiwāl): 106
	Form IV: 146
طيب	ṭaiyib: 106
طير	ṭāra: 146
	ṭair: 146
ظرف	ẓarf (pl. ẓurūf): 143
ظلل	Form X: 145
ظنن	ẓanna (u): 120, 82
	ẓann: 146
ظهر	ẓahr (pl. ẓuhūr): 131
	ẓuhūr (maṣd. I): 138
	Form IV: 146
	iẓhār: 123
عبد	‘abd (pl. ‘ibād, ‘abīd): 128
عجب	‘ajab: 121
	Form IV: 132
	a‘jabu: 149
عجز	‘ajūz (pl. ‘ajā’izu): 123
عجل	‘ajala(h): 135
عدد	‘adda (u): 139
	‘adad: 149
عدو	‘adūw (pl. a‘dā’): 140
عذب	Form II: 142

عرب al-‘arab: 107
‘arabīy: 108
عرف ‘arafa (i): 125
ma‘rūf: 108
ma‘rifa(h): 139
عرق ‘irq (pl. ‘urūq): 139
al-‘irāq: 56, 114
عزز ‘azīz (pl. a‘izza(h)): 114
عصر ‘aṣr (3 pls.): 124
mu‘āṣir (pl. Sound Masc.): 123
عصم ‘āṣima(h) (pl. ‘awāṣimu): 125
عفو ‘afā: 128
‘afw: 146
عقب ‘iqāb: 142
عقد Form VIII: 126
عقل ‘aql: 83
‘āqil: 129
علم ‘alima: 112, 125
‘ilm (pl. ‘ulūm): 126
‘ālim (pl. ‘ulamā’u): 123
‘ālam (pl. ‘awālimu): 124
ma‘lūm: 135
a‘lamu: 112
Form II: 65
mu‘allima(h) (pl. Sound Fem.): 123
Form V: 68
علو ‘alà: 106, 111, 138 (twice), 150
‘alīy: 111
عمر ‘amara (u): 72
‘umr(pl. a‘mār): 109
‘umaru 69
Form X: 72
عمل ‘amala (i): 130
‘amal (pl. a‘māl): 142
Form X: 130
عمم al-‘āmma(h): 149
عمى Form VI: 95
عن ‘an: 123, 128, 136
عند ‘inda: 107, 111, 148
عنوان ‘unwān, ‘inwan (pl. ‘anāwīnu): 144
عني ‘anà (ya‘nī): 130, 132, 146
عهد ‘ahd (pl. ‘uhūd): 142
عود ‘āda(h) (pl. Sound Fem.): 109
عوم ‘ām (pl. a‘wām): 109
عيد ‘īd (pl. a‘yād): 149
عين ‘ain (pls. ‘uyūn, a‘yun; a‘yān): 135
‘iyān: 146
غدو ghadan, al-ghada: 140, 142
غرب ghurūb: 136
al-maghrib: 132
غسل ghasala (i); ghasl: 128
غضب ghaḍiba; ghaḍab: 128
غفر ghafara (i): 72
Form X: 72
غلط ghalaṭ (pl. aghlāṭ): 126
غيب ghāba(h)(pl. Sound Fem.): 114
ghā’ib: 144
غير ghair: 112, 126
ف fa-: 116, 126, 77, 128, 135
فتح fataḥa (a): 116
miftāḥ (pl. mafātīḥu): 75
فرر farra (i): 144
فرس faras (pl. afrās): 130
فرض farīḍa(h) (pl. farā’iḍu): 149
فرع far‘ (pl. furū‘): 139
فرعون fir‘aunu: 146
فضل afḍalu: 107, 126
فعل fa‘ala (a): 39, 108, 128
فقد mafqūd: 146
فقر faqīr (pl. fuqarā’u): 136
فقط faqaṭ: 109
فكر fakara (u, i): 140
Form II, Form V, Form VIII: 140
فلح fallāḥ (pl. Sound Masc.): 56
فلس fils (pl. fulūs): 136
فور fauran, ‘alà (min) al-fauri: 109
فوق fauqa: 145
فوه fam (pl. afwāh): full explanations: 83
في fī: 44, 108
فيد fā’ida(h) (pl. fawā’idu): 132
Form X: 88

قبح qabuḥa: 66
Form II: 66
Form X: 72
قبل qabila: 72
qabla: 123, 144
qablu: 119, 123
qabīla(h) (pl. qabā'ilu): 138
Form II: 146
Form X: 72
قتل qatala (u): 44, 110
qatīl (pl. qatlà): 123
Form II: 66
Form III: 66
Form VI: 68
قد qad: 112, 72–3
قدر qadara (i): 118
قدس al-quds: 44
قدم qadīm: 110
Form II: 144
قرء qara'a (a): 107, 70
qirā'a(h): 108
qur'ān: 107
قرب qurb: 141
qarīb: 134
Form V: 136
قرد qird (pl. qurūd): 144
قرر Form II: 150
قرع qara'a: 116
قرن qarn (pl. qurūn): 132
قرى qarya(h) (pl. quran): 134
قصر qaṣr (pl. quṣūr): 123
qaṣīr: 140
قصو aqṣà: 146
قضي qaḍà (yaqḍī): 150
qāḍin, qāḍī (pl. quḍāt): 133, 92
qaḍīya(h): 133
Form VII: 95
قطر qiṭār (pl. quṭur): 134
قطع qaṭa'a: 105, 110
qaṭ': 145
qiṭ'a(h) (pl. qiṭa'): 106
قفل qufl (pl. aqfāl): 132
qāfila(h) (pl. qawāfilu): 122
قلب qalb (pl. qulūb): 127
inqilāb: 148
قلل qalīl: 129, 142
قلم qalam (pl. aqlām): 43, 109
قهر al-qāhira(h): 111
قود Form VII: 87
قول qāla (yaqūlu): 112, 115, 117, 131, 84–5
qaul (pl. aqwāl): 119, 86, 137
قوم qāma (yaqūmu): 72, 133
qaum: 132
Form IV: 143
قيل qāla (yaqīlu): 84–5
ك ka-: 130
كبر kabīr (pl. kibār): 106
akbar (etc.): 125, 79
Form V: 68
كتب kataba (u): 39, 51, 66
kitāba(h): 108
kitāb (pl. kutub): 46
kātib (pl. kuttāb): 122
maktūb (pl. makātību): 74
maktab(ah) (pl. makātibu): 75
Form III: 66
كثر kathura: 128
kathīr (and m.f. Sound Pl.): 112, 129
aktharu: 109
kathra(h): 149
Form IV: 144
كذب kadhaba (i): 116
kidhb, kadhib: 142
kadhūb: 144
كرم Form IV: 142
كسر kasara (i): 66
Form II: 66
Form VII: 71
كشف Form VIII: 134, 136
muktashif: 135
كظم kaẓama (i): 128
كفر kāfir (pl. kuffār): 69
كفف kāffatan: 150
كلب kalb (pl. kilāb): 43

كلل kull: 108, 142
kallā: 113
كلم kalima(h) (pl. Sound Fem.): 122
Form II
Form V } :68
kulla-mā: see كلل
كم kam: 112
كنس kanasa (i): 75
miknasa(h) (pl. makānisu): 75
كود kāda (a): full explanation: 150
كون kāna: 110, 69, 73, 132
كيف kaifa: 109
ل li (la):
preposition: 55, 111, 113, 132, 134, 135
conjunction: 114
"filler" particle: 77, 135
لا lā: 109, 121 (bi-lā), 70 (twice), 135
لألا li-allā: 120
لأن li-an: 114
li-anna: 112
لبس labisa (a): 69
libās (pl. albisa(h)): 69, 146
لذلك li-dhālika: 132
لزم lazima: 135
luzūm: 135
لسن lisān (pl. alsina(h)): 127
لعب la'iba: 115
لعن la'ana: 129
لغو lugha(h): 108
لقي laqiya: 94
Form III: 94
Form IV: 94
لكن see: ولكن
لكي li-kai: 114
لم lam: 114, 69
lima: 120
لما lammā: 109, 69
limā: 120
لماذا li-mā-dhā: 120
لن lan: 70
لو lau: 76, 144
ليس laisa: 117, 70, 82
ليل lail(ah) (pl. layālin): 132, 140
ما mā:
interrog.: 108, 135
neg.: 69, 70
relative: 126, 77, 148
compounds of: 120, 69, 77, 127, 128, 129, 138, 142, 148
after indef.: 113, 129
مائة mi'a(h): 113, 100
متى matà: 108, 77
مثل mithl (pl. amthāl): 138
محن imtiḥān: 143
مدد mudda(h): 109, 138
Form V: 142
مدن madīna(h) (pl. mudun): 55, 123, 138
مرء imra'a(h)
al-mar'a(h) } : 133
مرر marra (u): 146
marra(h): 122, 124
مرض marīḍ (pl. marḍà): 123
مرن tamrīn (and pls.): 148
مشي mashà (yamshī)
mashy } : 146
مصر miṣrīy (pl. Sound Masc.): 106, 55
مطر maṭar
Form IV } :67
مع ma'a: 111, 147, 148
مكك makka(h): 127
ملح milḥ
mallāḥ } :136
ملك malik (pl. mulūk): 107
malika(h) (pl. Sound Fem.): 55
من min: 106, 109, 115, 122, 125, 139, 142, 143, 148
man: 107, 114 (see alladhī), 128, 77
mimman (= min man) : 126
mimmā (= min mā): 148
منديل mandīl: 139

mīlād: 75
ولكن wa-lākin(na): 135
ولم walīma(h) (pl. walā'imu): 143
ولو wa-lau: 144
ولى Form V: 95
يا yā: 113
يحيى yaḥyà: 123
يدى yad (pls. aidin, ayādin / aidī, ayādī, also dual): 122, 128, 140, 146
يهد yahūd(īy): 149
يمم Form V: 144
يوم yaum (pl. aiyām): 108, 112, 115, 142
yaumīy: 124